BEHAVIOR AND GROUP MANAGEMENT IN OUTDOOR ADVENTURE EDUCATION

Outdoor adventure activities are becoming an increasingly popular part of physical education programs. The physical risks of these activities are often foremost in the minds of both instructors and participants, yet it is managing group behavior which can prove to be the most difficult. This is the first book for students and practitioners to address this essential aspect of outdoor adventure education (OAE).

Outlining key evidence-based training practices, this book explains how to interact with groups ranging from adolescents to military veterans within a variety of outdoor adventure education contexts. It provides practical advice on how to promote positive behavior, while also offering guidance on how to mitigate negative behavior and manage a variety of challenging behavioral issues. With ten chapters full of real world examples from rock climbing to wilderness trekking, it provides a comprehensive guide to understanding the complexities of behavioral group management (BGM) in theory and practice.

This book is vital reading for students training to be outdoor physical education instructors and for practitioners looking to enhance their group management skills.

Alan Ewert is a Professor in Outdoor Leadership at Indiana University, USA. He has also served in the position of Branch Chief of Recreation, Wilderness, and Urban Forestry Research for the USDA Forest Service. In that position, he was involved in helping initiate the development of a social science and human well-being program in the Forest Service. He has published numerous articles on the relationship between natural settings and human health in addition to a number of books on adventure education.

Curt Davidson recently received his PhD from Indiana University, USA, and studies the intersections of cognitive health, outdoor adventure, and social support. He has taught several courses at Indiana University, including graduate level Behavior Management and Adventure Education Facilitation. In addition, he has held positions as an outdoor instructor with over 12 programs including Outward Bound and Summit Adventure. His expertise in facilitation has led him to conduct multiple workshops for a variety of programs.

BEHAVIOR AND GROUP MANAGEMENT IN OUTDOOR ADVENTURE EDUCATION

Theory, Research and Practice

Alan Ewert and Curt Davidson

Routledge
Taylor & Francis Group

LONDON AND NEW YORK

First published 2017
by Routledge
2 Park Square, Milton Park, Abingdon, Oxon OX14 4RN

and by Routledge
711 Third Avenue, New York, NY 10017

Routledge is an imprint of the Taylor & Francis Group, an informa business

British Library Cataloguing-in-Publication Data
A catalogue record for this book is available from the British Library

Library of Congress Cataloging-in-Publication Data
A catalog record for this book has been requested

ISBN: 978-1-138-93523-5 (hbk)
ISBN: 978-1-138-93525-9 (pbk)
ISBN: 978-1-315-67753-8 (ebk)

Typeset in Bembo
by HWA Text and Data Management, London

CONTENTS

FIGURES

TABLES

CONTRIBUTORS

Pete Allison, Associate Professor for the Department of Recreation, Park, and Tourism Management at PennState, University Park, PA. Pete is also an Associate Professor for the Shaver's Creek Rock Ethics Institute.

Ken Glibertson, Professor for the Department of Applied Human Sciences at the University of Minnesota Duluth, Duluth, MN.

Aya Hayashi, Associate Professor in Outdoor Education for the Biwako Seikei Sport College, Shiga Japan.

Tom Smith, Executive Director of the Summit Adventure, Bass Lake CA.

Chad Spangler, Director of Veterans Programs at Outward Bound, Golden, CO.

Alison Voight, Coordinator, Therapeutic Outdoor Programs, and Assistant Professor for the Department of Recreation, Park, and Tourism Studies at Indiana University, Bloomington, IN.

Chun-Chieh Wang, Assistant Professor for the National Taiwan Sport University, Taoyun City, Taiwan.

FOREWORD

We live in an ever more complicated world. Each one of us navigates our way through this complicated world differently, it's what makes us human, makes us unique to one another.

Some appear to navigate the world more easily than others. Finding and working their way around, over and through the obstacles and barriers that are a constant part of the world we inhabit. Others struggle. And for some, their struggles are expressed in counter-productive and destructive behaviors where they limit and injure not only themselves but those around them. It's with compassion and hard work that we strive to create tools and techniques to help individuals successfully navigate their way in the world.

As the Executive Director of Outward Bound USA, one of the largest outdoor adventure education (OAE) organizations in the world, I have been fortunate to witness first-hand the positive impact that learning experiences in the outdoors have on individuals and groups. When skilled and compassionate instructors are coupled with intentional facilitation, the positive effect that wilderness and adventure learning has on personal growth and development can be significant.

Earlier in my career, I was on a multi-week expedition with a student who was physically gifted but socially and emotionally stunted. He had the strength, balance, coordination, and stamina of a high-caliber athlete. He was naturally gifted in the mechanical craftsmanship required to start a fire in wet weather and to find the best path to traverse a steep slope. However, he was argumentative, unwilling or unable to engage with his peers, isolated, withdrawn, and expressed himself either with sarcasm or anger.

The breakthrough came when, little by little, the group – in a wilderness setting – became more reliant on his physical and technical skills. And it was through their dependence on him that he found his self-worth and pride. And as he discovered his self-worth, he began to drop the false mask of arrogance and disdain for his peers and his instructors. As I came to know him better, I learned that his stunted emotional skillset was, in part, a result of his home life. His father was abusive and had left home leaving his mother to support a small family on her own. He had no role models and had no way of learning how to express difficult or negative emotions in a positive manner. He had no ability to express his fear, anxiety, and even hunger in a non-argumentative, positive manner. As a result, he isolated himself or acted out in a negative way at the first encounter of something, or someone, difficult.

That student, and that positive outcome, as well as the many other students out there, is the reason we need this book.

Of paramount importance for positive outcomes like the one above is having a staff that can successfully integrate both behavioral and group management skills and techniques while working with the individual student and group members. The positive outcomes for the students often include but are not limited to increased self-confidence, self-determination, resilience, and willingness to provide both leadership and consideration to their families and communities.

Outdoor Adventure Education (OAE) or, as it is sometimes referred to, wilderness-based learning is a powerful means to teach social and emotional skills that help individuals as they find and follow their path in life. The experiences that these types of programs offer can be truly transformative and enriching and can alter a person's life in a myriad of ways.

As with many other organizations offering OAE programs, we at Outward Bound often find ourselves asking how can we provide high-quality learning experiences for our students, and how can we increase our relevancy and impact to a broader number of students and members of our society.

These questions bring us to the theme of this book, namely, how can our staff and instructors proactively manage the varied behavioral and group management issues that often present themselves during an OAE program? Throughout this book you will find tools and techniques to help individuals who struggle to help themselves, individuals who know that they need help but don't know how to ask for it. This text will give you the skill set to help students figure out the underlying issues behind their behavior.

Instructors will discover techniques to help calm a student down, understand the behaviour, and alter it to a healthier approach. Administrators will enhance their understanding of the support system they provide to not only their students but also their students' families and instructional staff. They will also be able to figure out constructive ways to set the students up for a successful experience.

As the field of OAE evolves, we continue to break down barriers to make our programs more integrated with the functioning of our society. While working toward increasing student safety in the field, OAE is also striving to find creative ways to teach leadership, life-lessons, and emotional skills to help students find their way in an ever-changing world. Until this book, the field of OAE has searched for more relevant ways and techniques to manage and mitigate student behavior. At a time when school shootings, domestic violence, and an increase in mental and behavioral ill-health has been thrust to the forefront as issues within our society, this text seems more timely than ever.

It's difficult to be a youth in today's society. Information is constantly bombarding us, and there are fewer havens of rest and recuperation. This change in society is reflected in OAE programs. Students have been increasingly difficult to manage, drugs have been brought into courses, students are engaging in anti-social behavior, and are unwilling participants in the programs provided. Without effective tools and training, instructors may default to dismissing the student instead of proactively engaging and addressing the root cause of the negative behavior.

Outward Bound has been, and will continue to strive to be at the forefront of the OAE community. With this comes the ability to embrace new ideas melded to the work that is already taking place. This means giving our instructors and ourselves the ability to accommodate students with increasingly complex mental and behavioral issues. This means providing a safe haven to students who are otherwise cast out by families, schools, and communities. This book is a step in that direction, the path forward in which OAE becomes even more relevant, students are able to develop the skills and aptitudes needed to successfully navigate their unique path through the world, and where we, as educators, are able to serve them with the highest levels of competence and compassion.

Peter A. Steinhauser
Executive Director, Outward Bound USA

PREFACE

After accumulating over 40 years of experience, between the two of us, working with individuals and groups in outdoor adventure settings, it never ceases to amaze us what power there is in the combination of the outdoor setting, coupled with purposely designed challenging experiences and effective instructors, for positively changing people's lives. Outdoor Adventure Education (OAE) programs can significantly add to the mosaic of an individual's life in a myriad of ways, be it a singularly awe-inspiring vista, the incredible sense of achievement that a person feels after successfully completing an outdoor adventure, or the warm glow of camaraderie that a participant often experiences within an adventure team. It is a pattern that repeats itself many times over as individuals and groups engage in the adventure experience. We are struck by the prose of René Daumal, a French writer, who wrote:

> You cannot stay on the summit forever; you have to come down again. So why bother in the first place? Just this: What is above knows what is below, but what is below does not know what is above. One climbs, one sees. One descends, one sees no longer, but one has seen. There is an art of conducting oneself in the lower regions by the memory of what one saw higher up. When one can no longer see, one can at least still know.

For us, in this quotation the memory of what one "sees" higher up is the most important, in that it represents the changes and new belief structures that so often linger with individuals as they emerge from an adventure experience. Indeed, the very term adventure implies a "coming out" from some type of longer experience or trip. Our ancestors used a number of terms to describe these coming-outs, such as a walkabout, rite of passage, spiritual journey, or solo. In today's more empirical parlance we sometimes refer to this metaphorical event as a "temporal mobility." Whatever the term, the adventure experience often represents a going out and a coming back, but with a difference in the person often expressed in a variety of ways – physical, emotional, psychological, or sociological.

This "difference-making" can sometimes be influenced by issues that an individual brings to an OAE program or by something that happens during that experience. And it is here where Behavioral and Group Management (BGM) skills, techniques, and knowledge come into play. For often, the instructor of an OAE/BGM program or course will need to deal with behavioral issues expressed by the individual participant in addition to issues emerging from within the group. These issues span a wide gamut and include such concepts as PTSD, bullying, conflict with the group, substance abuse, authority dissonance, and hyperactivity. In some cases, parents send their children to OAE programs with the hope that they will be "fixed." As another example, military veterans often engage in OAE programs hoping to re-instill the many positive aspects of military life such as being part of a team, working with other veterans, and experiencing the physicality that OAE often involves.

What concerned us in the field of OAE was the abundance of sources of medical-related training for staff but the limitations currently available for training and skill development for BGM types of issues. It became clear that one small way to help start to rectify this imbalance was through this book. In reviewing the literature we found few other sources of information relative to BGM that looked at the issues from both an evidence-based and theoretical perspective, as well as offering some practical skills development for the instructor. There are many unknowns and gaps in our knowledge and this book does not represent an end-all or be-all for the area of OAE and BGM. Hopefully, what it does provide is a presentation of relevant material in a cogent manner that can serve as a foundation for further thought and dialogue surrounding this area of growing importance and visibility.

A. W. E. and C. B. D.

ACKNOWLEDGMENTS AND DEDICATION

While many people have aided us in a variety of ways to write this book, a special note of thanks go to Dr Alison Voight for her many editorial suggestions and the writing of Chapter 3 for this book. Also, we would like to thank Melissa Page for the organizational and editorial work she gave to this project. Without her help this book would have been a much more difficult climb to reach the summit.

The authors would like to dedicate this book to two groups. First, our families for the constant support and encouragement they gave us throughout this process. Second, we would like to dedicate this book to the many OAE/ BGM instructors and staff who give generously of their time, expertise, and involvement in helping their students have high-quality experiences, hopefully to better meet and conquer the challenges that they face.

A. W. E. and C. B. D.

1

OVERVIEW OF THE BOOK

As you read this, a broad range of individuals is engaged in some form of an Outdoor Adventure Education (OAE) experience. These experiences involve a wide range of activities including backpacking, rock climbing, mountaineering, white-water boating, or enjoying a restorative experience in an outdoor setting. Many of these experiences are offered through systematically organized programs. These programs have gained in popularity among a wide spectrum of users. For example, it has been estimated that in 2013, there were over 200,000 students attending Outward Bound worldwide, 4,000 students taking a NOLS course, and over 18,000 students engaged in some type of OAE college program. In addition, the American Camp Association estimated that there were over 40 million children and adults who attended camp last year. OAE programs are characterized as experiences that occur primarily in outdoor settings in which participants are often members of a small group and are faced with a variety of challenging tasks such as rock climbing, wilderness trekking, or white-water boating and from which they experience emotional, cognitive, social, and physical growth and development.

In another example, the Outdoor Source Book (Bunyan, 2011; IOL, 1998) reports that there are over 1,500 centers providing outdoor adventure experiences in the United Kingdom. This is in addition to the many other "providers" of adventure experiences. Numerous "Gateway" cities and towns have developed with a strong focus on providing for and marketing to the adventure experience. Examples of these locations include: Banff and Jasper; Alberta; Canada; Talkeetna; Alaska; Queenstown; Jackson Hole; Wyoming; New Zealand; Zurmat; Switzerland; and Glasbury, south Wales. These and numerous other locations speak to the degree and manner that outdoor adventure activities have permeated contemporary society.

While there are many motives for engaging in these programs, it is obvious that the field is oftentimes utilized to help teach life skills, pro-social behavior, and desirable character traits. Additionally, parents will often enroll their kids in OAE to "fix their problems" or to experiment with how the student performs without their current medication dosage. The average instructor and program is grossly ill equipped to manage these issues and student types with current levels of knowledge and training. This is evident from the increase in early dismissals and student expulsions from all types of programs.

Of paramount importance to many of these OAE programs is having a staff that can successfully integrate both behavioral and group management skills and techniques while working with the individual student and group members. In addition, OAE programs are often designed to facilitate group management and foster a successful experience for both students and groups of OAE programs. While, historically, a great deal of programmatic effort has been placed on the physical aspects of risk management in OAE, much less attention has been allocated to the various components of managing behaviors of the individual and group. Said otherwise, programs have made great training efforts to keep the client from falling off the cliff but much less attention to keeping that person safe emotionally and within a supportive group atmosphere.

For example, a breakdown of Outward Bound staff training indicted that only six hours were spent on behavior management and 12 spent on rock climbing site setup despite there being more behavior management incidents than rock climbing incidents (Davidson and Ottley, 2014). This imbalance of physical versus behavioral training effort toward staff development is reflected in the growing body of literature focused on physical risk management, with much less visibility for managing individual and group behaviors. This is not to say that programs believe issues related to behavior and group management are unimportant; what is lacking is a concerted effort to train staff in managing these types of issues and events. In addition, there is a growing need for evidence-based training practices specifically focused on issues of behavior and group management within an OAE framework. Thus, there is an unmet need in the OAE field for a book that focuses on various techniques, existing evidence, and intervention strategies related to educating staff on behavioral and group management issues.

Need for the book

Several trends are converging that speak to the need for a book on behavior and group management (BGM). First and foremost is the growing recognition of

FIGURE 1.1   OAE students on a winter backpacking course (photo: Ellen Henderson)

the prevalence of behavior and group issues concomitant with OAE programs and experiences. As previously alluded to, while the physical challenges are often first and foremost in the minds of both the staff and students, it is the behavioral and group issues that are often the most problematic. In a recent study, Davidson and Ottley (2014) found that issues requiring Wilderness First Responder training only accounted for 11 percent of the total number of reported incidents, while those issues involving behaviors or group issues accounted for double that number of incidents (22 percent). Thus, issues in OAE programs tend to be more behavioral and group management rather than physical or medical. This emerging trend speaks directly to the need for a book to be utilized as a training resource for program developers and staff trainers.

Related to the behavioral versus physical aspects of course or program incidents is the growing need for staff adequately trained in managing group and behavioral issues. Currently, there are few OAE-related books relevant to the topic. Training resources that do exist are primarily found in individual program staff manuals, oftentimes with significant gaps of information missing. Additionally, there is a relatively small body of academic and scholarly literature available but because of the lack of a book specifically addressing these issues, this availability is primarily restricted to academic journals and is inaccessible to practitioners.

A third trend that is converging in the direction of a need for a specific book is the widespread audience that is involved in behavioral and group management issues. While specific audiences will be covered in the following section, the range of behavioral and group management issues transcends a broad range of professional, academic, and practice-based groups. Simply put, we believe that behavioral and group management issues are increasingly important in both OAE programs and in society, in general. As such, it is important for those in the OAE field to become more conversant and attentive to these types of challenges and issues.

Who is this book intended for?

This book will resonate with a number of audiences, both within and outside of the OAE field. These audiences include: upper division undergraduate university, college, and community college students; university graduate students; program design specialists; scholars in OAE and related fields such as environmental education; field staff; academicians and researchers probably primarily in the OAE field; people seeking alternative behavioral and group management strategies/interventions; student services personnel; camp administrators and staff; managers of volunteer and semi-volunteer organizations (e.g. Peace Corp, SCA), recreation and park staff; adventure education leaders; environmental educators; etc. Finally, beyond the United States and Canada, there is a significant international audience, with numerous OAE programs in places such as Mexico, Singapore, New Zealand, Australia, Japan, Taiwan, Turkey, and Europe.

From this book, readers can expect to take away a number of theoretical and practical aspects, including the following:

1 A better understanding of what is meant and involved with behavioral and group management (BGM) issues within an OAE setting.
2 The underlying theories and constructs that can be helpful for staff and other individuals in dealing with BGM issues.
3 Specific techniques and procedures useful in OAE/BGM settings and with certain populations.
4 Issues relative to medications that are often used in OAE/BGM programs for specific behavioral applications.
5 How can specific issues such as rule violation be dealt with?
6 Other resources and literature that can be helpful in the OAE/BGM situation.

Gaps in our knowledge

Research in OAE was first compiled through Shore's (1977) work. In this effort, he described over 70 studies and papers that pertained to research efforts done on Outward Bound or similar types of OAE programs. From this and subsequent works (Ewert and Sibthorp, 2014, p. 161) a number of limitations in our level of understanding have emerged and this book is intended to reduce some of those gaps that are specific to OAE and BGM issues and situations. For example, as Shore reports even in 1977, the research-based evidence in OAE has primarily involved disciplinary issues such as self-concept and self-esteem, with much less attention being shown to understanding the effects of concepts such as program length, mix of activities, types of instruction, and type of course. With this in mind, Table 1.1 illustrates some of the questions we still have regarding both OAE and BGM experiences. Relative to this issue of understanding not only the outcome but also the process to achieving that outcome, and following the work by Ewert and Sibthorp, we would suggest the following levels of evidence that currently exist for the following process-related variables:

- Autonomous student experiences (e.g. solo, final expedition) – Medium
- Approaches to leadership training (e.g. leader of the day) – Medium
- Developing the therapeutic alliance – Low to Medium
- Mix of activities/length of activities – Medium
- Type of contracts with students (e.g. Full-value contract) – Low
- Types of activities – Medium to high
- Curriculum designs focused to a specific population – Low
- Specific OAE/BGM activities that are effective at helping students deal with SEEs (significant emotional events) – Low

And finally, and perhaps most importantly, there is a need for much more information on how OAE/BGM activities can transfer and stay meaningful to other parts of a student's life. Life skills such as team building and maintenance, leadership, communication, relationship building, tolerance of others, appropriate emotional responses, and developing intrinsic motivation (Raynolds *et al.*, 2007) represent a sample of the many skills and capabilities that students can develop through an OAE/BGM experience but about which the field has limited empirical knowledge.

The focus of the book

As will be described in Chapter 2, Outdoor Adventure Education (OAE) refers to educational experiences and activities that usually involve a natural environment or emulated natural environment that contain elements of real or perceived risk, in which the outcome is uncertain but can be influenced by the student and/or circumstance. Activities such as rock climbing, mountaineering, white-water boating, caving, and wilderness trekking are examples of OAE experiences. Because they often emulate a natural setting, climbing walls, ropes courses, alpine towers, and zip lines are often categorized as OAE activities.

Behavioral and group management (BGM) includes a broad list of issues and activities that can occur in an OAE format. A sample of these issues and activities can be seen in Table 1.2. In these cases, we are defining behavioral as particular actions or deportments that occur within and by an individual or within or by a

TABLE 1.1 Gaps in knowledge concerning OAE/BGM

- Durability of desired outcomes
- Transferability of OAE/BGM outcomes to "Real Life" settings
- Components of the program that influence outcomes
  - type of course
  - mix of activities
  - instructors/group
- Congruence between OAE/BGM effectiveness of activities and specific population
- Specific techniques and desired outcomes

TABLE 1.2 Examples of behavioral and group management issues

- Conflict in the group
- Runaways
- Bullying
- Homesickness
- The development of cliques
- Dysfunctional behaviors
- Inappropriate responses to authority
- Inappropriate emotional responses
- Passive aggressive behavior
- Bringing illegal or restricted substances to the course
- Suicidal ideation
- Low motivation
- Post-traumatic stress symptoms
- Substance addition
- Substance abuse
- Negative group culture
- Group think-related behaviors
- Low or negative motivation

specific group. Moreover, for this book, we have focused primarily on negative or undesirable types of behaviors and group management issues. Bullying type behavior is something that typically occurs at the individual level. The forming of exclusive cliques within a body of students could be considered a group management issue. Likewise, when we discuss OAE/BGM we are referring to actions that are of a BGM nature and that often occur within an OAE setting or program.

How the book is structured

As previously described, OAE programs generally provide more focus on physical risk factors, such as falling, loose rock, hazards associated with white-water, and medical issues connected to sanitation, than they do on behavioral and group management issues. This book is both timely and relevant to the broad field of OAE as BGM issues become more problematic. Adults face stress-producing factors which include job stability, changes in relationships, financial problems, and a lack of direction in one's life. For younger students, events such as bullying, family conflicts, parental divorce, drug use, and future goals add to both stress and uncertainty. While the goal of many OAE programs is to help students gain perspective and the tools important to deal with these stressors, many of today's clientele bring a variety of these issues with them to the OAE setting and, in turn, some of these attributes become BGM concerns that need to be dealt with.

This chapter has provided an overview of what we mean by the terms OAE and BGM, as well as the assumptions we have made concerning OAE and BGM, and the reasons why there is a need for this type of dialogue and information. In Chapter 2 the history of OAE/BGM is discussed from the perspectives of North America and Western Europe. A contrast is drawn between outdoor education and experiential education, both of which have connections with OAE and BGM. The chapter also discusses both the impact of OAE programs on participants and some of the different ways that OAE/BGM courses and programs are structured.

In Chapter 3, issues related to BGM are discussed through the lens of therapy and therapeutic intent. In line with this discussion, several theories are presented that offer the reader a linkage between the possible theoretical underpinnings of an OAE/BGM experience and applications for practice. Scenarios are added to the theory discussion as a way to consider how practical applications can integrate with existing theory.

The purpose of Chapter 4 is to explore a number of theories that we thought were most relevant and often associated with OAE/BGM. These theories are borrowed from the fields of psychology, social work, and counseling and are useful to provide a foundational understanding of individual and group behavior. A sampling of these theories includes Reinforcement Theory, Ecological Systems Theory, the Theory of Reasoned Action and Planned Behavior, and Stages of Change Model. We also discuss how an understanding of theories may be useful in designing a curriculum and dealing with BGM issues. Similarly, in Chapter 5, we discuss some of the constructs often linked to OAE/BGM. Constructs differ from theories in that a theory can be considered a proposed explanation or description of some phenomenon (Kane and Trochim, 2009). Constructs, on

FIGURE 1.2 OAE students engaged in a team-building exercise (photo: Pete Allison)

the other hand, can exist theoretically but are often abstract. A sampling of the constructs discussed in this book include resilience, empowerment, grit, and emotional intelligence, and they were included because of their prevalence in many OAE/BGM programs.

Chapter 6 is concerned with techniques typically used in OAE/BGM settings, a mix of relatively new techniques and those that have been used for a number of years. They include strengths-based practice, natural consequences, motivational interviewing, and meaning making. Expanding on the ideas presented in the techniques chapter are ideas and information useful for working with specific populations (Chapter 7). There we focus on populations such as adolescents, intact and non-intact groups, issues connected with Attention Deficit Disorder and Hyperactive Disorder, and military veterans. In a similar fashion, Chapter 8 discusses issues related to student medication management. Many instructors and group leaders will find this information to be particularly useful due to the increased presence of students and clients on specific medication and other prescribed drugs.

In Chapter 9, the concerns surrounding substance abuse, rule violation, and inappropriate behaviors are examined. Once again, the information presented in this chapter will be useful in a variety of OAE/BGM situations and settings. The concluding Chapter 10 provides the reader with a broad range of resources that appear in a variety of formats. The intent of this chapter is to provide a set of resources from which individuals working in an OAE/BGM setting can expand their information base and, hopefully, effectiveness.

Each chapter begins with an Overview and concludes with a section describing the Main Points made in the chapter followed by a number of dialogue questions designed to facilitate discussion, either in the classroom, field-location, or individual reflection. To aid in this dialogue, where appropriate, the chapters have a Scenario and subsequent questions, which are based on real-life events and reflect some of the issues described in the chapter. In addition, various chapters contain sidebars. The sidebars provide an example of a specific OAE/BGM program or technique that also highlights an issue discussed in the chapter. Moreover, the authors of the sidebars represent a wide diversity of backgrounds and experiences that serve to broaden both the reach and applications useful in OAE/BGM.

References

Bunyan, P. (2011). Models and milestones in adventure education. In M. Berry and C. Hodgson (eds.), *Adventure Education: An Introduction* (pp. 5–23). London: Routledge.

Davidson, C. and Ottley, G. (2014). *Examining Outdoor Training and Certification Standards by Incident Data*. Poster presented at the Wilderness Risk Management Conference. Stone Mountain, GA.

Ewert, A., and Sibthorp, J. (2014). *Outdoor Adventure Education: Foundations, Theory, and Research*. Champaign, IL: Human Kinetics.

IOL. (1998). *The Outdoor Source Book*. Penrith: Adventure Education.

Kane, M., and Trochim, W. M. (2009). Concept mapping for applied social research. In L. Bickman and D. J. Rog (eds), *Applied Social Research Methods* (pp. 435–474). Los Angeles, CA: SAGE.

Raynolds, J., *et al.* (2007). *Leadership the Outward Bound Way.* Seattle, WA: Mountaineer Books.

Shore, A. (ed.) (1977). *Outward Bound: A Reference Volume.* Greenwich, CT: Outward Bound.

2

INTRODUCTION TO OUTDOOR ADVENTURE EDUCATION AND BEHAVIORAL AND GROUP MANAGEMENT

Overview

Issues related to behavioral and group management (BGM) have been central to many programs since the very inception of outdoor adventure education (OAE). As a point of reference, many OAE programs and organizations have been specifically developed to address issues of behavioral and group management including special needs, delinquency, traumatic events, and other impacting occurrences. This chapter provides an overview of the development, intended purposes, and connections that OAE has to behavioral and group management issues.

Since the 1960s, there has been a dramatic growth in the number of people engaged in outdoor adventure education (OAE) and the number of organizations offering these types of experiences, both in North America and internationally.

Many specializations involving OAE – such as adventure education, challenge therapy, therapeutic adventure, and challenge courses – all serve a variety of diverse populations. The professionalization of adventure has yielded a growth in training programs ranging from degrees offered by colleges and universities, research units within governmental organizations, hospitals and outreach programs, the corrections system, K-12 schools, and a growth of adventure programs beyond the pioneering organizations of Outward Bound Schools and the National Outdoor Leadership School. The internationalization of adventure pursuits has also become quite sophisticated in program delivery, coupled with professional cooperation among colleagues worldwide.

Not surprisingly, with the growth of organizations associated with OAE, there have been concomitant changes in numbers of participants engaged in various forms of outdoor recreation commonly associated with adventure activities. From USA data using findings from the Outdoor Foundation, *Outdoor Recreation Participation Topline Report 2016*, nearly half (48.4 percent) of all Americans reported engaging in at least one outdoor activity in 2015. This aggregated into 11.7 billion outdoor outings with 142.4 million participants. Paddle sports including whitewater kayaking and sea/tour kayaking realized some of the biggest participation increases over this time frame. From a European perspective, a similar set of trends is also evident. While harmonization of data can be challenging, outdoor activities that appear most popular include hiking, studying and enjoying nature, and cross-country skiing (Bell *et al.*, 2007). Data have been fairly consistent regarding the continued growth of outdoor recreation activities within a variety of European countries. For example, visits to Finland's national parks increased from 714,000 in 1996 to 1,410,000 in 2005 (Metsähallitus, 2006). One development that is emerging and has increasingly

TABLE 2.1 Data from the Outdoor Recreation Participation Report, Outdoor Foundation, 2016

Activity	2015 participants aged 6 or older	3-year change
Backpacking	10,100,000	4.9%
Bicycling (Mountain)	8,316	2.8%
Canoeing	10, 236,000	1.3%
Climbing (Sport/Indoor/Boulder)	4,684	0.7%
Climbing (Traditional/ Mountaineering Ice)	2,571,000	5.5%
Kayaking (Sea/Touring)	3, 079, 000	8.0%
Kayaking (Whitewater)	2, 518,000	10.3%
Rafting	3,883,000	1.7%
Scuba-Diving	3,274,000	3.2%

appeared in Finland is the concept of "everyman's right" (Pouta *et al.,* 2000). This concept essentially implies that all forests, shores, and water areas, including those privately owned, should have open access to the public. Similar concepts can be seen in the United Kingdom and several other European countries and have interesting connotations for access for outdoor adventure activities in North America. Within the UK and Europe, Bell *et al.* (2007) report that there is an increasing number of people enjoying nature tourism activities such as Outdoor Adventure Education (OAE), and as these seek out new activities and technologies pressure will increase on natural resources and landscapes.

Professional development

What these numbers suggest, is that, far from being simply the realm of the daredevil or extreme sports enthusiast, activities commonly associated with OAE constitute a substantial portion of participants across the globe. In addition, adventure pursuits have also grown into different forms of professional delivery with each requiring slightly different schemes of training and serving slightly different audiences. For example, adventure education, outdoor education, environmental education, wilderness education, adventure recreation, and adventure therapy, have all become distinct aspects of the profession as people are taught in the outdoors and adventure is a primary or secondary part of the learning experience. Yet, the educational backgrounds of instructors in each of these areas often vary because of the need for a different skill set, knowledge, and audience. For instance, an instructor teaching a whitewater kayak class will focus on skill development involving both physical and psychological safety. This balance enables participants to effectively deal with fear while learning to read the river conditions and negotiating whitewater and other potential hazards. An instructor at an environmental learning center will use tools like a ropes course to build teamwork among the student group. Yet, their primary focus will be to use skills development and challenges such as ropes courses to help their students to be better able to study and explore nature.

Finally, an even more extensive set of skills are needed by those instructors that work with groups and individuals who have behavioral or group management issues. Whether the client be a youth with behavioral issues, a person who is physically challenged in some way, a group that has communication and conflict issues, or a myriad of other BGM-related concerns, instructors practicing in this realm often need an in-depth knowledge base of physical, human, and group-related KSAAs (Knowledge, Skills, Abilities, and Attitudes).

Comparing the different terms: outdoor education and experiential education

Before moving on to a more comprehensive discussion of adventure education, let us explore the companion fields of outdoor education and experiential education. Outdoor education is most commonly associated with the broad concept of teaching in or about the outdoors. Perhaps the best summation of this is the definition provided an elementary school teacher named L. B. Sharp (1947, p. 43) with his words, "Those things which can best be taught outdoors should there be taught." Donaldson and Donaldson added to Sharp's definition by adding that, "Outdoor education is education *in, about,* and *for* the outdoors." (1968, p. 63). Priest (1986, p.13) expanded on this definition by suggesting, "outdoor education is an experiential method of learning with the use of all senses." He outlines six primary points of outdoor education:

1   It is a method of learning.
2   It is experiential.
3   It takes places usually in the outdoors.
4   It is interdisciplinary.
5   It involves a multisensory approach to learning.
6   It is about the relationships between people and natural resources.

Gilbertson *et al.* (2006) also suggest that outdoor education takes place primarily, but not exclusively, through exposure to the natural or outdoor environments, with an emphasis often being placed on teaching about the relationships between people and the natural environment. They point out that two branches of outdoor education have emerged, environmental education and adventure education.

Gilbertson *et al.* (2006, pp. 5–6) described outdoor education as being comprised of three primary components: physical skills, interpersonal growth or educational skills, and ecological relationships. The primary method of presenting education including these components is experiential education. Adventure education, environmental education, interpretation, and ecotourism are aspects taught within outdoor education. As can be seen, according to Gilbertson's model, adventure education is closely aligned to outdoor education along three dimensions: ecological relationships, physical skills, and interpersonal or educational skills. In addition, an important component commonly associated with both outdoor adventure education (OAE) and outdoor education is the learning aspect through direct experience. It is here that experiential education comes into play.

> Experiential education is a method, a profession, and a philosophy. Philosopher and educational reformer John Dewey advocated the use of direct experience in education in his seminal book *Experience and Nature* [1938].
>
> *Gilbertson et al., 2006, pp. 9–10*

For Dewey, experiential learning is learning that occurs through an *authentic* experience. However, experiential education is more than simply having an experience in the outdoors, for in Dewey's conceptualization it must employ use of relevant learning theories and use systematic evaluation to determine their effectiveness. Thus, the role of the instructor in experiential education is to ensure that, through direct and structured experiences, the student is having a meaningful educational opportunity.

The Association for Experiential Education (AEE) defines experiential education as "a philosophy and methodology in which educators purposefully engage with learners in direct experience and focused reflection in order to increase knowledge, develop skills, and clarify values."

Building upon their definition, AEE provides a number of principles that serve to further specify the practice of experiential education. These principles include the following and in many cases are closely linked to the OAE instructional design for a broad variety of programs engaged in behavioral and group management (BGM) situations (see Gilbertson et al., 2006).

- Experiential learning occurs when carefully chosen experiences are supported by reflection, critical analysis, and synthesis.
- Experiences are structured to require the learner to take initiative, make decisions, and be accountable for results.
- Throughout the experiential learning process, the learner is actively engaged in posing questions, investigating, experimenting, being curious, solving problems, assuming responsibility, being creative, and constructing meaning.
- Learners are engaged intellectually, emotionally, socially, soulfully, and/or physically. This involvement produces a perception that the learning task is authentic.
- The results of the learning are personal and form the basis for future experience and learning.
- Relationships are developed and nurtured: learner to self, learner to others, and learner to the world at large.
- The educator and learner may experience success, failure, adventure, risk-taking, and uncertainty because the outcomes of experience cannot totally be predicted.
- Opportunities are nurtured for learners and educators to explore and examine their own values.
- The educator's primary roles include setting suitable experiences, posing problems, setting boundaries, supporting learners, insuring physical and emotional safety, and facilitating the learning process.
- The educator recognizes and encourages spontaneous opportunities for learning.
- Educators strive to be aware of their biases, judgments, and pre-conceptions, and how these influence the learner.
- The design of the learning experience includes the possibility to learn from natural consequences, mistakes and successes (Gilbertson et al., 2006).

Supporting both these definitions and the underlying principles is a long history of evolution concerning the Outdoor Adventure Education (OAE) field.

History of outdoor adventure education

Beginning with activities such as the camp movement and the development of outdoor education as a pedagogical method, there have been important connections to behavioral and group management. With the beginning in the UK of the Industrial Revolution in the 1700s, society began the transition from rural-based economies to urbanized settings. Not surprisingly, human activities and behaviors also changed. For example, types of recreation changed as a result of limited space available for recreation. Consequently, what was an everyday kind of experience – substantial levels of physical activity and access to outdoor space – evolved into a much more sedentary lifestyle often within a heavily urbanized environment with reduced opportunities for recreation in outdoor spaces. Not surprisingly, the health of urban youth began to decline, often as a result of lack of exercise and issues such as ever increasing air pollution. This was also the time when there began to appear a "disconnect" between humans and nature, particularly since increasing numbers of people were now separated from open space and activities typically done in natural settings. This disconnect continues to the present. Thus arose the beginnings of the Camp movement, with one part of this effort known as the "Fresh Air Fund" (Eells, 1986). The Fresh Air movement provided a camping experience in a northern New York state for youth living in heavily impacted urban parts of New York city and epitomized the growing belief that recreational activities done in small groups and within an outdoor setting would be effective at ameliorating many of the growing social ills of urbanized society such as youth gangs and crime,

FIGURE 2.1 A group of students find success on the summit of Mount Hood, Oregon (photo: Curt Davidson)

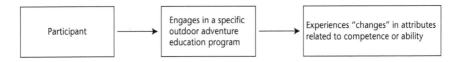

FIGURE 2.2 Underlying logic structure for outdoor adventure education

diminishing levels of health, and limited physical activity in non-polluted environments. The growth of movements such as the Fresh Air Fund provided a catalyst for the continued development of a belief that outdoor settings and structured activities could be beneficial in a number of ways for youth, and this led to the foundation of BGM programming.

It was also during this time that we saw the specific development of more formalized schools to teach physical skills but also attributes such as self-reliance, resilience, interdependence, and a sense of community through service to others. These are the very outcomes now sought out by a wide range of organizations catering to behavior and group management issues, both with individuals and groups.

The structure of many of these early programs dealing with behavioral and group management remains with us still, with programs currently operating under the belief that individuals participating in a specific program or experience can be "changed" through participation in that program. These changes then allow the person to better cope and successfully deal with other challenges in their lives. The logic underlying this structure can be seen in Figure 2.2.

This model can be further developed by calling to attention several other components that more directly relate to current societal needs such as specific behavioral and group management needs and impacts on society. This expanded model can be illustrated through Figure 2.3. In this model, we see a further specification of how BGM programs fit into a broader schema of providing for positive changes to both aspects of society (e.g. groups, communities, etc.) and the individual. Also acknowledged in this model is the intertwining of social needs and individual needs. Critical components to this model include how an OAE organization responds to the expressed individual and societal needs and how these "changes" translate into behaviors following the program or course. In turn, these new behaviors are depicted as impacting society and the individual in a variety of ways, some of which are shown in Figure 2.3.

Formalized schools in outdoor adventure education

One of the earliest programs that adhered to this expanded logic model as depicted in Figures 2.2 and 2.3 and that specifically dealt with behavioral and group management issues at both the social and individual levels (e.g. populations related to juvenile delinquents) was a program called Outward Bound. This represented the development of more formalized schools offering

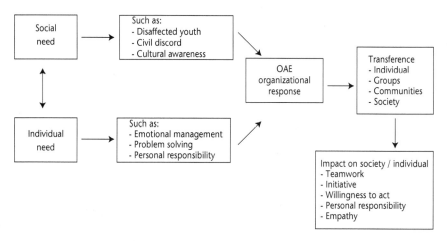

FIGURE 2.3 Expanded logic model of behavioral and group management models

adventure-based activities but for educational and personal development reasons in additional to recreational endeavors.

With the advent of World War II, the paths of three men crossed in Great Britain that led to the development of what could be argued, is the forerunner of most behavior and group management programs (BGMPs). It was a combination of the vision of Kurt Hahn, coupled with the financial expertise of Lawrence Holt and the managerial skills of Jim Hogan that turned vision into reality and led to the formation of Outward Bound (Wilson, 1981). Since its inception in Aberdovey, Wales, in 1941, as a training and educational system for strengthening an individual both physically and spiritually, Outward Bound has emerged as a leading organization in the field of Outdoor Adventure Education.

It was not until 20 years later, however, that the concept of Outward Bound (by then an institution consisting of 13 other schools throughout the world), finally reached the Western Hemisphere. Spearheaded by Charles Froelicher, the Colorado Outward Bound School emerged in 1962 with the purpose of:

> developing apparent and latent capabilities through experience, both strenuous and testing, which demand an increase of initiative, self-confidence, understanding and respect for others. Using life in the mountains as the defying force, the students are taught the importance of cooperation and self-discipline in learning to cope with the hazards and emergencies of mountain living. They become acquainted with the great rewards of difficult and sustained efforts well done, the important spiritual value of service to others and self-respect for a well-trained body.
>
> *James, 1980, pp. 8–9*

How this process actually works was described by Walsh and Golins (1976) in their description of what they called the Outward Bound Process Model.

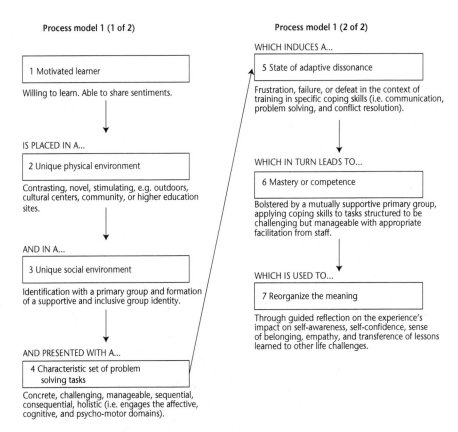

FIGURE 2.4 The Outward Bound process model

As illustrated in Figure 2.4, the model begins with learners being placed in specific and often unique natural environments in which the participants gain some specific training and are faced with a characteristic set of problem-solving tasks such as climbing a mountain, backpacking on a rugged trail, or canoeing down a white-water river. In dealing with these tasks, the participants are often faced with adaptive dissonance through the challenges and having to deal with adversity. Adaptive dissonance occurs when individuals encounter an imposing challenge toward which they have to develop and implement an effective coping mechanism. From successfully dealing with this adaptive dissonance, the individual develops a sense of mastery and competence that, through reflection and facilitation, can result in a reorganization of meaning and learning. In turn, this reorganized learning and subsequent meanings from the experience can be transferred into lessons and resultant behaviors for other life challenges.

With a descriptive motto of "to serve, to strive, and not to yield" Outward Bound in the United States and Canada has grown to include eight individual schools in North America and over 30 schools worldwide. Three years after the establishment of the first Outward Bound School in Colorado, in 1962, the National Outdoor Leadership School (NOLS) emerged, with the specific purpose of developing skilled outdoor leaders.

A broad spectrum of organizations and schools offering OAE experiences have since developed, with examples such as the Dartmouth Outing Club, Wilderness Inquiry, British Schools Exploring Society, and Duke of Edinburgh Award Scheme (see Allison *et al.*, 2011, for a description of the overseas youth expedition in the UK). Many of these programs operate under the assumption that wilderness and other natural or undeveloped landscapes offered a setting that could provide the emotional catharsis and physical challenge, which was increasingly lacking in contemporary, urbanized society. In a sense, adventure became likened to William James's "The Moral Equivalent of War" (Metcalfe, 1976, p. 5).

By the 1960s outdoor adventure activities such as backpacking and mountain climbing became accepted uses of back-country and natural environments. This usage, combined with the phenomenal growth of organizations (e.g. Association of Experiential Education in 1974; First North American Conference on Outdoor Pursuits in Higher Education in 1974) and events (Earth Day, May 1, 1970) catering to the outdoor adventure, resulted in the emergence of a new genre of recreationalists, a group which deliberately sought out the challenges and dangers often associated with the OAE.

BEHAVIORAL AND GROUP MANAGEMENT TRENDS AND ISSUES IN THE UK

Pete Allison, PhD, PennState University

This sidebar provides an overview as to current trends in the UK with regard to behavioral and group management work using outdoor and experiential learning. It is close to impossible to provide a comprehensive list of different organizations and their relation to theoretical assumptions or client groups. Instead this section highlights some differences between USA and UK practices and trends and directs the reader to several sources which may be of interest.

Introduction

Behavioral and group management using outdoor experiential learning in the UK structurally differs from the USA in the way it is funded and experienced by young people and is also influenced by the topography and relatively large population on a small land mass.

Funding for young people "at risk," which remains the dominant term, is directed from the governments primarily through youth work funding. For example, funding is directed towards young people aged 16–25 who are categorized as "Not in Employment, Education or Training" (NEET). Recent figures (2016) from the government indicate 12 percent (865,000) of all young people in this age category are NEET (http://researchbriefings.parliament.uk/ResearchBriefing/Summary/SN06705).

Against this backdrop it is not surprising that there are multiple initiatives that are broadly concerned with increasing the life opportunities for these groups which are often associated with poverty and lower class areas of communities (both urban and rural). It is also worth noting that there is a contrast here with the USA in that the focus in the UK is a social one – the issues are seen as social, not individual – problems or challenges for society to address. Thus, they are not normally seen as medical problems or issues to be addressed or funded by the National Health Service (NHS) or private health care providers.

The following two examples are used to highlight two different organizations that are large and leading practice in youth work. There are several other organizations listed at the end of the chapter which readers may be interested to learn about but space does not permit providing more details here.

The Prince's Trust

One example of an organization that works with young people who are disadvantaged is the Prince's Trust. A charity (equivalent of 501(C) 3 status in USA) started in 1976 by Prince Charles. The charity is primarily a youthwork organization which aims to develop confidence, motivation, and skills to allow people to gain greater control of their lives. The charity has eight main types of activity, of which two are particularly relevant to this book:

1   The Team programme is a 12-week personal development course, offering work experience, practical skills, community projects, and a residential week.
2   The Fairbridge programme is an individually tailored personal development programme for young people. It combines one-to-one support and group activities, delivered at Prince's Trust centres. The course starts with a five-day residential experience undertaking outdoor activities.

Both of these programmes involve outdoor activities which are seen to be part of a bigger programme of change. The second one features much individualized support to assist young people to think about their options and the passions that they have and then support them to take steps toward achieving those goals through courses, skill development, job applications, and hopefully ending with employment.

Staff who work on these courses are typically youth workers who have subsequently developed their outdoor skills to be able to lead outdoor activities as a medium for development, rather than outdoor instructors who have "turned their hand" to youth work.

Research and evaluation on the work of the Prince's Trust vary because of the diversity of people undertaking the programmes. Some people have offended and the focus of the programme is to reintegrate them into society while other programmes are earlier interventions with people who are considered to be "at risk" of offending in the future. In 2014 Arthur (p. iii) found that participation in the Prince's Trust Fairbridge programme "can potentially provide the starting block for positive change in the lives of participants" and reduce recidivism by

- acting as a catalyst for change in the lives of offenders;
- significantly improving confidence, listening and communication skills, tolerance, levels of self-expression, ability to cope with stress;
- enhancing participants' levels of engagement with further education and training;
- positively impacting on the emotional well-being of the participants;
- being responsive to the particular needs of participants.

Duke of Edinburgh Award

The Duke of Edinburgh Award (DofE) was founded by Kurt Hahn in 1956 as a badge scheme primarily focused at addressing five decays in society (Hahn, 1958, p. 4):

1   The decay of fitness due to our modern methods of locomotion.
2   The decay of self-discipline helped by stimulants and tranquilizers.
3   The decay of enterprise due to the widespread disease of *spectatoritis*.
4   The decay of skill and care helped by the decline in craftsmanship.
5   Above all the decay of compassion which [Archbishop] William Temple called spiritual death.

He believed in four pillars that could address these decays which remain today as the primary components of the awards:

1   Volunteering
2   Service
3   Physical activity
4   Expedition

The award has three levels (Bronze, Silver, and Gold), with the final award also requiring a residential experience. Outside the UK the scheme is known as the 'International Award' (available in the USA: www.intaward.org/united-states-of-america). Today 300,000 young people in the UK (one in eight of those aged between 15 and 16 years are undertaking a DofE programme) and 850,000 young people globally in over 140 countries are involved in the award. Since the start in 1956 over 8 million people have participated in the award.

Historically, the award was often criticized for being primarily focused on white upper middle class young people (Hunt, 1990), but this has changed and the award now involves all parts of society irrespective of class, colour, religion, or sex. For example, there are award groups in schools, youth groups, prisons, engineering organizations (apprentice schemes), and many more. The DofE heavily relies on volunteers throughout society, which is considered a strength in drawing together communities around a common positive cause.

Discussion

I have described two organizations which take different approaches to youth work in the UK, using some outdoor experiential education. Many organizations could have been detailed here but I selected two that are national and that take differing perspectives on similar issues. They are similar in that they both see behavioural issues as essentially a problem to be addressed by society. The former relies heavily on taxpayer's money while the latter receives very little and relies heavily on fundraising activities and volunteers.

What is not evident here is the success measures of such programs. While some research has been undertaken, the evidence is best characterized as isolated (e.g. Campbell et al., 2009) and often superficial. Much debate is possible on what are appropriate measures and methods to assess outcomes, given the complexity of the problems the programs are attempting to address. The Prince's Trust is primarily focused at a harder to reach population while the Duke of Edinburgh award takes an enrichment model and works with all young people to help them to gain greater control of their lives regardless of socio-economic status.

Perhaps one of the biggest challenges to be addressed is that the conceptualization of NEET (detailed above) has what might be charitably understood as an unintended consequence in that it provides what Roberts (2011) refers to as a 'tidy pathway' but creates a 'missing middle' of young people who are in employment, education, or training but do not benefit from youth work funding. The binary which NEET categorization inevitably creates does not necessarily reflect the needs of young people who are experiencing transitions from youth to adulthood and often rapidly changing circumstances.

One aspect of practice that is not evident in the UK is Wilderness Therapy. One organization (Venture Trust) is the closest to the USA practices. The reasons for the lack of Wilderness Therapy in the UK are multi-factorial but include the conceptualization of the challenges (social rather than psychological), the absence of the wilderness that is found on larger land masses, and the slow change from historical social stigma associated with therapy in UK society.

Theoretically much of the outdoor experiential education practice in the UK with young people considered to be "at risk" relies on experiential learning cycles and some psychology theories such as cognitive behavioural theory (CBT), growth mind set (Carol Dweck), and concepts such as risk and resilience. These concepts have come under some critique – for example, Foster and Spencer (2011) found that risk and resilience were inappropriate ways to understand young people's lives and suggested that narrative might be a more humane and fruitful conceptualization for both theory and practice.

As might be expected, there is a mixture of practices and many of the outdoor youth work organizations focus on the outdoor component of their work. The balance of practices in different organizations varies – how much indoor/outdoor work they do, how experiential or otherwise, how related to state education. There has also been some discussion of the value of risk in such practices; for example, Nichols (1999, p. 101) questioned the use of risk with young people who "already face a disproportionate amount of risk in their lives."

There are many organizations in the UK involved in youth work in some way or another. The following list provides a starting point for readers to find further information (a great deal is available on the internet). Inclusion or otherwise in this list is not an endorsement in any way but rather intended to provide some initial pointers to practices in the UK.

- Brathay Hall
- British Exploring Society (Dangoor Next Generation Programme)
- Catch 22
- National Citizenship Service
- Ocean Youth Trust
- Outward Bound (particularly the Skills for Life courses)
- UK Youth
- Venture Trust
- Youthlink NI
- Youthlink Scotland

Acknowledgment

This section was supported by the GACR project Models of bodily experience in the theoretical foundations of experiential education and its kinanthropological context (GAČR 16-19311S).

FIGURE 2.5 OAE students after the successful completion of their course (photo: Pete Allison)

The connection between adventure and behavioral and group management

We have examined how Outdoor Adventure Education (OAE) developed from something done for recreational purposes to an approach that typically focuses on issues related to health and wellbeing, personal growth, or activities and experiences with therapeutic intent. This diversity of purpose has both programmatic and theoretical implications. For example, according to Ewert and Wu (2007), adventure experiences typically conducted through education or therapeutic-based organizations such as schools, universities, or international organizations such as the National Outdoor Leadership School (NOLS) or Outward Bound (OB), often include structured activities such as group initiatives or similar activities that promote teambuilding, trust, personal growth and development, and the development of individual decision-making and judgment, and can be thought of as Educational Adventure Program or EAP. On the other hand, experiences that tend to be more recreational and/or involve the process of providing services, assistance, or information (e.g. training, equipment, food, route information, and guiding) are often referred to as Guided Trips (GTs). (See Figure 2.6.) The history of OAE has been built through both of these types of programs and how an individual views adventure education often depends on whether they are part of an educational adventure program or a guided trip. Moreover, from the perspective of behavioral and group management, different "types" of programs often result in different types of outcomes, some of which are appropriate for behavior and group management, some of which are less so. Many of the differences between EAPs and GTs are illustrated in Table 2.2.

TABLE 2.2 Comparison of GTs and EAPs

Issues	Guided Trips (GT)	Educational Adventure Programs (EAP)
Programming issues		
Goals/objectives	Delivery of quality experience	Facilitation of learning experience
Focus of program	Outcome	Process
Motivation	Outcome	Process
Locus of decision-making	Guide	Instructor → student
Judgment	Mountain sense (intuition)	Linear process
Risk	Higher	Structured
Clientele	Exclusive/affluent thrill seekers	More inclusive
Leadership composition	Lone, independent	Instructor team
Group size	Small	Medium
Environmental impact	Considerable (i.e. expedition guiding)	Small
Environmental ethics	Minimum impact	LNT
Types of the activities	Diverse	Diverse
Locale	International/national/local	Local/national
Access to natural resources	Permit/concession	Permit
Programming evaluation	Informal	Formal
Professional Issues		
Leadership training	Implicit/apprentice	Explicit/leadership curriculum
Technical training	Advanced	Intermediate
First aid/SAR training	WFR	WFR
Internal regulation (certification)	AMGA, IFMGA	WEA
(accreditation)	UIAGM, AMGA	AEE
External regulation	Laws and regulation	Laws and regulation
Governing body	Often internal regulation plus land management agency	Often only land management agency
Conference		AEE, WEA, ICORE
Research/publication	Rare	JEE, etc.
Industry	Tourism (adventure tourism)	Education
Market outlook	Increasing	Increasing

continued…

Table 2.2 continued…

Issues	Guided Trips (GT)	Educational Adventure Programs (EAP)
Individual issues		
Driving force	Love for the outdoors/a way of life	Love for the outdoors/ change agent
Career development/ advancement	Equipment design, development, and testing, consultant, lecturer, writer, film maker/assistant	Program director
Job season	Seasonal "the circuit"	Seasonal
Turnover ratio	High	High
Benefits/salary	Minimal	Minimal
Role of leader	"Choreographer of social experience"	Facilitator of learning experience
Client/student expectations	Pressure from clients to reach summit	Expectation from students for high-quality learning experience

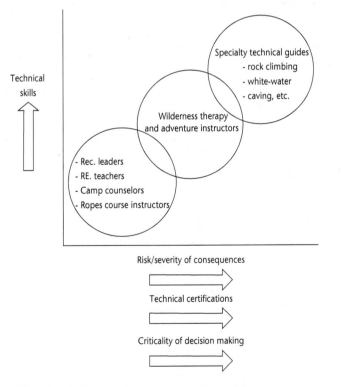

FIGURE 2.6 Evolving differences in types of OAE practitioners

Beyond whether an individual is on an EAP, a GT, or simply out with a group of friends, family, or by themselves, what is the connection between an adventure experience and behavior and group management? For example, some evidence currently exists that suggests that participation in an OAE experience can improve both attitudes and behaviors at the workplace and that these changes can be seen by fellow workers (Rhodes and Martin, 2014). It seems clear that there are multidimensional aspects to this question and that adventure serves a number of roles in contemporary society. Moreover, although there is much overlap, these roles can often be clustered into the categories of learning physical skills, experiencing challenging landscapes, testing one's self, or being part of a team or group of people engaged in a common purpose. What then are some of the impacts for individuals and groups as a result of participating in an OAE program?

Impact of outdoor adventure education programs

There exists a substantial literature concerning the positive impacts that OAE programs can have on both groups and individuals. For example, in their landmark study of the impacts of out-of-class experiences such as Outward Bound, Hattie and colleagues (1997) found at least 40 distinctive outcomes. Ewert and Sibthorp (2014, pp. 127–8) categorized outcomes from OAE experiences as Interpersonal (or how a person acts) and Intrapersonal (individual and developmental types of outcomes). Specific examples can be seen in Table 2.3. Outcomes commonly associated with behavioral and group management situations included cooperation, interpersonal communication, social competence, behavior, relating skills, and recidivism. Other outcomes that could be added to this list include emotional maturity (Hayashi and Ewert,

TABLE 2.3   Interpersonal and intrapersonal outcomes

Interpersonal	*Intrapersonal*
Group outcomes • cohesion • sense of community • collective efficacy	Self-systems • concept • efficacy • confidence • awareness • motivation
Leadership	Skill building • problem-solving
Group functioning	Attitude
Behaviors	Leadership
Communication	
Organization	
Tolerance	

2006), effective leadership (Palmer *et al.*, 2001), social cohesion (Rogers *et al.*, 2016), and aspects of group development (Ewert and Heywood, 1991).

Similarly, Bunyan (2011) developed the dynamic adventure model in which selected characteristics of what he terms an "adventure environment" can combine to create a Dynamic Development Climate, which in turn leads to personal growth and development. The characteristics described in the Bunyan model include overcoming fear, having a supportive group, leadership, physical exercise, and having a natural environment as the setting. See Figure 2.7.

Using natural environments as the setting for OAE programs has a long history, with early programs featuring OAE activities, such as the Boy and Girl Scouts, Girl Guides, the Gunnery School for Boys, and the Duke of Edinburgh Award Scheme, all drawing heavily on natural landscapes as vehicles to help facilitate the achievement of program goals and aspirations. Brownlee (2015) refers to these natural settings as "platforms for adventure activities" and in this case emphasizes the role that parks and protected lands play in adventure experiences.

A number of scholars have proposed that a major factor in the efficacy of BGM programs is simply being in contact with the natural environment itself (Bardwell, 1992; Mitten, 1994). A number of theories provide explanations on how this contact with nature provides benefits in various adventure-based activities and experiences. Two of the more salient theories include the Psychoevolutionary Theory (PET) and the Attention Restoration Theory (ART). The assumption underlying these theories and BGM programs is that simply being exposed to the natural environment (e.g. wilderness) will result in positive changes. As such, the natural setting serves as a somewhat passive connection in PET and ART.

Expanding on this concept has been the suggestion that structured programs or activities work to "focus the power" of nature, and that highlighting this relationship could work to further enhance health-related outcomes (Mitten,

Possible ingredients of adventure

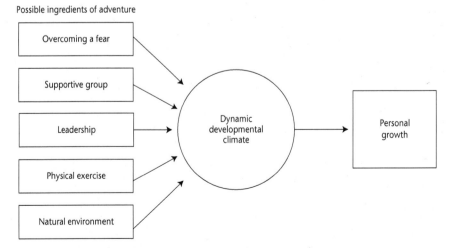

FIGURE 2.7 The dynamic adventure environment model

2009). Termed Intentionally Designed Experiences (IDEs), these specially designed activities can enhance the beneficial aspects of contact with nature (Sheard and Golby, 2006). Moreover, the idea of IDEs is that programming in the natural environment can, and should be, purposeful in its planning and implementation in order to achieve specific benefits. In this way, specifically designed experiences and programs conducted in outdoor natural environments provide a synergistic effect that enhances the impact of each one (setting and program). Figure 2.8 illustrates how these different components fit together.

As can be seen in Figure 2.8, and relative to outcomes commonly associated with BGM programs conducted in natural settings, the type of benefits resulting from participation in an IDE can be separated into two orders or levels. First order benefits can be considered major outcome variables (often personal growth related) that occur from participation in an IDE and include achievement, restoration, empowerment, and resilience. Second order benefits emerge from the occurrence of these first order outcome variables and include

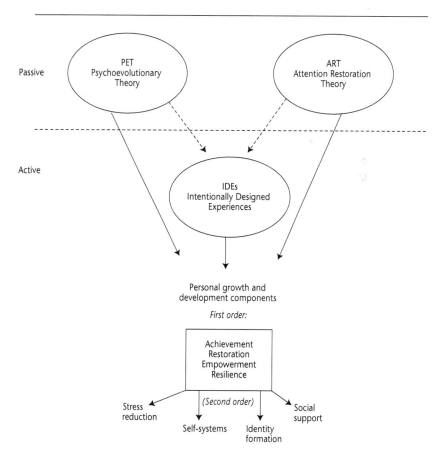

FIGURE 2.8 Intentionally Designed Experiences and personal development outcomes

benefits related to self-systems (e.g. esteem, concept, awareness, and personal efficacy), stress reduction, identity formation, and social support.

The idea of the IDE posits that the purpose, type, and specifics of the program, as well as the type of clients, all influence the outcome. The IDE is an active mechanism that, depending on its design, incorporates many of the theoretical underpinnings of the human–nature benefit interaction involving constructs such as ART and PET into a program or experience that ultimately contributes to health and/or quality of life.

Ecological systems thinking and BGM

Many, if not most, BGM programs using adventure-based activities typically occur in natural and outdoor settings. In addition, we discussed the synergistic role that both setting and activity play when combined in a purposeful way to facilitate specific outcomes. Outcomes within a BGM context can be thought of as multidimensional and varied. Moreover, they can be categorized in individual-based and other-based. Table 2.4 provides an overview of a sample of these specific BGM-related outcomes. Clearly, there is overlap between those outcomes that are primarily applicable to the individual and those that have primary meaning for the group. In addition, Table 2.4 only represents a sample of the many possible outcomes that can be achieved from a BGM-related course.

Outcomes are influenced by a multitude of both internal and external variables. For example, internal variables include those factors that are directly related to the individual or structure of the program. Examples of these internal variables would include personality, past experiences, attitudes, and other intrinsically located factors. Other internal factors that are related to the structure of the program include instructors, programmatic activities, curriculum, and mechanics such as food, sleeping accommodations, etc. Consider that a specific BGM program or course may consist of a number of segments, often based on

TABLE 2.4 Specific outcomes related to BGM programs

Individual-based	Other-based
Spiritual	Social competence
Emotional	Communication
Intellectual	Social awareness
Physical	Group emotional
Compassion	Intelligence
Resilience	Teamwork
Self-regulation	Group achievements
Sense of achievement	Social intelligence

the major type of activities being engaged in, such as rock climbing, rafting, solo, final expedition, or backpacking. These segments can last for one to a number of days. Moreover, each segment can also be divided into sessions, days, or discrete events. For example, rock climbing on day 1 might consist of belay practice, rope management, and nomenclature. Day 2 might require anchor building, basic climbing moves, and beginning top rope climbing, and so on. The point is that each segment is nested into a larger course format and can be divided up into specific days, events, or specific activities. The interactions of the individual in these various segments and specific events can be crucial to BGM types of issues and situations. Not surprisingly, these nested characteristics add to the inherent complexity often associated with BGM courses or experiences that have a BGM issue. An example of a hypothetical BGM course with nested components can be seen in Figure 2.9.

External variables refer to those factors and events that are often beyond the control of the program and/or staff and include obvious issues such as weather, unplanned or unexpected events, and conflicts in the group. Other external factors that can alter a course or its outcomes can involve interaction with other groups, or medical or other issues such as logistical challenges (e.g. resupply is late).

These variables collectively serve to influence the outcomes experienced by individual participants and are often thought of as "confounding" the outcomes of a program (Heppner *et al.*, 2007). That is, these confounding variables complicate the picture in ascertaining what actually caused the outcomes that were observed. In addition, the outcomes ascribed to a specific program or

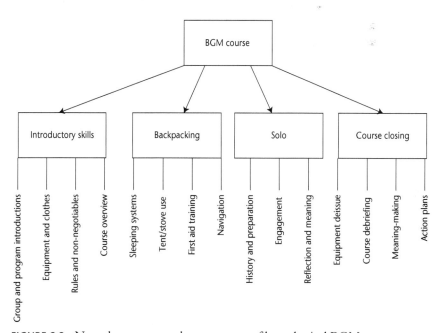

FIGURE 2.9 Nested segments and components of hypothetical BGM course

experiences consist of two types: expected and actual. While often overlapping and congruent, the numerous characteristics and variables illustrated in Figure 2.10 provide an example of the many components of the ecology of the BGM and OAE situations. For example, inclement weather may be a particular challenge to an individual with a specific type of personality or background. Likewise, programs may be limited in their ability to deal with a challenging weather situation (e.g. sleeping bags are too "lightweight"). There may be a medical emergency that alters the conduct of the course or changes the tone of the experience. Despite these issues, just completing the course may provide a sense of achievement to the individual which results in feelings of empowerment, an enhanced level of resilience, or sense of rejuvenation.

Thus, the ecology of a BGM/OAE program is multifaceted, often somewhat indeterminate, and subject to a variety of influences from multiple sources. Successful BGM programs often have built up a history of dealing with a broad spectrum of issues and events, from which they often have the ability to identify a correct course of action which results in the student achieving a set of desirable

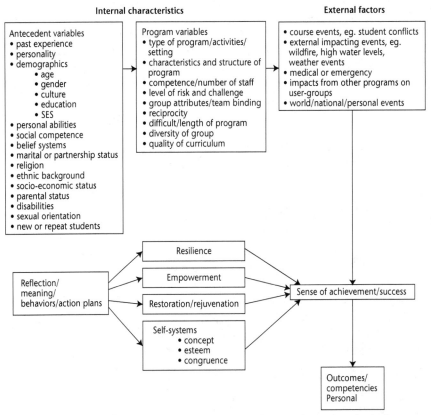

FIGURE 2.10 Nested segments and components of a hypothetical ecological system in OAE

outcomes from the experience. Related to this history is the presence of highly trained and experienced staff who have the ability to successfully deal with unexpected situations while still achieving the program's and student's stated or desired goals and outcomes.

Conclusion

In this chapter, we have explored the history of OAE programming as well as the impacts of OAE programs upon individuals and groups. We continued this exploration by looking at some of the process models that have served to shape how specific programs are designed and structured. In addition, we examined the issue of program outcomes and how these outcomes can be influenced by the ecology of the experience. That is, the numerous variables that can influence both a program and the participants in adverse and positive ways. In subsequent chapters we will go into greater detail regarding the underlying theories, processes, and techniques useful for the BGM situation in OAE settings.

Main points

- Since their inception, central to many Outdoor Adventure Education (OAE) programs has been dealing with participants who have behavioral and group management (BGM) issues.
- In support of the popularity of OAE activities and subsequent programs is the growth of recreational endeavors that can be categorized as adventure-based activities, both in North America and globally. This increased involvement by the public has resulted in broadened support for the outdoor environmental resources including wilderness areas, land acquisition for parks and forests, and the acceptance of adventure activities, such as rock climbing, as legitimate leisure pursuits.
- There is a broad rubric of terms that deal with activities often done in the outdoors, such as outdoor education, experiential education, and adventure education.
- The history of OAE includes an awareness of the importance of outdoor and natural environments for both physical and emotional health.
- Outward Bound developed in 1941, and became one of the foremost outdoor adventure programs, with schools spread across the globe. From this type of educational approach, emerged the Outward Bound Process Model.
- Outdoor Adventure Education programs can often be categorized into Guided Trips (GT) and Educational Adventure Programs (EAP). Each plays an important role in providing an adventure experience for individuals and groups. Moreover, there is an ongoing need for leaders and instructors in the area of OAE.
- With the inception of Outward Bound and the National Outdoor Leadership School, the training of leaders for adventure-based programming assumed

greater importance in the recreational and educational systems of a large number of countries, including the United States, Canada, Great Britain, Australia, and New Zealand.

• Numerous beneficial outcomes have been documented from participation in OAE programs, many of which can be specific to BGM types of courses. These outcomes are often influenced by a broad array of internal and external variables and factors such as personality of the individual participant, group dynamics, and weather.

Discussion questions

1   Adventure has often been thought of as a recreational pursuit but is this a good disciplinary frame for it? Are there more appropriate academic disciplines from which to base the study of adventure?

2   The "Golden Age of Mountaineering" in the 1700s and 1800s was partially responsible for ushering in the importance of adventure as an end in itself. That is, adventuring could result in intrinsically meaningful outcomes. What do you think are some outcomes that you have seen or experienced yourself from engaging in an adventure activity or program? Are these outcomes always positive?

3   Are there some specific OAE activities such as rock climbing that are particularly relevant to behavioral and group management issues? How do you think an OAE course specifically focused on BGM issues would differ from other OAE programs?

References

Allison, P., Stott, T., Felter, J., and Beames, S. (2011). Overseas youth expeditions. In M. Berry and C. Hodgson (eds), *Adventure Education: An Introduction* (pp. 187–205). London: Routledge.

Arthur, R. (2014). *Evaluation of Prince's Trust Fairbridge Programme – Holme House Prison Project*. Middlesbrough: Teeside University, Social Futures Institute.

Bardwell, L. (1992). A bigger piece of the puzzle: The restorative experience and outdoor education. Paper presented at the Coalition for Education in the Outdoors, *Research Symposium Proceedings* (pp. 15–20), Bradford Woods, IN, January 17–19.

Bell, S., Tyrväinen, L., Sievänen, T., Pröbstl, U., and Simpson, M. (2007). Outdoor recreation and nature tourism: A European perspective. *Living Reviews in Landscape Research*, 1, 1–46.

Brownlee, M. (2015). Parks and protected areas: A platform for adventure activities. In R. Black and K. Bricker (eds), *Adventure Programming and Travel for the 21st Century* (pp. 53–67). State College, PA: Venture Publishing.

Bunyan, P. (2011). Models and milestones in Adventure Education. In M. Berry and C. Hodgson (eds), *Adventure Education: An Introduction* (pp. 5–23). London: Routledge.

Campbell, J., Bell, V., Armstrong, S. C., Horton, J., Mansukhani, N., Matthews, M. H., and Pilkington, A. (2009). The impact of the Duke of Edinburgh's Award on young people. (Unpublished) http://nectar.northampton.ac.uk/2447.

Donaldson, G. W., and Donaldson, L. E. (1968). *Outdoor Education: A book of Readings.* Minneapolis, MN: Burgess.

Eells, E. (1986). *A History of Organized Camping: The First 100 Years.* Martinsville, IN: American Camping Association.

Ewert, A., and Heywood, J. (1991). Group development in the natural environment: Expectations, outcomes, and techniques. *Environment and Behavior,* 23(5), 592–615.

Ewert, A., and Sibthorp, J. (2014). *Outdoor Adventure Education: Foundations, Theory, and Research.* Champaign, IL: Human Kinetics.

Ewert, A., and Wu, G.-J. (2007). Two faces of outdoor adventure leadership: Educational adventure programs and guided trips. *Journal of Wilderness Education Association,* 18(1), 12–18.

Foster, K. R., and Spencer, D. (2011). At risk of what? Possibilities over probabilities in the study of young lives. *Journal of Youth Studies,* 14(1), 125–143.

Gilbertson, K., Bates, T., McLaughlin, T., and Ewert, A. (2006). *Outdoor Education: Methods and Strategies.* Champaign, IL: Human Kinetics.

Hahn, K. (1958). Address at the forty-eighth annual dinner of the old centralians, London. *The Central: The Journal of Old Centralians*, 119, 3–8. Retrieved 16 September 2016, from www.KurtHahn.org/writings/writings.html.

Hattie, J., Marsh, H., Neill, J., and Richards, G. (1997). Adventure education and Outward Bound: Out-of-class experiences that make a lasting difference. *Review of Educational Research*, 67(1), 43–87.

Hayashi, A., and Ewert, A. (2006). Outdoor leaders' emotional intelligence and transformational leadership. *Journal of Experiential Education,* 28(3), 222–242.

Heppner, P., Wampold, B., and Kivlighan Jr., D. (2007). *Research Design in Counselling.* Boston, MA: Cengage Learning.

Hunt, J. (1990). *In Search of Adventure.* Guildford: Talbot Adair Press.

James, T. (1980). *Education at the Edge.* Denver, CO: Colorado Outward Bound.

Metcalfe, J. (1976). *Adventure Programming.* Austin, TX: National Educational Laboratory Publishing.

Metsähallitus (2006). Institutional homepage. http://metsa.fi.

Mitten, D. (1994). Ethical considerations in adventure therapy: A feminist critique. In E. Cole, E. Erdman, and E. Rothblum (eds), *Wilderness Therapy for Women: The Power of Adventure* (pp. 55–84). New York: Harrington Press.

Mitten, D. (2009). Under our noses: The healing power of nature. *Taproot Journal,* 19(1), 20–26.

Nichols, G. (1999). Is risk a valuable component of outdoor adventure programmes for young offenders undergoing drug rehabilitation? *Journal of Youth Studies,* 2(1), 101–115.

Palmer, B., Walls, M., Burgess, Z., and Stough, C. (2001). Emotional intelligence and effective leadership. *Leadership and Organization Development Journal,* 22(1), 5–10.

Pouta, E., Sievänen, T., and Heikkilä, M. (2000). National outdoor recreation demand and supply in Finland: An assessment project. *Forestry,* 73(2), 103–105.

Priest, S. (1986). Redefining outdoor education: A matter of many relationships. *Journal of Environmental Education,* 17(3), 13–15.

Rhodes, H. M., and Martin, A. J. (2014). Behavior change after adventure education courses: Do work colleagues notice? *Journal of Experiential Education,* 37(3), 265–284.

Roberts, S. (2011). Beyond "NEET" and "tidy" pathways: Considering the "missing middle" of youth transition studies. *Journal of Youth Studies,* 14(1), 21–39.

Rogers, S. D., Loy, D., and Brown-Bochicchio, C. (2016). Sharing a new foxhole with friends: The impact of outdoor recreation on injured military. *Therapeutic Recreation Journal*, 50(3), 213–227.

Sharp, L. B. (1947). Basic considerations in outdoor and camping education. *The Bulletin of the National Association of Secondary-School Principals,* 31(147), 43–48, The Department of Secondary Education of the National Education Association, Washington, D.C.

Sheard, M., and Golby, J. (2006). The efficacy of an outdoor adventure education curriculum on selected aspects of positive psychological development. *Journal of Experiential Education,* 29(2), 187–209.

Walsh, V., and Golins, G. (1976). *The Exploration of the Outward Bound Process.* Denver, CO: Colorado Outward Bound School.

Wilson, R. (1981). *Inside Outward Bound.* Charlotte, NC: East Woods Press.

3

THERAPEUTIC CONSIDERATIONS IN BEHAVIOR AND GROUP MANAGEMENT

Overview

Successful management of groups in an outdoor adventure context remains a critical component of safe and effective programs. As is the case with outdoor adventure activities, there lie many important areas related to managing or facilitating groups, with the obvious factor of risk taken into consideration. But in addition to risk management, there are the underlying components of theory-based programming, to further validate and clarify what we do. This chapter discusses the management of groups from the perspectives of human behavior, communication, and behavioral change that is based on two significant theories: *behavioristic theory* and the *cognitive behavioral change process*. Both theories provide a strong foundation for better understanding the significance of human behavior, how it can be changed relative to facilitated outdoor adventure experiences, and how theory-based programming can aid in the successful fulfillment of program goals. Several scenarios are also presented throughout the chapter to better illustrate these points.

(Almost) every outdoor leader wants to be regarded as a successful, competent, and well-liked person. But most of these leadership qualities must come with the background, experience, and effort to accomplish this status. A leader may be highly trained at outdoor activities, from setting up a belay system, or repel site, to canoeing on white water, but the management of a group, where positive outcomes are the goal and valuable experiences are learned, requires much more than just being extremely skilled.

Anyone leading a group of persons, whether it is two or twenty, in an outdoor pursuit or program is responsible for those persons. More specifically, that leader is responsible for the "management" of his or her group. While the term management may sound contrived, or even somewhat negative (e.g. "handling" people), it is a critical component of a leader's success in moving the group towards its goals. In particular, managing a group sometimes involves a delicate "dance" between a group's behavior, or actions, and how the leader reacts to this behavior, and/or directs the behavior. In turn, a group's behavior is often the best form of communication for a leader, whether overt, spoken, or tacit.

Behavior is communication

The *behavior* of individuals in a group is a clear example, or one method, of communication. Anyone who has led a group of participants, where despite their best efforts the group simply did not "gel" or become a cohesively functioning group, understands this. The clients of the group are clearly communicating something, whether it's as minor as disliking the food choices, to more complex displays such as disruptive, oppositional, moody, or even dangerous behavioral signals. Moreover, while it may not always be feasible to change the functionality or management of a group into a highly dynamic and productive one, understanding what lies *behind* dysfunctional behavior, and managing that behavior, is critical in meeting program outcomes (Voight and Ewert, 2015).

Management of a group of persons is an interplay between the group's objectives and goals, and the personal dynamics of the participants' individual behavioral characteristics. Often, participant behavior can be one of the single most important factors linked to the attainment – or prevention – of both individual and program goals. How program goals are established is most often reflected in the specific nature or philosophy of services offered at an agency. Programs in outdoor education can be depicted based on four or five program "types," or broad categories represented along a continuum (see Figure 3.1), from "Recreation" to "Primary Therapy" (Gass et al., 2012; Gillis, 1992).

As can be seen from Figure 3.1, goals can range from a recreation-based focus to more stringent objectives in a primary therapy-type of program in certain settings (e.g. Wilderness Therapy). Education has been added to this continuum, as an additional program type (see Gass et al., 2012), most closely aligned with after-school programs, or other social skills programs such as special education using adventure education or therapy as a main focus. The behavioral

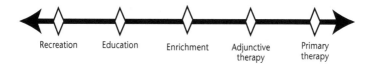

Recreation　　Education　　Enrichment　　Adjunctive　　Primary
　　　　　　　　　　　　　　　　　therapy　　　therapy

FIGURE 3.1 Outdoor adventure types of programs and services along a continuum

management of clients will directly correlate to the program's staff and their educational credentials, expertise, the activities engaged in, and the ultimate goals of the program as dictated by the "type" of program previously indicated. As an additional note of clarity in this chapter, individuals participating in outdoor adventure or education programs are referred to as clients, participants, or students, in a general sense, and are used interchangeably.

Group management

The majority of outdoor recreation and outdoor education programs, for the past several decades, facilitate learning outcomes and program goals using the "group process" (Walsh and Gollins, 1976). The group process allows for multi-level learning opportunities, including dyads, triads, etc., and, as is often the case, groups of four or more participants. Groups can provide for unique interactions among the members, as well as unique challenges to a leader (Shank and Coyle, 2002). But when teaching groups of persons outside of a traditional learning environment, such as a classroom versus a remote wilderness area, varied and differing management techniques become of paramount importance.

Critical to effective management is having a sound understanding of the motivation behind the underlying behavior of your participants. A leader who can interpret a participant's behavior, beyond the overt manifestation of the behavior, can better manage it and (re)direct it (as deemed necessary) toward the most efficacious and successful outcomes of an activity, not only for an individual participant's sake, but also for that of the group (Gilbertson *et al.*, 2006; Voight and Ewert, 2015). For instance, the following scenario exemplifies this argument.

An outdoor leader confronted with a very oppositional client may think, "I know that my client has trouble in school because of a learning disability, and this outdoor adventure activity is challenging the client in ways that are very frustrating for him/her. So the lashing out and disruptive behavior is coming from a place of deep, unresolved anxiety for my client. I understand the reason for the behavior, and I need to redirect my client to a challenge that is more manageable for my client; and ultimately will provide a sense of accomplishment for him/her."

This understanding, or being able to "read" an individual or group, as some might say, can come from several sources. Certain outdoor leaders may regard personal intuition as a primary method for understanding and managing groups, while others may indicate that years of experience account for the best source of "interpreting" and managing group behavior. While these may all be true, an additional, and perhaps even more important method or source of interpreting individual client behavior, would be understanding the *theoretical* attributes which underlie human behavior.

WORKING WITH SPECIAL POPULATIONS IN TAIWAN

Chun-Chieh Wang, PhD, National Taiwan Sport University, Taiwan

Highly valuing Confucianism, Taiwan attaches great importance to education. Each level of the social construct such as governments, institutions, communities, schools, and families is devoted to education; unfortunately, the educational system emphasizes academic performance which often needs to be achieved by rote learning. Rote learning refers to learning by memorizing things without full comprehension. Students use the skill to score high rather than taking the time to internalize what they have learned from school. This pattern has been adopted as a major learning approach in school compared to experiential education (EE), which has been applied for troubled youths in Taiwan. For the past ten years, EE programs have been utilized to work with youth at risk and to deal with personal issues such as self-centeredness, emotion management, dropping out from school, or substance abuse problems. From the decade-long experience, Taiwan has developed three types of EE programs:

1   Day program. This one-day program usually consists of one-day-per-week group sessions and lasts for at least three weeks. Programs depend mostly on applications of activities such as cooperative games, challenge courses, hiking, and rock climbing. These types of activities are for program providers who would like to develop their students' trust, communication, and cooperation through various conditions where their mental, social, and physical skills are challenged.
2   Short-term residential program. Primarily, this program refers to educational sections taking place in camps. The length of this kind of program is usually between two and nine days, including multi-day trips for activities like cycling or backpacking. Since people will stay together for days, instructors usually focus on using group processes to see how these youth function and work together as a group.

3   Long-term residential program. These programs usually run more than nine days and include multi-activities or multiple-day activities. Considering the potential risk of certain adventure activities, a specified level of skill learning or training is required for the participants in advance of their participation in the program. In addition, of great importance is the relationship between the students and instructors. Often, this connectedness between group members and leaders develops through time. The relationship makes it possible for subjects to feel the care from the instructors, sense the alliance among the group, and learn the modeling from the leaders.

Usually, in Taiwan, the EE programs with special populations are conducted by outdoor adventure specialists, often in conjunction with a counseling psychologist or social worker. Most of these programs are funded through non-profit organizations such as City People Foundation. The City People Foundation has two programs: one is Symbiosis camp program for youth at risk; another one is Sunflower program for girls who have been sexually assaulted.

Symbiosis camp program is a summer camp, which began in 2004. They work with counseling offices at high schools and target high-risk adolescents. In these programs, adolescents participate in adventure activities such as rock climbing, kayaking, cycling, and mountaineering. The program is designed to last up to 28 days and focuses on helping with issues related to self-efficacy, self-concept, social adjustment, and communication.

The Sunflower program is a long-term residential program with underage girls who are victims of sexual assault. In the summer of 2014, the program started by building kayaks and then training these girls to sea kayak around Taiwan Island over a period of 60 days. Through the 720-mile trip, these girls were challenged to build up their confidence and prepare themselves for their later lives.

As more and more organizations began to use Outdoor Adventure Education techniques and experiences, outdoor adventure professionals in Taiwan founded the Asia Association for Experiential Education (AAEE) in 2006. It is the largest EE organization in Asia and helps address educational needs among Chinese societies such as Mainland China, Hong Kong, and Macao. AAEE is a platform for people who view EE as core value to connect with and communicate to others. AAEE in Taiwan will continue to develop in the field of Experience Education and hopefully, in the future, we can develop more connections and interactions between the western and eastern EE programs.

FIGURE 3.2 Excited students during a BGM course (photo: Chun-Cheh Wang)

Theories supporting human and behavioral change

There are several major theories that may specifically apply to client intervention or behavioral change management in outdoor adventure programming, as well as other group contexts such as adventure therapy, at-risk youth programs, therapeutic outdoor recreation, and recreation therapy. In particular, two widely accepted and utilized theories in the practice of group management include "behavioristic or behavior modification" and "cognitive behavioral change process" (Long, 2011; Stumbo and Folkerth, 2013; Waughfield, 2002). Each of these two specific theories of human behavior, and their relationship to client management, will be discussed in more detail in the following section.

Behavioristic theory

As an outdoor group leader you may already have very particular beliefs about human nature and/or human behavior, and the type of impact you can have on participants as a leader; how you might transform and redirect immature or negative behaviors, feelings of self-doubt, or other insecurities in the wake of outdoor challenges presented to your group members.

If you have studied or are familiar with the tenets of behavioristic theory, you adhere to the belief that most behavior is *learned* – whether the behavior demonstrated is highly destructive, self-defeating, aggressive, extraordinarily optimistic, or unremarkable with regards to confronting challenges and embracing outdoor adventure activities. Leaders who enfold behavioristic principles believe that, since behavior can be learned, then *it can also be unlearned or changed* (Watson, 1913). The following scenario depicts how adopting a behavioristic approach to client management might be implemented.

> As an outdoor leader at the early "forming" stages of a group, you notice one particular client that seems to stand apart from the group, through his/ her loud and rather aggressive behavior. You summarize that this participant seems to be demanding attention, and will do or say things that ensures this happens. You say nothing at first, to see if it will resolve itself without your intervening. But as time passes, the client's loud and overt actions are starting to become disruptive to the group. Using the premise of the behavioristic theory as a framework for action, you believe that the client's behavior can be redirected, or changed. You establish activities that allow the client to be rewarded for positive behavior, ignoring negative behavior (where it is safe to do so), and give attention and praise for non-disruptive actions. A participant can begin to internalize that there are better, alternative forms of getting attention, perhaps for the first time in his or her life.

Negative patterns of behavior can take a lifetime to learn, but the context of an outdoor adventure group and concomitant challenges can indeed be highly effective in altering unfavorable behaviors in exchange for more rewarding ones (Bandura, 1977; Walsh and Gollins, 1976). Several specific techniques that can be used in behavior modification and would be beneficial for an outdoor leader to become familiar with might include shaping, modeling, positive and negative reinforcement, ignoring, bargaining, contracts (i.e. full value contract), and more. While describing in detail each of these behavioral modification techniques is beyond the scope of this chapter, it would be extremely advantageous for an outdoor adventure manager or leader to be familiar with the theoretical premise underlying these techniques, how they can be applied, and their purpose in the successful obtainment of program goals.

Cognitive behavioral change process

The second theory widely utilized in the practice of group management that will be discussed in this chapter is referred to as the "cognitive behavioral change process." In addition, it should be noted that there are several important concepts and related theories that are associated with the principles of behavioral change. It behooves a group leader to be familiar with these theories of behavior in order to be effective in group management, not only from the perspective

FIGURE 3.3 A group of students receive instructions on rock climbing anchor construction in the Utah Desert (photo: Curt Davidson)

of better understanding your clients, but also using these to assist in program planning and evaluation, and justification to outside parties (more on outside parties later in the chapter).

The basic premise of the cognitive behavioral change process is that how a person thinks or feels will be the underlying reason for how that person reacts emotionally and behaviorally in varying circumstances (Long, 2011). This theory consists of three basic factors that ultimately dictate a person's behavior. It posits that a person has certain preconceived thoughts or beliefs about experiences that he or she may have encountered in life, and define these beliefs as "antecedents." The second component of the cognitive behavioral change process is the actual behavior demonstrated by the participant, or the "action" taken. The final factor of the process is described as "consequences," which depending on a person's thoughts can reinforce his or her original belief system, or the antecedents.

The cognitive behavioral change process may seem similar to the Theory of Reasoned Action, also referred to as the Theory of Planned Behavior described by Ajzen (1991). More specifically, the theory of planned behavior looks not only at the beliefs or attitudes (antecedents) a person may ascribe to, regarding a particular behavior, as well as what others in a social context think about the behavior; but it also examines the perceived control one feels he or she may have regarding engaging in a certain behavior. This, in turn, affects the *intention* one may hold, and consequently the likelihood of actually engaging in the behavior.

In other words, the stronger the intention to do so something, the stronger the inclination to perform the behavior.

Another theoretical concept related to the cognitive behavioral change process, one which is often considered a cornerstone of intended outcomes in outdoor adventure programs, is the construct or theory of self-efficacy. While this may be a highly familiar concept to most leaders, it is directly connected with the cognitive behavioral change process theory, in that it examines how persons may feel about themselves, their capabilities in given situations, and how participants may react when faced with challenges in an outdoor adventure context. The following scenario illustrates how the cognitive behavioral change process may be used to help facilitate behavior of one, or several, group participants in an outdoor adventure activity.

> The group that you are managing has an individual who does not seem to be joining in with the others. He is about 13 years old, and often stays off by himself, or when asked to perform certain duties or challenges during an outdoor climbing tower activity strongly declines to participate. He sometimes makes a big joke about the climbing, and likes to attract negative attention, saying it's a "stupid thing to do anyway." When pressed to join in, he may lash out by yelling at peers who are trying to encourage him. Based on his assessment prior to joining the group program, it was indicated that he had a lot of difficulties in school; failing classes, etc. At least every time he tries something he tends to fail at it. He may have a learning disability, but was only recently tested. His parents, as he himself disclosed, "don't think he's worth much," and he can't do much because he's not "too bright." So the client has learned to internalize his struggles for most of his life; and relating this to the cognitive behavioral change process, the client is demonstrating his "antecedent" or beliefs about his abilities – that he is no good at trying things, a failure. So his "action" (by not participating) reflects these beliefs, and the action (behavior) is to back away, or lash out at others. The "consequences" of his actions are likely to reinforce his beliefs or antecedents. In other words, instructors and/or peers may reject him, exclude him, make fun of him, or ignore him, etc. But if an outdoor instructor can facilitate, or introduce a course activity related to the climbing tower, where the client's beliefs are changed in a positive context – where he tries an outdoor challenge and succeeds, or feels good about his effort – the consequences or outcomes can be altered, and as such, so too can the negative beliefs a person has about himself.

While there are other significant theories that can be directly linked to the principles of the cognitive behavioral change process, such as attribution theory, empowerment theory (Zimmerman, 1990), self-determination theory, learned helplessness, etc., the common denominator is that these theories attempt to

FIGURE 3.4 Outward Bound students engage in stacking their rafts, a common activity used for group problem solving (photo: Curt Davidson)

explain human behavior. When a manager or leader of a group of participants recognizes or better understands what may be an underlying reason or motivation for a client's behavior, it can greatly assist in the delivery and design of programs, establishment of goals, and successful outcomes. Further still, when successful outcomes are met or achieved, through challenging outdoor activities, specifically structured, or "scaffolded" challenges (Walsh and Gollins, 1976) in a way to move participants towards positive self-regard, a client may be induced to internalize these behavioral changes in his or her everyday life on a long-term basis.

Linking theory with practice

The link between leadership management and theoretical knowledge is a stronger one than a leader might at first presume. Understanding the theoretical aspects that underlie human behavior is a critical component of service delivery (Voight and Ewert, 2015). Without this background knowledge, a client's behavior can result in frustrations, misunderstandings, poor communication, misreading behavioral cues, and/or anger on behalf of the leader. The following scenario illustrates this point:

A participant is demonstrating defiant, disruptive, and non-cooperative behavior. Rather than becoming angry herself, a good leader attempts to try and understand the origins of the behavior. Questions she may ask herself are, "What might be some underlying motives for acting out?" e.g. Uncontrolled impulsivity? Poor social skills or communication skills? "What does the participant gain by this behavior?" e.g. Attention? Release? "Or what might the participant be communicating?" e.g. Frustrations? Anger?

While attempting to understand motives behind disruptive behaviors may not always be feasible, using grounded theory helps the leader to make an assessment of the participant's behavior, and will provide a framework from which the leader can decide on the best course of action, or intervention, to challenge or ameliorate the behavior.

Rationale for theory-based practice

Linking practice with established theories of human behavior and behavioral management can not only provide a significant framework from which to practice leadership management, but also provide a solid justification and rationale to outside parties. Who might these outside parties represent? Table 3.1 delineates some of those interested parties, and the corresponding rationale for demonstrating a program based on theoretical underpinnings, rather than what has always been done in the past (i.e. what has been convenient, or based on staff interests or skills), without a solid justification beyond an historical precedent.

These interested parties can be significant players in any organization or agency, and may include supervisors, sponsors, insurance companies, funding bodies, families, legislative bodies, and so forth, as indicated in Table 3.1. As is often the case, agencies and programs in the outdoor education/adventure arena need to demonstrate that their programs are worth the investment of their clients' money – that there will be demonstrable change for the better in the adult clients, or in their child participants' lives through overall development, learning, enhanced self-confidence, and/or increased self-efficacy behaviors. One of the most salient mechanisms in demonstrating effectiveness and professional underpinnings of a program is being able to provide causal evidence of leadership techniques linked to behavioral theories that are used in service delivery.

For example, when working with young girls who may have self-worth and self-esteem issues, theoretical literature, such as Bandura's (1986) social learning theory, has indicated that through the process of reflection, generalization, and application instructors can assist individuals in making positive changes in their lives based on increased self-efficacy (Kottman *et al.*, 2001). Many outdoor adventure programs provide an excellent platform for increasing self-efficacy through small group tasks, incremental challenges, and adaptive thinking through application (Walsh and Gollins, 1976; Gass *et al.*, 2012).

Leaders involved in the management and leadership of participants in outdoor (adventure) activities should be somewhat familiar with several salient theories of human behavior that may impact their program delivery. This becomes even more significant if an outdoor leader is dealing with a specific population for which a strong understanding of the theory of human behavior would be extremely beneficial in accomplishing successful outcomes for the client (e.g. youth at risk, families in crisis, clients who have experienced Post Traumatic Stress Disorders (PTSD) or addiction, etc.). For more information regarding the facilitation and management of specific groups in outdoor adventure activities see Table 3.2.

TABLE 3.1 Examples of interested parties and the rationale for theory-based programming

Responsible or interested party	Theory-based programming rationale
Supervisor/Manager	Relating best practices for program delivery associated with theoretically-based applications establishes a strong foundation for achievement of program goals and validation of activity programming. This can also assist managers with client assessment and staff's ability to function and facilitate programs at a high quality level.
Insurance companies	Justification for third-party payment for services based on theoretical/research studies which can define and delineate what outdoor programs are, what they can accomplish, and how a positive impact on client change, especially for youth programs, can be achieved. Theory-based programming can also contribute to a body of knowledge and research for purposes of replication of results, and generalizability to other programs and populations.
Funding bodies	Theory-based practice can lend credibility and validity to possible outside funding sources, such as grants, and other subsidies or scholarship programs, etc. Demonstrated success of theory-based programs and achievement of goals contribute to a knowledge base of the field, rendering them more likely to be funded and supported.
Families	Can justify, at a more complex level, the program offerings and the rationale behind program objectives to parents or guardians. Theory-based programming establishes a more robust platform for program goals, and achievement of positive outcomes for parents.
Legislative bodies	Theory-based programming can establish precedent for successful outdoor adventure programs helping to garner interested legislative bodies regarding land use and access, as well as city councils, parks, boards, and other state or local governing bodies.

Conclusion

Successful outcomes for individuals participating in outdoor adventure programs can be as diversely defined as the number of persons engaged in the activities. But while there is often no one single definition of success that applies to each client, there must be tangible evidence that positive change has occurred for participants, and that participation in your outdoor adventure program has been beneficial in some capacity. One common element, which has been linked to successful outcomes for participants, is how the programs are *facilitated* and/ or *managed* by outdoor leaders (Priest and Gass, 2005; Priest *et al.*, 1999). As previously indicated, behavior demonstrated by clients is communication. But this communication must be understood by outdoor leaders, and facilitated in such a way as to bring positive changes not only to the group, but to an individual as well. Having a sound understanding of the motivation behind client behavior can be substantially aided by the incorporation of theoretical concepts in the planning of goals and outcomes. Moreover, behavioral theories such as the cognitive behavioral change process, and the behavioristic theory, lay the groundwork for the underlying belief that participants' behaviors and thoughts can be changed or improved where needed or desired through skillful management by outdoor leaders. A theoretical framework can provide a strong foundational building block from which to strengthen and evaluate our programs, where changes can be assessed and measured, and ultimately assist in the prediction of participant behavior, the replication of successful program interventions and activities, and the generalizability to other outdoor programs (Voight and Ewert, 2015). Finally, as program outcomes become validated and replicated through theory-based practice and ongoing evidence-based research, solid justifications can be made to funding sources, both outside as well as inside an outdoor education agency for continued financial support, and enhancement of our status as a profession.

Main points

- Behavior is communication. Managing groups in an outdoor adventure context requires a leader who is attentive to the behavior of the individuals of the group and understands how to best interpret the underlying meaning of that behavior.
- Management of a group of persons is an interplay between the group's objectives and goals, and the personal dynamics of individual behavioral characteristics that facilitates the attainment of the program's goals.
- The goals of outdoor adventure programs may be represented along a continuum, which can range from recreational, enrichment, educational, to adjunctive and primary therapy. An outdoor leader's understanding of participants' behavior, and the facilitation of that behavior, can better lead to the achievement of program goals.
- Relative to the experience and intuition of the outdoor leader, group management can be greatly enhanced by understanding the critical importance of the theoretical attributes which underlie human behavior.
- Two widely accepted theories which are often used in the practice of group management and participant behavior are the theories of "behavioristic or behavior modification," and the "cognitive behavioral change process."
- The basic tenet of behavioristic theory is the belief that most behavior is *learned*, whether the behavior demonstrated is highly destructive, or extraordinarily optimistic, or unremarkable when confronting challenges and embracing outdoor adventure activities. Leaders who subscribe to behavioristic principles believe that since behavior can be learned, then it can also be unlearned or changed.

TABLE 3.2 Group management considerations for specific populations in outdoor adventure activities

Groups with specific needs	Mobility	Communication	Risk
Sensory issues (Visual & hearing)	• Know preferred method of mobility—cane, guide dog, or sighted guide for visual impairments. • Will guide dogs be an issue? (Legally they must be allowed, but sometimes they may create unexpected barriers.) • When hiking, walking, biking, climbing, canoeing, etc., alert blind person to sounds as needed (i.e. oncoming traffic, trains, nature sounds of birds or animals, other visitors, dogs, etc.)	• Provide verbal cues at every level of the activity for blind; describe natural features, animals, birds, vistas, equipment, etc. • Modeling or touching of objects will enhance an outdoor experience (i.e. belay device, natural artifacts, rock faces, for visual loss). • Keep camp areas well lit at night as compensation for reduced hearing abilities & access to conversations, lip reading, etc. • Provide additional written & visual cues needed for the deaf. • Establish signals for the deaf during activities for communication and for safety, i.e. hand, head, with canoe paddles, etc. • Tap shoulder gently to get deaf person's attention.	• Be very clear about all possible dangers inherent in the outdoor adventure activity: low branches; uneven terrain; cliffs; crevasses; etc. • Do not assume person is unable to do tasks; allow for dignity of risk • Activity demonstration will allow hearing-impaired to make informed decisions about risks
Mobility limitations	• Know best method of mobility for person with limitations. • What equipment adaptations are needed, if any. • Consider transportation needs & access possibilities between outdoor sites and facilities (cars, golf carts, etc.). • Will the person need more assistance during the activity? • Could the outdoor site be modified or another area substituted for easier access?	• Keep communication open about problems or issues: pain; fatigue; anxiety. • Never assume persons with similar mobility issues have the same level of ability, needs, or disability.	• Be sure participants understand level of skill and strength needed for activity. • Allow for dignity of person to attempt risk/activity. • Pre-assess for strength, agility, and endurance. • Have advanced exit strategy, if possible.

Older adults	• Pace may need to be slower. • Allow for extra time if persons want to rest more or go slower to accommodate physical decline. • Know distances between sites, resting areas, level of emergency care available. • If desired, can activity or outdoor location be modified for easier access?	• Inform older adults, in advance, of distances during outdoor activities, hikes, etc., time & endurance needed, level of skill needed to do adventure activity, etc. • Are there hearing or vision issues? • Never assume older persons are incapable or need help. Always ask first. • Do not patronize.	• Biggest diversity in this population; do not make broad assumptions of people. • Assessments are critical to discern skill level, agility, & endurance. • Knowing participants' medical history and/or medical needs is advised. • Staff with medical training for cardiac events is beneficial.
Cognitive/emotional issues (traumatic brain injury; intellectual disability, PTSD, etc.)	• Usually not an issue unless indicated by the person. • Consider any balance issues when conducting outdoor activities. • Consider coordination issues. • Choose a less challenging site for adventure activity if desired for positive outcomes.	• Don't treat adults as children; create trust. • Repeat information as needed; simple, step-by-step instructions are best. • Model desired behavior. • Are instructions well understood by participant? • Repeat/train skill process if necessary for successful involvement. • Expect appropriate behavior.	• Activity demonstration will allow person to better understand & judge level of involvement and risk. • Point out potential hazards within outdoor sites (i.e. getting lost, dangerous areas, poisonous vegetation). • Re-check questionable choices/decisions of person.

Please note: Each person is an individual first, and no two limitations, however similar, reflect the same level of function. The best way to manage any group with varying levels of ability is to always ask if assistance is needed, and then how to best accommodate persons, involving them in advance, in the planning, if possible.

- The second major theory discussed in this chapter was the cognitive behavioral change process. This particular theory posits that how a person thinks or feels will be the underlying reason for how that person reacts emotionally and behaviorally in varying circumstances, and consists of three basic factors that ultimately dictate a person's behavior: antecedents, actions, and consequences.
- Significant interested parties in any outdoor organization or agency where sponsorship or funding is involved may include supervisors, sponsors, insurance companies, funding bodies, families, and legislative bodies, such as city councils or boards. Outdoor education/adventure programs must be able to demonstrate that their programs are worth the investment of their clients' money through the effective achievement of program goals and outcomes, such as enhanced self-confidence, and/or increased self-efficacy behaviors.
- Being able to provide causal evidence of leadership techniques that are linked to behavioral theories used in service delivery will greatly substantiate the validation of program outcomes, justify financial outlays, and better cultivate the field of outdoor adventure education as a profession.

Discussion questions

1   As a manager or leader of an outdoor group, communicating with your group or with individuals becomes paramount for successful outcomes. Describe how behavior becomes communication, and give one or two examples of participants' behavior communicating in an outdoor adventure context. How might poor communication, or misunderstanding a participant's behavior, compromise group outcomes?
2   Adhering to the behavioristic theory, describe how undesirable or negative behaviors might be unlearned or changed in an outdoor adventure program.
3   Consider the theory of the cognitive behavioral change process, and define its three basic components. Also describe how the application of this theory would assist with facilitation and better understanding of a client who was very reluctant to try new or adventurous challenges due to his or her beliefs that they would only fail if they did try.
4   Explain why basing outdoor program goals, activities, and facilitation techniques on sound theoretical concepts would be beneficial to outside funding sources, or other interested parties.

References

Ajzen, I. (1991). The theory of planned behavior. *Organizational Behavior and Human Decision Processes*, 50, 179–211.
Bandura, A. (1977). Self-efficacy: Toward a unifying theory of behavioral change. *Psychological Review*, 84(2), March, 191–215.

Bandura, A. (1986). *Social Foundations of Thought and Action: A Social Cognitive Theory*. Englewood Cliffs, NJ: Prentice-Hall.

Gass, M., Gillis, H. L., and Russell, K. (2012). *Adventure Therapy: Theory, Research and Practice*. New York: Routledge.

Gilbertson, K., Bates, T., McLaughlin, T., and Ewert, A. (2006). *Outdoor Education: Methods and Strategies*. Champaign, IL: Human Kinetics.

Gillis, H. L. (1992). Therapeutic uses of adventure challenge-outdoor-wilderness: Theory and research. In K. Henderson (ed.), *Proceedings of the Coalition for Education in the Outdoors Symposium* (pp. 35–47). Cortland, NY: Coalition for Education in the Outdoors.

Kottman, T., Ashby, J. S., and DeGraaf, D. (2001). *Adventures in Guidance: How to Integrate Fun into your Guidance Program*. Alexandria, VA: American Counseling Association.

Long, T. (2011). Cognitive-behavioral approaches to therapeutic recreation. In N. J. Stumbo and B. Wardlaw (eds), *Facilitation of Therapeutic Recreation Services: An Evidence-Based and Best Practice Approach to Techniques and Processes* (pp. 289–306). State College, PA: Venture.

Priest, S., and Gass, M. (2005). *Effective Leadership in Adventure Programming* (2nd edn). Champaign-Urbana, IL: Human Kinetics.

Priest, S., Gass, M., and Gillis, H. L. (1999). *Essential Elements of Facilitation*. Online at: https://openlibrary.org/publishers/Tarrak_Technologies

Shank, J., and Coyle, C. (2002). *Therapeutic Recreation in Health Promotion and Rehabilitation*. State College, PA: Venture.

Stumbo, N., and Folkerth, J. (2013). *Study Guide for the Therapeutic Recreation Specialist Certification Examination*. Urbana, IL: Sagamore.

Voight, A., and Ewert, A. (2015). Integrating theory with practice: Applications in adventure therapy. In C. Norton, C. Carpenter, and A. Pryor (eds), *Adventure Therapy around the Globe: International Perspectives and Diverse Approaches* (pp. 243–250). Champaign, IL: Common Ground Publishing.

Walsh, V., and Gollins, G. (1976). *The Exploration of the Outward Bound Process*. Denver, CO: Colorado Outward Bound School.

Watson, J. B. (1913). Psychology as the behaviorist views it. *Psychological Review*, 20, 158–177.

Waughfield, C. (2002). *Mental Health Concepts* (5th edn). Albany, NY: Delmar.

Zimmerman, M. A. (1990). Taking aim on empowerment research: On the distinction between individual and psychological conceptions. *American Journal of Community Psychology*, 18(1), 169–177.

4

RELEVANT THEORIES AND THEIR APPLICATION IN OUTDOOR ADVENTURE EDUCATION AND BEHAVIOR AND GROUP MANAGEMENT

Overview

The purpose of this chapter is to explore the relevant theories associated with behavior management strategies and the theoretical underpinnings of behavioral mitigation techniques. Selected theories were chosen based on their relevance to managing the types of behaviors experiential education instructors may need to address during their programs. With a working knowledge of these theories, EE facilitators will have an increased ability to identify and understand behavioral issues that may occur on their courses and how to best manage these behaviors. Likewise, these theories provide a theoretical foundation on which to base potential intervention strategies when issues inevitably arise with participants or students. These theories are borrowed from the various fields of psychology, sociology, and social work and can provide insight into why a student is exhibiting a particular behavior, and procedures that can be taken to intervene, and help them have a successful EE experience.

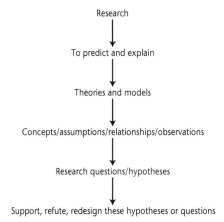

FIGURE 4.1   The role of research in general with particular relevance to understanding human behavior and mitigating and managing behavior and group management situations

Similar to other fields, the role of research in OAE has typically been concerned with developing theories and then testing and observing these theories. Whether empirically based or more grounded in naturalistic and other forms of qualitative inquiry, researchers always strive to develop information beyond what we may already know. The pathway described in Figure 4.1, represents a typical linear progression of research commonly seen in OAE settings.

In addition we often make a variety of assumptions and look for relationships when researching a particular phenomenon. In this case, assumptions can be thought of as statements about the nature of a phenomenon that are presumed to be true, if only temporarily (e.g. the longer and/or more intense the OAE experience, the greater the effect). On the other hand, relationships represent the type and strength of the connection between two or more variables (e.g. adults have an inverse relationship to risk-taking behavior).

In addition, there is the problem of confounding variables in OAE. In this situation, confounding variables are variables that obscure the effects of another variable. Thus, it becomes unclear whether the actual treatment caused the effect. Moreover, to be a confounding variable there must be an association between the confounding variable and the independent variable which is of interest and directly associated with the outcome or dependent variable.

And finally there is the question of causality. Many theories seek to identify either the variables or process by which a particular phenomenon actually occurs. However, to be "causal" the following criteria must be satisfied.

1   There must be a temporal order in the way the variables interact.
2   There must be a logical association between the variables.
3   Plausible alternative explanations must be considered.
4   The outcomes must make sense within the broader theoretical framework.

TABLE 4.1 Ranges of theories

Empirical generalization	Patterns concerning two or more easily observed concepts (e.g. gender or skill level)
Middle-range	More abstract and focus on a specific and substantive topic (e.g. self-efficacy is important in OAE participant behavior)
Theoretical framework	Also known as a paradigm or general orientation toward a specific subject (e.g. outdoor adventure education is a potential change agent)

Thus, theories are often an important component of finding explanations as to why and how things happen in an OAE/BGM setting. Theories can be defined as a collection of explanatory statements about observed and inferred relationships among variables (Von Neumann, 2007). Theories can be thought to have different ranges depending on the overall impact or "reach" of the theory. For example, in Table 4.1, theories can be categorized as simply an empirical generalization, a middle-range theory, or a theoretical framework. Most of the theories discussed in this chapter fall into a middle or theoretical framework range.

With a solid foundation in the theories behind OAE/BGM, an instructor should be able to come up with a rational plan for preemptively establishing a positive group culture, maintaining that culture, and providing intervention strategies when students deviate from the desired behaviors. These theories will also provide a functional knowledge for understanding why students may be exhibiting undesirable behavior. Also, behavioral intervention plans should be rooted in these theoretical ideas to achieve maximum functionality and benefit for both the student and the staff of the EE program. Always keep in mind that the end goal is to help the student have a successful OAE experience and to learn how to transfer their newly found behavioral strategies back into their home life.

Reinforcement theory

To begin, one useful theory that is a logical starting place for this discussion is Reinforcement Theory (Premack, 1965). Reinforcement theory has been used to explain human attraction, train students on a variety of outcomes, and even treat diseases (Berger and Calabrese, 1975; Kingham, 1958; Stipek, 1993). Reinforcement theory can be used as a motivator to encourage or discourage behavior through operant or classical conditioning (Bolles, 1972). Classical conditioning is the type of reinforcement that is behind a phenomenon such as when a teacher offers extra credit for perfect attendance and thus students are more likely to attend class. Operant conditioning is typically the type of reinforcement used to mitigate behaviors. There are two types of operant conditioning: reinforcement and punishment (Mazur, 2002). Reinforcement is typically used to fortify good behavior, like when teachers give candy to their pupils for getting good grades in school. Punishment is typically used to decrease negative behavior, such as when a teacher gives a student detention for passing notes in class.

Reinforcement theory was first "discovered" by the famous Russian psychologist Ivan Pavlov who used food and bells to condition dogs to salivate, thus using the theory to reinforce a desired behavior (Grant, 1964). Since then, it has provided a reason for many types of human behavior such as rewarding good children to incarcerating prisoners (Mazur, 2002). It plays a critical role in society and provides a basis for understanding behavior. It also provides a structure educators can use to modify and change behaviors they, and a society at large, desires or conversely need to eliminate.

Reinforcement theory plays a huge role in the AE process, particularly when programs desire to change attitudes and behaviors. For example, Success Oriented Achievement Realized (SOAR) is a typical program in the OAE field that works with students with ADD, ADHD, and LD. The program takes students into a novel setting (the outdoors) and works with them to change their behaviors and attitudes with respect to their cognitive limitation. A student who has trouble keeping their belongings organized is a typical example of a student SOAR would serve in their program. For this student they would teach him or her strategies for keeping their belongings organized, and then through reinforcement theory, continually check the progress of that student, using consequences or rewards for the student's performance on the task. An example of a reward might be verbal praise. A typical consequence for a student who

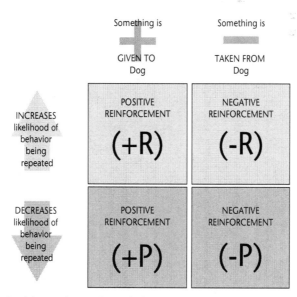

FIGURE 4.2 Positive and negative reinforcement and how "conditioning" can be used to increase or decrease behaviors

does not stay organized is that they have to spend more time organizing their belongings in their tent before they are allowed to join the group for activities.

Programmers should consider the use of reinforcement theory when considering how to maintain the long-term impacts that OAE programs afford their students. For example, one way reinforcement theory can be utilized on a macro level is with the use of post-course intervention techniques. This idea encompasses that by utilizing techniques to contact students at various time intervals after their course, such as via Facebook or phone calls, organizations can reinforce the outcomes that the students have learned by making them recall and remember the various course experiences and discussions that led to their learning. The application of reinforcement theory in this way provides a theoretical framework in which the post-course intervention are a valuable extension of a standard AE course.

While much is known about the use of reinforcement theory in traditional education, little research has explored the use of the concept in AE settings. Some potential areas for investigation include the use of booster maintenance sessions and retention of AE outcomes over long periods of time. Additionally, reinforcement theory might play a larger role in AE programming than in everyday life because of the novel environment in which AE programming takes place. For example, because students often experience increased amounts of stress during AE programming, the potential exists for a more impactful environment to reinforce behaviors, increasing the magnitude of the treatment for the students throughout the AE experience (Baldwin *et al.*, 2004).

Understanding the role Reinforcement Theory plays in AE programming is critical to perpetuating AE and the related field of wilderness therapy. It may provide a crucial piece of understanding about how the AE paradigm may be an effective way to address or change people's behaviors. This may be even more critical to understand for programs in the Wilderness Therapy Arena because their whole premise is to change the destructive habits of their clients (Russell and Hendee, 2000). It would seem that this theory provides an excellent lens through which AE researchers can examine the field and assess what is happening to their students during and after their AE experience. Practitioners can also use this theory to train instructors on managing behaviors and instill in their students the values and beliefs held by their organizations.

Ecological systems theory

Based on the systems theory, and how organisms adapt to their environments, one of the leading theories that can help instructors understand student behavior is Bronfenbrenner's Ecological Systems Theory (EST) (Paquette and Ryan, 2001). This theory posits that an individual is influenced, and thus is a product of, multiple layers of their environmental surroundings. This layering effect can influence a person's attitudes, beliefs, behaviors, and social capital among other things.

FIGURE 4.3 OAE students engaged in a service project during the course (photo: Curt Davidson)

This theory is particularly useful for understanding a person's background as they come to a program and can help staff anticipate the antecedents a student is likely to come with. For example, a person who comes from an inner-city, low socio-economic background would have a drastically different ecological system than a person who comes from a wealthy, upper class background. EST can help an experiential educator to understand a person's background and empathize with that person based on what they know. This theory is particularly useful for understanding how and where a student has learned a behavior, and then using that information, an informed decision can then be made concerning how to approach that student with relevance to modifying their behavior. The caveat to using this theory to make informed decisions is the folly of making assumptions and prejudiced decisions or inferences based on a person's perceived EST.

A person is thought to have five different ecological systems of which they are a part. The microsystem is the first and most influential system. This level

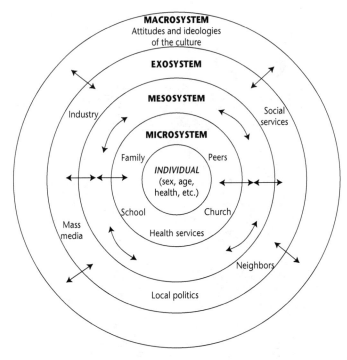

FIGURE 4.4 An individual's ecological system and the relationship and interactions of the subsystems

consists of factors of influence such as family, school, and peers. It is important to understand that these are all things that a person directly influences, and are directly influenced by. For example, an only child's microsystem is significantly different from a person who grows up with five other siblings. This would directly affect how much attention they have received from their parents, how they access resources like food, and enhance or limit the types of social interactions they have had growing up. This type of system difference can affect almost anything including cognitive function, personality, or social awareness.

The next level is the mesosystem. This level is a little more abstract but is essentially the idea that when two microsystem level components interact with each other, there is some influence for an individual. A common mesosystem interaction happens between parents and their child's school system. A child with very involved parents may call the school when their son or daughter gets cut from a sports team. The result may be that their child is placed back on the team. A lesser involved parent may not call the school and their son or daughter has to deal with the fact that they will not be on the sports team that season. In this way, two micro-level system components have interacted, thus altering the child's state. Keep in mind that these mesosystem interactions happen all the time and have significant influence over the way a person views the world system of which they are a part.

The following level is the exosystem which consists of large-scale systems such as the current educational system or government. A great example of this is capitalism, where a person is, generally, free to go and start a business of their choice. This perception of freedom can be influential in a person's development, locus of control, or outlook on life. Contrast this with a person who grows up in communist North Korea where a person has little influence over the type of career they may choose. These exosystem components are part of the foundational context in which all other components exist and affect a person on many levels including locus of control, optimism, and worldview.

The exosystem is closely related to but different from the next system: the macrosystem. This level is made up of overarching cultural beliefs that influence a person. For example, the idea that murder in western society is wrong and should not be engaged in for personal gain is a commonly held value. As a result, most people do not engage in this activity (thankfully). These overarching cultural beliefs are particularly important when working with international students whose cultural beliefs may be slightly different than those of the institution or educational staff.

Finally, the chronosystem makes up the last component of a person's ecological system. This is the idea that the time period in which a person exists plays a role in their developmental process. For example, people who grew up in the Depression are often thought to be more frugal and resourceful than the millennial generation. This is because they grew up in a time when resources were scarcer or more difficult to obtain. These types of time periods should be considered, particularly when staff are serving various ages in populations and adjusting their courses to address relevant issues.

EST plays a huge role in the development of a person's ideas, beliefs, and attitudes. This theory can provide a context for how program staff design an experience, understand their clientele, and help educators prepare curriculum for incoming students. Further, it can be useful for understanding the context in which a student views a problem. For example, if a student grows up in an abusive household, they may respond to yelling and a threatening staff member in a much different way than a person who grew up without that negative influence. Staff should alter their behavior with such students, and use the lens of EST to develop a thoughtful plan to help facilitate success for students.

Theory of reasoned action and planned behavior

The Theory of Reasoned Action and the Theory of Planned Behavior are two very similar theories. These theories comprise a system to help explain why people behave the way they do based on motivations and attitudes. First, the theories posit that people behave based on their perceived attitudes about that behavior. For example, if a student believes it is in their best interest to listen to a lesson on how to light a stove, they will likely choose to be attentive. Relatedly, the person must also believe that their behavior will have the outcomes they

FIGURE 4.5 OAE students navigate a white-water river (photo: Ryan Hines)

desire. In the example of stove lighting, the desire to learn that skill must be present in the student or created by the instructor (i.e. explaining that they will be responsible for cooking their food while on course).

The second component to these foundational behavioral theories is the social desirability component. This is the idea that a person acts on a behavior with the assumption that the behavior is desirable to certain others. For example, a student who is openly defiant to an instructional person during an OAE experience is operating under the assumption that there is some desire for him or her to do so by the other students present on the course. Further, a rational actor in a situation must also have the motivation to comply with the social norms of the group. This theory can be used to explain why the group contract is so important and it is so critical to get investment and buy-in from all students when going through that process (see Chapter 5).

These theories are of particular relevance to OAE instructors because they can be used to manipulate students with behavioral issues. Further, it is helpful for understanding how a student can be motivated to stop disruptive behavior and thus comply with more positive group norms. For example, if a student is acting out of context with the group and constantly not complying with rules set forth by the instructional staff, they can use the lens of reasoned action or planned behavior to evaluate and thus sway that student to act accordingly. One technique for this is to merely have a conversation with that student about how the other students, as well as the staff, are not finding their behavior acceptable. This approach plays into the social desirability angle of the theory of reasoned action.

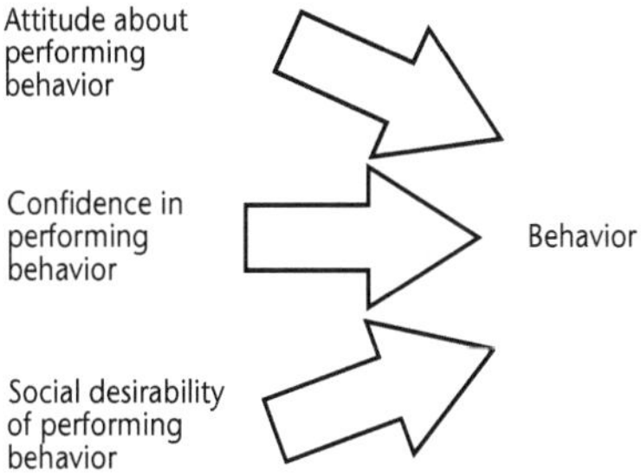

Attitude about
performing
behavior

Confidence in
performing   Behavior
behavior

Social desirability
of performing
behavior

FIGURE 4.6   How planned behavior and reasoned action become applied behavior

Another strategy for utilizing these theories is to provide a larger context and big picture benefits perspective to participation in OAE programming. For example, oftentimes, instructors will be cryptic about what events transpire on their course and what the purpose of participation is so that the student "discovers" the benefits for themselves. No doubt this approach has value, however it may be more beneficial, especially with problematic or behaviorally difficult students, to be straightforward with them about the benefits and gains they can see from investing in the OAE process and program.

These two theories differ in one final component. The theory of planned behavior posits a third component to predict and understand behavior and that is the idea of control over their behavior. Said differently, a person must feel that they are competent and confident of performing their behavior. This plays a role in the OAE process when a student fails to act in a desired way. Instructional staff should consider the possibility that a person may not feel confident that they can act in a way that the staff desires and thus it needs to be explained how they would like him or her to behave. This may be the result of a number of historical variables but can often stem from negative relationships in the person's home environment.

The theory of reasoned action and the theory of planned behavior are useful in many ways for understanding individual and group behavior. These theories provide rationale for establishing a positive group culture right from the onset of the course. It is also useful for considering the motivations and behaviors of individuals, and how different intervention strategies may be operationalized

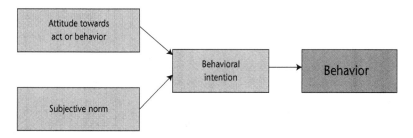

FIGURE 4.7   Attitudes and norms and their influence on behavioral intention and behavior

to mitigate the undesirable behavior from various students. They are often the theories behind direct intervention strategies that will be discussed in Chapter 5 such as the behavioral contract. An understanding of these theories and that a person is usually a reasonable and rational actor is imperative to understanding and mitigating behavior in OAE programs.

Stages of change model

The stages of change model is a theory created to help understand how people modify behavior. It can be useful to help understand that change in behavior is a process, and not an instantaneous transition. This model produced a line of thinking to break down how a person experiences change, thus helping the facilitator to focus on where that person is within the states of change, and how best to meet their needs. In this way, they can also help the person move through the process, thus increasing the likelihood of change and assuaging the process for the individual (Norcross *et al.*, 2011). The following section will explore this important model.

Stage one is considered the "precontemplation" stage. In this phase, a person may or may not even know that an issue or problem exists. Let's use the example of a student who wants to be a more effective communicator. While in this stage, an instructor can play a critical role in the entrance into the stages of change model. OAE programs have been found to be really effective at bringing about awareness to people of habits they did not even know they exhibited. This process usually happens through peer to peer feedback and skilled facilitation from the instructor. In this example, the instructor may use these techniques to bring awareness to the student pertaining to their lack of communication skills.

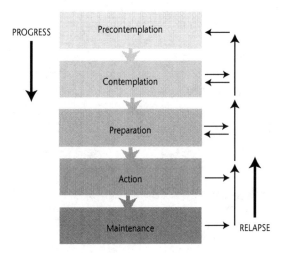

FIGURE 4.8   The stages of change model and direction in which an individual moves through each stage

The next stage is the "contemplation" stage. This stage is important because this is where a person invests in the action of change. Referring back to the example of the student with poor communication skills, the student will see the benefits to enhancing their communication. An instructor during this stage should focus on the positive benefits to implementing the behavioral change – for example, in this scenario, explaining to the student that through increased ability to communicate, they will experience a greater sense of empathy from others because of their behavioral adaptation.

The next stage that a person will enter into is the "preparation" stage. During this stage, the intention to change the behavior becomes clear to the student. At this point, the person with poor communication skills would acknowledge and be ready to pursue the necessary steps for modifying their behavior. The student will begin preparing themselves and others for the change they are about to make. In this phase, the instructor should consider using a supportive and encouraging leadership style so that the student does not lose motivation to make the change. Reminding them of the positive benefits to changing would also be a positive technique for the instructor to consider.

Taking direct actions will move the student into the "action" phase of the model. In this way, the student should have a plan to implement the behavioral changes they are considering. For example, speaking up more during debriefs, giving more feedback, and voicing their opinion during group decision-making exercises would all be positive and reasonable actions for the student with poor communication skills to consider. During this phase, instructors should consider how they can continue to support the student, but also suggest strategies for the student to make the behavioral change. For example, sitting down and making a development plan with the student with time-critical and strategic goals would be a huge help for the student during this action phase. Further, teaching them effective strategies for changing their behavior is appropriate at this stage since they are investing in the process. An instructor should consider teaching the student effective communication strategies in the case of our example.

The following stage is the "maintenance" phase of change. During this stage, it is imperative that the student figures out a way to continue the positive behavior they have worked hard to bring about. In the communication example, this would mean that the student needs to find ways to continue being an effective communicator, and to transfer those skills when he or she goes back home. With certain behavioral modifications, this may mean achieving time oriented, target goals as they develop. For other behaviors this may mean simply not relapsing back into the undesired behavior such as is the case with drinking, smoking, or substance abuse.

This particular stage is difficult for the OAE field because of the short-term nature of our experiences. Wilderness therapy companies have found success with follow-up intervention strategies (see p. 56). However, when the student is placed back in their original ecological system, it is often extremely difficult for them to maintain the positive behavioral changes they have experienced on the OAE course. Instructors should consider doing all they can to make sure the students are prepared for this process of reentry, and to anticipate the difficulties they may experience in maintaining their positive changes after returning home. Likewise, administrators and programmers should consider this, and continue to develop innovative ways to help ensure the lessons from the OAE experience are maintained.

Finally, the last stage of the model is the stage that we hope the students never enter into: relapse. It is important to keep in mind that if the student does experience relapse, that does not mean the instructors, or OAE experience, were ineffective at changing their behavior. In this stage the student may find themselves falling into the same old habits. The relapse stage is most disastrous with destructive behaviors such as drug abuse or self-harm, however it is discouraging no matter what, if the student was making efforts to change their behavior. During this phase, it is important to remain positive and encouraging and never express disappointment in the student. Coaching the student back into the contemplation stage is critical at this juncture and reminding them that they changed once, and can do so again is imperative for their health and wellbeing.

As stated earlier, this model is useful for understanding how people change on both large and small scales. The model is particularly useful for identifying where people are at as they become aware of changes that need to happen in their life. In fact, this may be the single most important thing OAE programs accomplish since it is difficult to get a student to completely change their behavior in the short time of an OAE program. Additionally, it is useful for the instructor to adjust their leadership style or mentoring approach to help encourage the student into the subsequent behavioral change phases.

De-escalation

Sometimes, through a series of events and the added stress of being outside their natural surroundings, students have episodes in which they lose control of their reactions and emotions. During this time a student may exhibit any of the following behaviors: yelling; physical violence; property destruction; or self-harm. These behaviors are often extremely difficult to manage but it is not outside the instructor's ability to do so. There are a few simple techniques that you can utilize to de-escalate the situation and help the student resolve their emotions and deal with them in a more positive manner. It is important to remember that these people are often acting this way because they do want to help, but are just not expressing that in the most productive avenue.

A person in a position of authority, such as that of an instructor, often reacts by yelling back or telling the agitated student to sit down, calm down, and be quiet. This is counterproductive to the situation and these types of reactions should always be avoided. Keep in mind that the person is trying to communicate their needs. They are doing so in a way, however, that is often not ideal for our culture and society and is certainly not productive within the "normal" means of communication. Also, it is important to remember never to shout back at the person. Speaking in a measured, soft tone is often the only measure necessary to get the person to calm down and start a dialog that resolves the situation.

Next, utilizing empathetic listening techniques will help the person calm down and feel that they are being heard. This might involve asking questions, summarizing what you know about the situation, asking for clarification, or just providing space for the person to vent. During this time, to help protect the ego of the person, consider moving them away from the group, or the group away from them. After the situation is over, this will help them assimilate back into the group with minimal embarrassment. Additionally, this creates a safe environment in which the person can feel like they will not be judged and can communicate their needs.

There are physical considerations that can lead to effective de-escalation techniques as well. Both for your safety and the safety of the agitated person, consider giving them at least two arms lengths of space between yourself and them until they start to calm down. Also, keep your hands at your side, with your palms facing toward the other person. This presents an air of openness and a position that lacks judgment. Standing face to face and squarely with the agitated person is also a less threatening stance and may help the person calm down and start a dialog. Bending your knees slightly will help the person perceive that you are at ease and that they can start to let their aggression down.

Next, starting a dialog about the needs of that person and the reality of the situation is key to moving beyond the explosive situation. Express and repeat short phrases, such as, "I'm here to help," "this is a safe place," and "tell me how I can help you right now," since the person's agitated state may not allow them to effectively hear what you are saying. Allowing people to make choices will also help them feel like they are in control of the situation and ultimately will lead them back to regaining their composure. For example, an instructor may ask "do you want some food or drink right now," presenting a simple decision the agitated person can make that helps them regain a sense of control over the situation they are dealing with.

As with most behavioral intervention strategies, it is imperative to remember to get to the root of the problem. Oftentimes, what immediately triggered the escalated situation is not the primary motivation for the agitated behavior. After initially calming the person, find out what the underlying problems are, and how their needs are not being met. As an instructor, if you address this element of the situation, you are much more likely to avoid future escalated situations. Finally, come up with a plan for helping them assimilate back into the group. Make sure to include the individual in this plan. Some common strategies that may work include allowing that individual to explain what happened or having the instructor speak on that person's behalf. This is also essential to ensuring that they have a successful remainder of the course.

De-escalating agitated students can be a daunting prospect. These situations are often uncomfortable and can be scary depending on how the student is acting. As with most things, practicing these skills in staff training can help prepare you to deal with the reality of these situations. Also, learning from your experiences will help you become better at de-escalation as you handle more of these situations.

SCENARIO

Reed was a 15-year-old boy, returning camper to his EE Program. He had been attending the camp for two years, and staff were informed in his pre-course meeting by his parents that he had grown a significant amount through the program. He was prone to anger outbursts, and had a difficult time getting along with peers, but bonded well with older staff. Reed also had a hard time being rational when escalated, oftentimes breaking and throwing things when he got worked up. Reed was diagnosed with ADD, and no other diagnoses, just known issues with anger and self-control.

James was a 14-year-old camper, first time at SOAR. He was very helpful and obedient, showing a great deal of leadership the first few days at camp. As camp proceeded, James started to lose motivation to stay engaged in the program, oftentimes becoming defiant when asked to wake up in the morning, complaining during physical activity, and was notorious for lying about his family's wealth and his own possessions, telling the other campers that he had saved up enough money to buy a viper sports car. James had ADHD, and no other diagnoses.

Sean was the oldest boy in the group, at 16 years old. He was physically larger than the other kids, standing at 6'1" and 250lbs. This was his first year at the program, and he struggled with blurting control due to autism. Although very high functioning, he often talked over other participants and staff to make satirical jokes. Sean was also the leader in the group, stepping in between arguments and disagreements without prompting, for better or worse.

Starting on day one, Reed made it very clear to the staff and participants that he always made an "enemy" at camp, and his goal was to not make an enemy. The rest of the boys wanted to make a rule in the full-value contract to not exclude others, which Reed was adamantly opposed to, stating "man that stuff happens anyway." Throughout this whole discussion, Reed continuously spoke over other participants and staff, until pulled aside and asked to wait five seconds before speaking. Sean, similarly, was unable to refrain from joking about inappropriate political topics, and was asked, with no avail, to rein it in and focus for a few minutes. James was taking notes on the full-value contract, coming up with the majority of rules and helping staff out. One staff set a time limit, telling the boys that if they could focus for three minutes, they could be done and continue with their evening.

Reed has a series of outbursts, the biggest leading up to this scenario on day one of their three-day canoe portion of the course. He was upset by the fact that the group could not paddle against the wind on the lake, and was forced to stop for the night at their lunch spot. He jumped in a canoe, trying to paddle against whitewater-capped waves about four feet from the shore. The lifeguard in the staff pulled his boat back in, and a staff member took him aside after he began lashing out at other campers, calling them "weak, insufferable idiots."

The staff and participants go on a one-day trail ride with both of the horse wranglers. That given day was a staff member's day off, due to this there were two staff members, and two wranglers. About 30 minutes into the trail ride, one of the other participants, who was extremely allergic to horses, began to have an intensified allergic reaction, and the lead medic decided that it was essential to stop and hike him back down to camp. The group stopped the horses, and began to rope up and start on eating lunch to keep the rest of the group occupied. As the staff were occupied James made an offhand comment and Reed looked escalated, but then walked away. Then, James asked him why he wasn't saying anything, and Reed ran, full-speed, and tackled him to the ground, attempting to hit him before staff and Sean pulled him off of James. The staff who was tending to the participant having an allergic reaction ran over, not knowing who had done what, and pulled James away from Reed and started to ask him what had happened, while Reed was escorted to the other side of the field by a tree to calm down. Reed was hitting his head and sobbing, while James was yelling. The wranglers pulled Sean aside along with the rest of the group. Sean was yelling at Reed, further instigating the situation, while Reed was still escalated. Staff attempted to quiet Sean, to no success. The staff notified their course director, who had the director come up to escort down the participant who was having an allergic reaction, along with one of the wranglers and the staff who was tending to him. The course director came up to escort down Reed, who was with staff on base for the rest of the day.

Discussion questions

1   How could reinforcement theory have been utilized with the establishment of norms to prevent this episode?
2   Full-value contracts are useful tools when administered appropriately. What are some key points to include in the formation of the FVC when creating it with the students?
3   Using the theory of reasoned action, what assumptions can you make about the behavior of the student who attacked James?
4   At the conclusion of this situation, it's likely some de-escalation tactics would be useful to calm Reed down. What are key points when de-escalating someone after a physical fight?

Conclusion

Hopefully, in this chapter you learned some relevant theories to help you mitigate student behavior. If you base your actions for dealing with behavioral situations on one or more of these theoretical ideas, you will be successful at mitigating student behavior, helping them make a plan to improve their behavior, and teaching them life lessons about what is and is not acceptable behavior. Further, a working understanding of these theories will help you prevent problematic behavior, and to be a more impactful instructor for the students you are serving. There are a host of other valid theories out there, and the more you know and base your actions on these tried and true methods, the better instructor you will be.

Main points

- Reinforcement Theory is the foundation of all behavioral change and is inherent in any type of system where an outside force is trying to change behavior. Reference this theory when you consider reward/punishment techniques.
- Ecological Systems Theory is useful to understand a person's attitudes, values, and beliefs. It may also serve to help inform your decisions when chosing an approach to mitigate and manage student behaviors.
- The Theory of Reasoned Action is that all actors in a situation behave in a way that is congruent with the inherent knowledge that they know the consequences to their actions.
- The Theory of Planned Behavior is the foundational theory for understanding why a student is behaving in a particular way, and can help you understand why they are doing this. The behavior is likely the result of the student making an attempt to meet one of their needs.
- The Stages of Change Model is useful to help a student through overcoming and changing a negative behavior. Consider guiding them through these stages and help them to understand where they are in the process.
- The maintenance stage, of the stages of change, is the most difficult stage. Be sure to leave the student with a detailed plan of how they can continue the positive steps they've made while on their OAE experience.

Discussion questions

1 How does Ecological Systems Theory inform our practice both when preparing for students to arrive on course, and in preparing them to return home?
2 What are three critical techniques to remember when trying to de-escalate a student?
3 What can you or your program do to help a student in the maintenance phase after they have returned home from your OAE program?

References

Baldwin, C., Persing, J., and Magnuson, D. (2004). The role of theory, research, and evaluation in adventure education. *Journal of Experiential Education*, 26(3), 167–183.

Berger, C. R., and Calabrese, R. J. (1975). Some explorations in initial interaction and beyond: Toward a developmental theory of interpersonal communication. *Human Communication Research*, 1(2), 99–112.

Bolles, R. C. (1972). Reinforcement, expectancy, and learning. *Psychological Review*, 79(5), 394.

Grant, D. A. (1964). Classical and operant conditioning. In A. W. Melton (ed.), *Categories of human learning* (pp. 1–31). New York: Academic Press.

Kingham, R. J. (1958). Alcoholism and the reinforcement theory of learning. *Quarterly Journal of Studies on Alcohol,* 19, 320–330.

Mazur, J. (2002). *Learning and Behavior.* Upper Saddle River, NJ: Pearson Education.

Norcross, J. C., Krebs, P. M., and Prochaska, J. O. (2011). Stages of change. *Journal of Clinical Psychology*, 67(2), 143–154.

Paquette, D., and Ryan, J. (2001). Bronfenbrenner's ecological systems theory. *Children*, 44, 1–105.

Premack, D. (1965). Reinforcement theory. *Nebraska Symposium on Motivation,* 13, 123–180.

Russell, K. C., and Hendee, J. C. (2000). Wilderness therapy as an intervention and treatment for adolescent behavioral problems. In A. E. Watson, G. H. Aplet, and J. C. Hendee (eds), *Personal, Societal, and Ecological Values of Wilderness: Sixth World Wilderness Congress Proceedings on Research, Management, and Allocation* (vol. 2, pp. 136–141). Proc. RMRS-P-14. Ogden, UT: US Department of Agriculture, Forest Service, Rocky Mountain Research Center.

Stipek, D. J. (1993). *Motivation to Learn: From Theory to Practice.* Needham Heights, MA: Allyn & Bacon.

Von Neumann, J., and Morgenstern, O. (2007). *Theory of games and economic behavior.* Chicago, IL: Princeton University Press.

5

SELECTED CONSTRUCTS USEFUL IN BEHAVIOR AND GROUP MANAGEMENT

Overview

By way of example, this chapter explores specifically selected psychological and sociological constructs that are often used, either explicitly or implicitly, in BGM types of programs. Of particular interest are the constructs of resilience, grit, self-determination theory, emotional intelligence, social support, and restoration. Each of these constructs is thought to be relevant to those programs having behavioral and group management issues within an OAE setting.

Relevant terms

It is important to understand what we mean by concepts and constructs. By concepts we mean elements or components of a theory that are typically based on something factual (e.g. number of people on a course). Constructs on the other hand imply a component of a theory that is hypothetical or inferential (e.g. motivations of the participants). Similarly, construct validity tells us how well our theories translate into actual anticipated outcomes. The constructs of resilience, grit, emotional intelligence, self-determination, empowerment, and social development were selected as constructs important to OAE/BGM because they serve as the underlying goal or parameter for many programs. That is, while there might not be a "theory of grit" to guide our thinking, developing grit among our students is often one of the underlying constructs that guide how we design a program and how to deal with our students.

Resilience

A number of authors have suggested that adventure-based programs can be effective in enhancing levels of resilience because of (a) spending extended time in pristine environments, (b) separation from normal life, (c) social support, and (d) the intensity and challenging nature of the experience (D'Amato and Krasny, 2011; Ewert and Yoshino, 2011). One of the assumptions underlying these studies is that the challenging situations often inherent in adventure experiences may help participants develop adaptive systems that will aid them during future uncertain and demanding events. While much of the work on resilience focuses on traumatic situations, or recovery from highly stressful life experiences (Ai and Park, 2005; Linley and Joseph, 2004), it has also been acknowledged that resilience is a common trait that can arise from everyday situations (Masten, 2001). Recently, a number of researchers have been interested in the development of specific interventions to build or increase resiliency. These interventions include work site training (Waite and Richardson, 2004), clinical interventions for youth (Waaktaar *et al.*, 2004), and military soldiers and veterans (Ewert *et al.*, 2011).

Resilience has been conceptualized as experiencing growth through a disruptive event (Richardson, 2002). Disruption is followed by a phase of reintegration. It is within reintegration that a variety of possible outcomes exist. An individual may reintegrate resiliently, reintegrate back to homeostasis or baseline, reintegrate with loss, or dysfunctionally reintegrate. Resilient reintegration represents the experience of growth or insight through the disruption, rather than simply getting through the experience, or experiencing some sort of loss. Richardson (2002) suggests that knowledge of this process may empower people to make conscious choices regarding the way they experience a disruption, and that training experiences may serve to catalyze this process.

The idea of utilizing specific training or experiences to enhance resiliency is of particular interest to the outdoor adventure field. Adventure programs often utilize a variety of activities, such as peak ascents, high ropes courses, or rock climbing, that can be both challenging and stressful to participants. Additionally, social and emotional aspects of participation, such as living and working in a group or being away from home, may also be stressful. The idea that these experiences can ultimately result in positive growth and development has been a cornerstone of both research and practice in the outdoor adventure literature for several decades (e.g. Neill and Dias, 2001; Walsh and Golins, 1976).

FIGURE 5.1 Students learning to snowshoe in Michigan (photo: Ryan Hines)

Relative to the adventure education field, three primary questions arise from work on resiliency. First, does participation in an adventure education course increase resiliency? Second, *how* do adventure-based activities enhance the resiliency development process? And third, what variables influence the role that adventure programs play with respect to resiliency?

Beyond just being stressful, OAE activities can also contribute to the development of resilience in the following ways:

1 Participants can develop positive views of themselves through their achievements while participating in the experience.
2 While engaging in an OAE, students often develop a more realistic perspective of their capabilities.
3 Through the use of challenging activities, participants can develop an enhanced locus of control.
4 Through group participation, communication skills are often enhanced through OAE.

Thus, the research literature and subsequent practice suggest OAE types of activities and experiences can be effective in promoting resilience in an individual. One way in which these changes can take place is illustrated in Table 5.1, where a combination of antecedent variables such as personality and past experience combine with selected internal and external factors to determine any changes in the level of resilience experienced by an individual. Adventure activities, such as skill acquisition and practice that serve to boost an individual's confidence, awareness of self, such as strengths and abilities in addition to the presence of a supportive group, can provide the catalysts important to enhancing levels of resilience.

TABLE 5.1 Selected constructs and associated activities

Resilience	Grit	Emotional intelligence	Self-determination	Empowerment	Social support
Personally challenging experiences	Goals by end of course	Group activities	Physical activities requiring skill development	• Development of learning and skills	• Group activities that build trust and reliance on others
• Physical	• Daily challenge of outdoor living	Communication and Belaying trust building	• Climbing	• Development of action plans for future behavior	• Facilitated debriefs
○ rock climbing	• Facilitated debrief	• Lowering	• Boating/rafting	• Times for reflection such as mini-solo, quiet hikes	• Small group activities
○ long hikes	• Journal prompting	• Small team activities	• Anchor-building	• Guided facilitation focusing on personal strengths and abilities	• Rafting
○ mountaineering	• Scaffolded	• Facilitated debrief	• Survivor skills	• Leadership activities such as leader of the day (LOD)	• Tandem canoe/kayaking
○ final expedition	• Activities with incremental success	• Reflection activities to examine student's role in the group	• Facilitated debrief	• Autonomous activity (e.g. final expedition)	• Belaying
• Reflective	• Personally challenging experiences	• Simulated activities (i.e. mock job interviews)	• Leader of the day	• Natural consequences journal prompting	• Lowering
○ solo with structure	• Share examples and role models who show grit	• Help students identify their emotions	• Navigation		• Trust falls
○ letter to self	• Reframe problems	• Have discussions about emotions felt on course	• Strengths-based approach		• Community-oriented activities (sharing circles)
Strengths-based approach to course journal prompting facilitated debrief	• Teach strategies for perseverance like incremental goals	• Teach de-escalation techniques	• Create "life plans" or "life mission statements"		• Facilitated time for students to get to know each other
	• Encourage pro-social habits	• Teach problem solving skills	• Great goals		• Team activities (i.e. rafting, belaying others)
	• Facilitated discussion on knowing when to quit	• Role-model pro-social behavior	• Celebrate course accomplishments with strengths-based approach		• Independent travel (minimal instructor role)
			• Role-model pro-social behavior		• Duo (think solo but in pairs)
					• Role-model pro-social behavior

Grit

Grit is defined as the passion for achieving long-term goals and perseverance to accomplish projects that last a month or more (Duckworth and Quinn, 2009). The modern concept of grit in the literature is relatively new and has a growing body of research (Duckworth and Gross, 2014; Hoerr, 2013; Von Culin *et al.*, 2014). The concept of grit moves beyond mere perseverance to encompass both resolution and energy to accomplish longitudinal projects more than a month in duration, with an emphasis on goal attainment (Robertson-Kraft and Duckworth, 2014). By this definition, a person who works on a project for two months and completes it, contrasted to a second person who works on a project for one month and gives up, from losing passion to work on that project, would be said to have more grit. In this way, grit can lead to the accomplishment of goals, which is also an important aspect of character education, how children find success, and an outcome of many OAE programs (Hattie *et al.*, 1997; Tough, 2013).

Grit is different from perseverance in the sense that it is perseverance in the form of interest and effort, and not merely perseverance through hardship, such as loss of a loved one (Von Culin *et al.*, 2014). Von Culin et al. (2014) found that achievement and success is a product of this type of perseverance instead of a random product of ability, chance, or luck. Grit has also been shown to be a significant predictor of success in academic and vocational types of pursuits, including a higher grade point average for students and workplace retention (Duckworth *et al.*, 2007, 2009; Duckworth and Quinn, 2009; Fillmore and Helfenbein, 2015). As opposed to talent, grit is a better predictor of success among a variety of ages and settings, and can thus be thought of as a consistency in what people think, the way they act, and the way they feel about pursuing a project or task.

The theory of planned behavior can be useful for providing a theoretical framework to understand the construct of grit (Ajzen, 1991). This theory posits that a person's behavior is based on their intentions, norms that surround the action being contemplated, and control the actor senses they possess over their situation. For example, if a person wishes to lose weight, they may join a gym because it's a normal course of action within our society for achieving this goal, they have the capital in both social and economic terms to engage in this activity, and the act of joining aligns with their ultimate intention of weight loss in a rational way. Within this framework, grit can be defined as the way in which a person is unwavering in his or her intentions, belief in the norms, and knowledge to pursue a goal set forth by themselves or an external other (Von Culin *et al.*, 2014, p. 2).

While achievement is also an important component of grit, the two terms are not synonymous. For the purpose of youth development through interventions like OAE, achievement is the idea of accomplishing a task regardless of complexity or length (Li and Pan, 2009). This is an increasingly important distinction between the two concepts, even though both are considered as desirable attributes for young people to possess in modern society (Perkins-Gough, 2013). Grit can be thought of as a mediating variable for achievement, where through various amounts of grit an individual accomplishes a task or goal. In this way, possessing "true grit" makes a person more likely to follow through and accomplish a task than another person with "less grit."

The concept of grit is comprised of two different sub-constructs, that of interest and effort in long-term goals (Duckworth and Quinn, 2009). Interest and effort, as they are known to make up the construct of grit, share a strong correlation. Analysis of this correlation was conducted by Duckworth *et al.* (2009) and were shown to be strongly correlated ($r = .59, p < .001$).

Interest as applied here is the idea that a person maintains attention long enough to complete a given task. For example, in learning to play chess a person must maintain interest over a long period of time, allowing them to learn the intricacies of the activity. In this way, a person who successfully accomplishes this goal is thought to have an adequate amount of grit to sufficiently learn the game of chess. However, the demarcation between "knowing chess" and "not knowing chess" is difficult to determine. For this reason, grit has largely been associated with projects with a finite ending such as school graduation (Perkins-Gough, 2013). In contrast to accomplishments that can happen over any person's timespan, it would only take the same person a short length of time to learn how to lace their hiking boots, for example.

Effort is the second component that comprises the construct of grit (Duckworth *et al.*, 2007). Effort can be defined as a person's long-term commitment and energy expenditure to complete a project (p. 1089). If a person is known to be gritty, they will continue to put forth continued, sustained effort towards accomplishing a long-term goal. Again, this is of particular importance when working towards a goal with no tangible ending point. In this context, it is important to consider the definition of grit again as a person's ability to maintain that effort for a significant duration of time. Findings from a recent study indicate that grit is a product of engagement and meaning as opposed to pleasure (Von Culin *et al.*, 2014). That is, a person is more likely to engage in the pursuit of a long-term goal based on the amount of meaning they find in the accomplishment of that task (p. 307). For example, graduating from college is an outcome that often has significant meaning for people because it indicates a level of status within society as well as a practical achievement. This type of pursuit could be an indicator of grit because of the meaning people ascribe to the accomplishment, as opposed to the pleasure they derive from pursuing the goal.

Outdoor Adventure Education programs lend themselves to this idea of grit as a sustained effort because of the natural interest and inherent fascination people have in challenging and potentially dangerous activities like rock climbing and white-water paddling (Wöran and Arnberger, 2012). Furthermore, OAE program participants require long-term interest and effort, as the theory of grit states, merely to complete the experience. This is particularly true of longer OAE programs, which can last up to an entire year. Additionally, daily persistence and recommitment to the program is crucial for students to find success in their course or experience of any length. Each day students must wake up and face the day's challenging activities, be it putting on their backpack, hiking up a mountain, or becoming resigned to the fact that they are stranded in the wilderness with the group of which they are a member. Because of this dichotomy of persistence on a daily basis and over the duration of the course, these OAE experiences are thought to be effective at instilling grit and resilience in participants. Furthermore, evidence from previous studies suggests that traits like grit and resilience can then be transferred back to their everyday life when they return home (Holman and McAvoy, 2005; Rhodes and Martin, 2013; Sibthorp, 2003).

Returning to the example of learning an instrument, there is no point in time where one suddenly "knows how to play" the instrument, but one learns instead over a sustained period of time. Similarly, a person also must put in effort to learn to play an instrument. In this way, grit manifests itself in the form of practicing regularly to develop the skill of playing the instrument. Initial effort may wane, and it might become more difficult for a person to continue their effort towards learning. This person might be said to lack in grit because of the lapse in the effort they are putting into a given task. With this in mind, OAE programs that are longer in length may be more effective at instilling character traits such as leadership and self-concept since there is a longitudinal temporal component to the idea of grit and more time for the treatment to be effective (Hattie *et al.*, 1997). Said differently, it is possible that to enhance levels of grit, defined as interest in a project that takes 30 or more days, one could argue that this skill would require a similar timeframe to be acquired (30 days or more).

Scholars and practitioners are beginning to understand the importance of grit and what it might mean for the lifelong success of their students (Hochanadel and Finamore, 2015; Hoerr, 2013). Hoerr (2013, p. 14) found that most of his students learn grit through extracurricular activities such as traditional sports and practicing for these competitive activities. The repetitive nature of sports, such as practicing every day, may be where individuals acquire grit. Outdoor Adventure Education programs could serve the same function with repetitive tasks such as pitching a tent every day or having to go to the creek to access a water supply. These activities, unlike traditional sports, do not require athleticism and may serve a wider range of abilities than the realm of sports that are traditionally present in school systems. The process of making common tasks more painstaking, like having to hike to get water, may thus be a contributing factor to a student gaining grit through the OAE experience.

Grit has been found to be a significant predictor of a number of traits, including grade point average and cardiac-based exercise (Bowman *et al.*, 2015; Duckworth *et al.*, 2007; Silvia *et al.*, 2013). Robertson-Kraft and Duckworth (2014) further explored the idea of grit as a predictor of teacher retention in low-income schools. These studies imply that grit can be expanded beyond merely standard educational issues and suggest that grit may also be useful in understanding success and goal orientation in a number of different venues related to personal maintenance, goal orientation, and success attainment. Silvia *et al.* (2013) suggested that grit has significant influence over one's personal health and wellbeing. This has implications for a number of fields that directly influence a person's health or other facets of a person's life such as the way they find happiness or life satisfaction (Cohn *et al.*, 2009; Singh and Jha, 2008; Von Culin *et al.*, 2014).

Grit has been conceptualized as a passion and interest to pursue a specific goal over the course of 30 days or more (Duckworth *et al.*, 2007). The temporal component of grit is an important element to consider, given that passion and interest in a goal can be short-term as well. However, the "month or more" portion of grit is manifest from the desire to have a construct that predicts success more effectively than "talent" (Perkins-Gough, 2013). For example, Duckworth and colleagues (2009) found that grit was a better predictor of graduation from West Point Academy than talent (Duckworth and Quinn, 2009; Robertson-Kraft and Duckworth, 2014). This idea is therefore an important consideration for this study, given that many OAE programs are shorter than a month. However, conceptually, this does not mean that grit cannot be impacted by a shorter treatment. Investigation into this idea is an important component of this research. One study has already illustrated that grit can be effectively enhanced by a treatment that is shorter than a month (Gamel, 2014). In her doctoral dissertation, Gamel investigated the enhancement of grit through a seven-day character education program that took place at a summer camp which sought to teach life skills to youth. In her work, she found that, despite this treatment lasting for seven days, subjects did show significant increases in levels of grit (2014, p. 65). This study is foundational to this current work because it establishes a theoretical rationale that grit, which is specific to a 30-day timeframe, can be influenced by shorter treatments. This is of paramount importance because there are few OAE courses that last for more than 30 days. Although the literature tends to suggest that longer experiences are more impactful than shorter experiences, these authors could find no other literature that suggests a necessary or threshold timespan that is required for the instillation of character development traits such as grit (Ward and Yoshino, 2007).

In the United States, as education and youth development is often a topic of interest to politicians, government at all levels is interested in character traits such as grit, tenacity, and perseverance and how society may supplement the current educational system to instill these types of character traits into young people (Shechtman *et al.*, 2013). Shechtman *et al.*'s 2013 report makes the case for furthering character development in young people and how these traits, more so than grade point average, have become increasingly important for predicting success in college, careers, and other facets of their lives (p. 112). This report alludes to the idea that finding concrete avenues for enhancing character development traits is essential to the development of healthy future generations.

Recent literature has drawn attention to non-cognitive developmental traits such as grit in the forefront of fields ranging from education to philosophy (Peterson, 2015). A number of scholars and educators believe grit is an important trait for a young person to possess (Duckworth *et al.*, 2007). For example, possessing grit may help a student do well on standardized tests, complete a course, stay in an extracurricular activity, or have the perseverance to resist a negative behavior like gang membership (Peterson, 2015; Tough, 2013). Due to the current line of thinking, and the aforementioned studies that suggest grit is instrumental in the success of young people, instilling grit through character development is a worthwhile endeavor. This study is therefore important because of the potential for discovering a program, such as OAE, that effectively instills grit, interest, and effort into young people, which would be beneficial both to youth and the societies in which they are members.

It should be noted that the concept of grit, due to popular culture or preconceived notions, and as it exists currently in the literature, is not a product of an individual suffering a hardship (Perkins-Gough, 2013). The concepts of how individuals deal with adversity, setbacks, hardships, or other negative factors in their lives are better suited to be explored through the lenses of hardiness, resilience, or a host of other related perspectives. The exploration of this idea, that grit is the passion for pursuing long-term goals, makes this project unique because it is not limited to only how an individual deals with setbacks, such as those encountered with resilience, but also seeks to address how the levels of passion they have about accomplishing goals they put their mind to affects their personal development. Thus, grit remains central to the idea that it is a predictor of pursuing a goal that benefits or satisfies the intrinsic needs of a person (i.e. becoming an accomplished athlete).

THE OUTDOOR ORIENTATION PROGRAM AS THE INITIATION FOR THE COLLEGE LIFE

Aya Hayashi, Biwako Seikei Sport College, Japan

With a growing rate of students going to higher education (54.5 percent in 2010), "First Year Experience (FYE)," which is a freshman orientation program, has gained popularity over the last ten years in Japan (Yamada, 2012) in order to respond to various types of students. In 2007, 97 percent of institutions in Japan offered some type of FYE. However, few schools have offered outdoor orientation programs. Biwako Seikei Sport College (BSSC) has developed a four-day adventure-based outdoor orientation program called Freshman Camp (FC) for all freshman students (over 300) since the founding of the College in 2003. The goal of the FC is to build interpersonal relationships and to foster environmentally desirable behavior, as the bases for improving competencies of sport professionals. It is the first class (one credit) offered right after the entrance ceremony. Although they had gained admission, the accomplishment of the camp means literally becoming a student of the BSSC, that is, the initiation. Anecdotal evidence shows that 40 percent of graduates think FC was their most powerful class in four years and helped their transition to college and the development of friendships. Several research projects have been conducted to prove the effects, for example, the development of emotional intelligence

(Kurosawa, 2004). Hayashi and Ewert (2013) conducted a long-term study to prove the effect of FC on college adjustment, then found the development of social provision (lasts over two years) and its positive relationships with college adjustment. The program is shown in Table 5.2. These successful program implementations have been made by the actualization of the school mission, careful consideration of students' characteristics, and utilization of the local natural environments, with strong cooperation among faculty members and student staff.

TABLE 5.2 The program of Freshman Orientation Camp at the BSSC

	Day 1	Day 2	Day 3	Day 4
AM		• Outdoor cooking (B&L) • Initiative games by classes	• Breakfast • Bus to trailhead • Mountain-climbing by classes	• Breaking down the camps, cleanup • Reflective activities • Closing
PM	• Opening • Icebreak games • Tent & tarp setting • Cooking dinner • Night hike	• Class recreation activities (competition) • Ori for mountains • Outdoor cooking (D&L)	• Lunch in mountains • Goal at the hotspring • Back to the camp • Dinner party (BBQ) • Camp fire	

School mission

The mission of the school is fostering compassion under the theme of living together with nature. A simple life in the natural environment and physically and emotionally challenging activities that require cooperation with each other help students to find out how they are regarded by others and the natural environment. It is meaningful that they start building the new relationships all at once by sharing fun, anxiety, difficulty, excitement, and achievement together.

Student characteristics

Since the school has only one department that is Sport major, all students are athletes who love competition and physical activities. However, many of them have very strong anxiety about getting along with other students, since it strongly affects their sport accomplishment. The progression for the activities with support from faculty members and student staff is the key to lead them. Many students hesitate to talk to new friends at first. However, through icebreaking activities, building their camp by group, cooking together, trying initiative games, and competitive class recreation, they become ready for the challenge together. After completing successful mountain climbing, they become very close to each other and get motivated for upcoming college life with their new friends.

Natural environment

The school is located between Lake Biwa, which is the biggest lake in Japan, and the Hira Mountain Range. The lake is called "Mother Lake" since it provides drinking water for 14 million people. The students stay three nights in the tents set just by the lake. They experience the beauty of the environment as well as the severity of the area (strong wind and cold in early April). They climb the highest mountain in the area which is often still covered by snow, then on the way down the mountains, they find their school on the mountain range fed by the moonlight off of the shining lake. Through adventurous experiences, the feeling of attachment to the area has grown and they feel "home" where they are accepted.

Support from faculty members and senior students

Since the Freshman Camp (FC) is the important part of the First Year Experience (FYE), all class teachers from the faculty take part in at least some part of the program and share the experience with freshman students. It presents very meaningful opportunities for teachers to build relationships with individual students. In addition, many senior students support the program, for example, students who major in outdoor education take the role of teaching outdoor skills during the FC, and students who major in athletic rehabilitation take care of injuries of freshman students. The support from senior students helps freshman students have the ideas about their near future in college life. Tackling the FC with students and faculty members together is the way to recognize the mission and direction of the school.

I obtained the invaluable friends and self-confidence through the FC. I confirmed that accomplishment of challenges bring me positive change. Now I understand that the FC was the start for my growth. (Comment from a graduate in 2015).

Self-determination

One of the commonly sought goals in OAE/BGM programs is the facilitation of the development of personal motivations that are more intrinsic rather than extrinsic. Linked to a number of related factors such as resilience, "grit," perseverance, and emotional intelligence, intrinsic motivation refers to engaging in behaviors because they are meaningful and valued by the individual as well as satisfying in and of itself, as opposed to engaging in an activity or behavior in order to satisfy a more external demand (e.g. friend wants you to do it, or it's expected of you, etc.). In a process called "internalization" an external motivation such as it is expected can be integrated into an individual's set of internal motives. Thus, in the BGM case and specifically with teenagers or adults having issues with authority, transforming rule compliance from an external motive (e.g. the police will arrest me if I run over this mailbox) to an internal motivation (e.g. I shouldn't run over the mailbox because it's the wrong thing to do and that is not who I am) can be a positive change for the individual.

The construct of self-determination is concerned with the motivations underlying the choices people make when they are not exposed to external influences or interference. Based on the work of Deci and Ryan (2002), the actual theory of self-determination focuses on the degree that a person's behavior is self-motivated and self-determined. Within the OAE/BGM setting, participants are often faced with situations that demand personal initiative and self-responsibility rather than being directed by the dictates of others. From the perspective of OAE, three caveats pertain to the use of the construct of self-determination:

1   Participants can develop the ability to master and control their own emotions and drives.
2   Participants have the inherent tendency toward personal growth and development.
3   Personal growth and development are inherent but not automatic (Deci and Vansteenkiste, 2004).

Moreover, Self-Determination Theory (SDT) is based on three inherent needs that, if present, will facilitate personal growth and development: competence; relatedness; and autonomy. Competence refers to the desire to seek to control and gain a sense of mastery over the outcome of the experience. Relatedness is the desire to interact and experience caring for others. Finally, autonomy is the need to be an active causal agent in one's life and act in accordance with an individual's own belief system.

Past research has suggested that persons high in self-determination may have a more enhanced ability to deal with solitude, practice mindfulness, employ self-regulation in areas such as education, modifying substance abuse such as alcohol use, and the use of environmental behaviors.

There are a number of attributes commonly associated with OAE that serve to enhance aspects of self-determination. For example, perceived control is often present in OAE settings in a variety of ways, particularly as students gain skills and practice using those skills. This sense of control serves to influence the sense of self-determination, particularly with respect to competence and autonomy.

Based on the three components comprising self-determination – competence, autonomy, and relatedness – a sample of OAE/BGM activities that could serve to enhance self-determination include:

- Skill development and practice
- Autonomous activities such as solo, unaccompanied travel, and reflection time
- Experiences necessitating group cooperation and high levels of communication, such as ropes courses, peak climbs, or white-water rafting.
- Activities involving "reciprocity." Reciprocity implies that people have different strengths and capabilities, and as such, specific individuals can help others in areas they are skilled in such as land navigation, and receive help in areas they are less skilled or capable (e.g. cooking).

In sum, OAE activities and experiences can be useful in the BGM situation for a variety of reasons including physical challenges, emotional demands, and group needs. Of particular importance in the BGM situation is considering how to structure the activities and outcomes in ways that enhance an individual's sense of self-determination.

FIGURE 5.2 Cooking in a natural shelter provides fun and variety to the OAE course (photo: Ryan Hines)

Emotional intelligence

Emotional Intelligence (EI) is defined as "the subset of social intelligence that involves the ability to monitor one's own, and others' feelings and emotions, to discriminate among them, and to use this information to guide one's thinking and actions" (Salovey and Sluyter, 1997). More recently, Bradberry and Greaves (2005, p. 24) defined EI as "how we manage behavior, navigate social complexities, and make personal decisions that achieve positive results." Studies have shown that people with high levels of EI have generally shown greater mental health, leadership abilities, and overall job performance. Thus, EI becomes an important construct regarding how OAE/BGM participants manage their behavior, deal with social issues, and make personal decisions that impact their lives.

Previous studies have examined both the development of EI through participation in OAE (Hayashi and Ewert, 2006) and the role that levels of EI play in the enhancement of leadership skills (Hayashi and Ewert, 2013). Relative to the development of leadership skills Hayashi and Ewert (2013) found that higher levels of EI resulted in more effective leadership skills such as maintaining a sense of optimism, flexibility in decision-making, trust, and generating enthusiasm.

Within OAE/BGM, what makes EI a particularly valued construct is that, unlike IQ which is considered relatively fixed, EI is considered a "trainable" attribute (Dulewicz and Higgs, 2004). Many of the activities and experiences created in OAE/BGM programs facilitate the development of a variety of attributes and characteristics commonly associated with EI, such as self-awareness, self-regulation, social skills, empathy, and intrinsic motivation. In addition, the practices of reflection, reoccurring feedback, consequential outcomes, and a small group setting that commonly occur in OAE/BGM experiences help facilitate the development of learned skills such as self-awareness and empathy for others.

In sum, Emotional Intelligence (EI) is a useful construct in OAE/BGM settings. First, many of the activities used in these programs are suitable for enhancing levels of EI. Second, at both the individual and societal levels, EI has some important, even profound, attributes, for example (Mayer, 2008):

1   Better social relations among children and teens, with EI often being associated with more effective social interactions and inversely correlated with anti-social behaviors.
2   EI in adults is linked to enhanced perceptions of social ability and more successful interpersonal relationships. In addition, individuals with high EI are perceived by others as being more pleasant, socially skilled, and empathic to be around.
3   EI has been correlated with greater achievement in academics.
4   EI has been positively correlated with higher life satisfaction, self-esteem, and lower levels of insecurity or depression.

Social development

The Social Development Model (SDM) provides a basis for understanding how relationships and socialization impact behavior (Catalano and Hawkins, 1996). Understanding the SDM can be essential to the intricacies of behavior and group management. The primary goal of many OAE programs is to alter personal relationships to increase more desirable behaviors such as levels of trust and communication in an individual's social system. The SDM provides a framework which suggests that individuals develop social support by offering inclusion in pro-social behaviors and positively reinforces individuals through feedback from peers and trained professionals (Hawkins, Catalano, and Arthur, 2002). Outdoor Adventure Education lends itself to this model because it is based on feedback and processing of the experience. For example, after rock climbing, students will participate in a group discussion to provide feedback about how they performed. This feedback often consists of praise from fellow participants and instructional staff based on their performance. This type of positive, feedback-laden discussion is typical of most OAE course components and OAE programs.

The SDM model suggests that OAE programs may be an ideal place to increase trust, communication, and relationship quality among participants. Moreover, Outdoor Adventure Education courses are structured as safe environments where sensitive and deep types of information may be safely disclosed. This environment, which is usually facilitated by the instructional staff, creates forums in which this information disclosure may happen. Such forums may be absent in an individual's life and therefore a novel experience for them. For example, inclusion in pro-social behavior occurs every time a student engages in a discussion about their relationships with others (i.e. their parents). These discussions often lead to a breakdown in communication and social support barriers. This behavior is praised by the instructional staff and other group participants, thus positively reinforcing this behavior. From this it is likely that the student will continue having similar discussions while engaging in deeper, more meaningful conversations. This also facilitates trust as communication topics get more frequent and more sensitive, requiring more trust between the OAE students and instructional staff, which is critical for behavior modification.

Due to the foundations the SDM has in areas such as criminology, it may also be relevant for extinguishing negative behaviors in individuals (Wiesner and Capaldi, 2003). For example, if a student who has problems following directions from authority figures observes other students following similar directions from their instructional staff with ease, the former may then follow directions more closely and easily to conform to the norms of the group. Likewise, he or she may also get feedback from instructors or fellow participants on this negative behavior, thus increasing the likelihood that this behavior will be modified during and after the course through the SDM model and other intervention strategies.

The SDM model also suggests that individuals will act accordingly to group social norms while participating in OAE courses (Catalano and Hawkins, 1996). Because it encourages positive behavior during the course, including enhancing the peer to peer relationships through positive interactions, it may also suggest that these behaviors will persist after the OAE program has ended. Additionally, the SDM model has also been proven to be relevant and appropriate in recreation and leisure settings including OAE programming, making it ideal to utilize as the framework for this study (Duerden and Witt, 2010).

Social support

Another important concept relative to behavior and group management is the conceptual nuance of social support among participants in OAE courses. While social support has been defined as using others as a resource for coping and problem solving, as well as general sources of support and comfort (Cutrona, 1990), it has been more specifically identified as "information leading the subject to believe he or she is cared for and loved, esteemed, and a member of a network of mutual obligations" (Cobb, 1976). Social support is therefore instrumental in the wellbeing of an individual which can then lead to the development of pro-social and desirable behaviors. Literature has posited that a person who has a positive social support structure is more likely to have a positive view of themselves and others, positive help-seeking habits, and higher emotional support systems in place (Mikulincer and Florian, 1995; Mikulincer et al., 1993).

Social support and social bonding are obviously important components in the OAE experience. The development of social support, while participating in a course, can lead to definite increases in positive norms in post-course behavior (Catalano and Hawkins, 1996). For example, if a participant has a strong social support system, the student is more likely to disclose problems or issues he or she is facing, which then leads to a more healthy and desirable approach to mitigating these problems in the future. While existing literature has shown that positive changes in social support happen during participation in an OAE experiences, there are significant gaps in research as to exactly what these changes are, how they affect a participant's experience, and what lasting effects they may have. By filling this gap in understanding, increased knowledge about social support and its effects on participants may be applied to other EE outcomes that are being addressed.

Social support is often thought to be composed of three separate components; trust, communication, and relationship quality (Ommen et al., 2008). Multiple studies have shown that these three variables can be effective indicators of social support (Cutrona, 1996; Kirmeyer and Lin, 1987; Richman et al., 1998). It is imperative that instructors who wish to enhance the quality of life for their student, and positively manage and mitigate behaviors, help students to build a stronger sense of social support. This can be done by building trust, communication, and strong social bonds within the group members. Further, facilitate discussions based on how this social support constructs were enhanced, and challenge the students to think about how they might duplicate this process with friends and family back home.

Conclusion

Constructs are distinguished from terms such as theories and concepts in that they represent something that may be extremely important but is either hypothetical or inferential. While you might be able to see specific behaviors of students, you can only really hypothesize or infer what their motivations might be, thus, suggesting that the term motivation is a construct. The constructs selected for discussion in this chapter were chosen because of their prevalence and often importance in the area of OAE/BGM. For example, numerous programs are intentionally designed to enhance a person's level of resilience.

Often related to resilience are the constructs of grit and self-determination. Grit is connected to perseverance and a willingness to stay with a given task over a relatively long period of time. Self-determination, on the other hand, typically involves three components often seen in OAE/BGM programs: developing a sense of mastery and competence; relatedness or opportunities to help others; and autonomy which implies having a sense of control in one's life. Other constructs that have been discussed involve emotional intelligence and social development. Emotional intelligence involves being able to regulate one's own feelings and beliefs and, ultimately, behavior. Often present in OAE/BGM programs are opportunities to experience social development and social support. Both social development and social support are examples of tangible ways in which OAE/BGM programs often work toward altering negative behaviors and belief systems, through providing opportunities to work as a member of a small group, effective group and instructor facilitation, and receiving ongoing feedback. Moreover, social support is supported by three components: trust; communication; and the building of quality relationships – once again, factors that are often in play in OAE/BGM programs.

Main points

- Constructs differ from theories in that they represent part of a theory that is hypothetical or inferential. For example, reinforcement theory infers how people develop beliefs about themselves. These beliefs are constructs in that they are hypothetical.
- Resilience is often thought of as a "bouncing back" from an adverse situation or traumatic event. OAE/BGM programs often develop experiences that help an individual develop and enhance their levels of resilience.
- In a similar fashion, many OAE/BGM programs design curricula and experiences that help an individual develop a sense of empowerment, i.e. a sense that they can change their lives for the better.

- Grit is a relatively new construct that is characterized by developing a sense of perseverance and willingness to engage in a behavior that can produce a beneficial outcome but only after an extended effort.
- Research is increasingly consistent regarding the positive relationship between Emotional Intelligence and leadership and societal traits.
- Social development involves the twin constructs of social bonding and social support. OAE/BGM can be especially effective in creating settings where individuals can bond with one another and develop aspects of trust.

Discussion questions

1   In what ways do you think constructs differ from theories?
2   How might you enhance social support amongst your students while they are participating in your OAE experience?
3   Why do you think enhancing grit through OAE experiences can be beneficial for students when they return back home? How do OAE experiences actually build grit in students?
4   How can building social support enhance student's pro-social and desirable behaviors?
5   How can the Social Development Model enhance your understanding of how to structure an OAE experience to encourage pro-social behaviors in your students?

SCENARIO

This incident occurred on a seven-day rafting trip on the Deschutes River. The students of the course were comprised of Grieving Teens, and there were eight students in the patrol. The idea around Grieving Teens is to create a space for peer-to-peer support of teens who are experiencing the lifelong grieving process, usually involving the loss of a parent or sibling. With this unique course type, instructors decided to take a laid-back approach in setting the tone for the course and to create a comfortable, relaxed culture for students.

The primary actor in this scenario is Owen who lost his father, with whom he was very close, eight months prior to the course's start, to an abrupt and short battle with cancer. Owen spoke openly about the loss of this relationship, and shared how he had always assumed his father would see him off for prom, and be cheering him at his high school graduation. At 18 and in such a large transition, Owen was upset about the loss and was often angered and agitated when talking about his father's death.

On day two of the OAE Course, Owen was working in the assigned job role of "Gear Technician" along with another male student, Troy, and an instructor, Holly. Troy and Owen instantly formed a close bond, identifying over their similar athleticism and recent experiences in graduating high school. As the three were loading equipment into a boat, Holly instructed the boys on where to place the dry bags. The boys suggested another location which was less ideal for loading, and therefore rejected by Holly, which resulted in slight tension although Holly explained the reasoning.

Throughout the next 24 hours, the boys approached the male instructor, Anthony, about their reaction to their interaction with Holly. They expressed their opinion that she was aggressive and they were unable to understand the lingering tension. Anthony assured the duo that Holly was in fact friendly and would be open to discussing these feelings. The boys continued to talk about the situation with one another without speaking to Holly. As co-instructors, Holly was aware of the conversation Anthony had with the students. Mutually, it was decided Holly would allow the boys to approach her, as a learning opportunity in communication for the students. Holly observed that each interaction with the boys, especially with Owen, was strained and tense. Her words were misinterpreted by Owen, due to her use of sarcasm which was the catalyst for the tension and issues that prevailed.

As instructors checked in with other students, they were made aware of other issues with the group culture. Owen was using his age as the eldest to take minimal ownership in group responsibilities. He explained to the younger boys about hazing. Owen had become a natural leader within the group, as the biggest and oldest, and his ability established himself as the alpha-male. He chose to move slowly, always consulting others about what to wear daily, and was always the last to join a group meeting. One night, at the conclusion of an evening meeting, Holly was taking volunteers for the next day's jobs. Owen and Troy were whispering on the side, so Holly assigned them the role of cleaner. They rolled their eyes to express their disgust with this decision. As Holly was checking with the students before bed that evening, she approached the boy's camp where they were negatively talking about her and how "she always ruined their vibe."

Holly calmly confronted the pair, and it was clear Owen was the main aggressor. He would not speak rationally and quickly escalated the conversation, becoming angry at Holly and saying she was "extremely unhelpful and judgmental." That night, he had shared with the group about his loss of his father and his currently strained relationship with his mother. She had breast cancer at the time of the course, to compound the issue of losing her husband. Recently, Owen's mother had been asking for more of Owen's help around the house in chores such as taking out the trash. Owen felt that, at this time of his life, he should be out with friends. He said verbal arguments with his mother occurred daily over chores. As instructors talked, they linked Owen's relationship with his mother to his relationship to Holly in each having strong elements of power struggle. Their relationship continued to be strained for the remainder of the course.

Discussion questions

1 How might have using sarcasm in this scenario impeded the instructor's rapport with the student?

2 What actions could have been used to help prevent this scenario and the lack of rapport between the instructor and student?

3 What actions and theories could you draw on, moving forward in the course, that could be taken to start to rebuild the rapport?

4 How is Bronfenbrenner's Ecological Systems theory applicable to this situation?

5 How might this scenario affect other group members' experience and what techniques could you use as the instructor to mitigate the negative group culture that seems to be occurring?

References

Ai, A. L., and Park, C. L. (2005). Possibilities of the positive following violence and trauma. *Journal of Interpersonal Violence,* 20(2), 242–250.

Ajzen, I. (1991). The theory of planned behavior. *Organizational Behavior and Human Decision Processes,* 50(2), 179–211.

Bowman, N. A., Hill, P. L., Denson, N., and Bronkema, R. (2015). Keep on truckin' or stay the course? Exploring grit dimensions as differential predictors of educational achievement, satisfaction, and intentions. *Social Psychological and Personality Science,* 6(6), 639–645.

Bradberry, T., and Greaves, J. (2005). *The Emotional Intelligence Quick Book.* New York: Simon & Schuster.

Catalano, R. F., and Hawkins, J. D. (1996). The social development model: A theory of antisocial behaviour. In J. D. Hawkins (ed.), *Delinquency and Crime: Current Theories* (pp. 149–197). New York: Cambridge University Press.

Cobb, S. (1976). Social support as a moderator of life stress. *Psychosomatic Medicine,* 38(5), 300–314.

Cohn, M., Fredrickson, B., Brown, S., Mikels, J., and Conway, A. (2009). Happiness unpacked: Positive emotions increase life satisfaction by building resilience. *Emotion* (Washington, DC), 9(3), 361–368.

Cutrona, C. E. (1996). *Social Support in Couples. Marriage as a Resource in Times of Stress.* Thousand Oaks, CA: Sage.

Cutrona, C. E., and Russell, D. (1990). Type of social support and specific stress: Toward a theory of optimal matching. In B. R. Sarason, L. G. Sarason and G. R. Pierce (eds). *Social Support: An Interactional view* (pp. 319–366). New York: Wiley.

D'Amato, L. G., and Krasny, M. E. (2011). Outdoor adventure education: Applying transformative learning theory to understanding instrumental learning and personal growth in environmental education. *Journal of Environmental Education,* 42(4), 237–254.

Deci, E. L., and Ryan, R. (eds) (2002). *Handbook of Self-Determination Research.* Rochester, NY: University of Rochester Press.

Deci, E. L., and Vansteenkiste, M. (2004). Self-determination theory and basic need satisfaction: Understanding human development in positive psychology. *Ricerche di Psichologia*, 27, 17–34.

Duckworth, A., and Gross, J. (2014). Self-control and grit: Related but separable determinants of success. *Current Directions in Psychological Science*, 23(5), 319–325.

Duckworth, A., and Quinn, P. (2009). Development and validation of the short grit scale (grit-s). *Journal of Personality Assessment*, 91, 166–174.

Duckworth, A., Peterson, C., Matthews, M., and Kelly, D. (2007). Grit: Perseverance and passion for long-term goals. *Journal of Personality and Social Psychology*, 92(6), 1087–1101.

Duckworth, A., Quinn, P., and Seligman, M. (2009). Positive predictors of teacher effectiveness. *Journal of Positive Psychology*, 4(6), 540–547.

Duerden, M., and Witt, P. (2010). The impact of direct and indirect experiences on the development of environmental knowledge, attitudes, and behavior. *Journal of Environmental Psychology*, 30(4), 379–392.

Dulewicz, V., and Higgs, M. (2004). Can emotional intelligence be developed? *International Journal of Human Resource Management*, 15(1), 95–111.

Ewert, A., and Yoshino, A. (2011). The influence of short-term adventure-based expereinces on levels of resilience. *Journal of Adventure Education and Outdoor Learning*, 11(1), 35–50.

Ewert, A., Van Puymbroeck, M., Frankel, J., and Overholt, J. (2011). Adventure education and the returning military veteran: What do we know? *Journal of Experiential Education*, 33(4), 365–369.

Fillmore, E., and Helfenbein, R. (2015). Medical student grit and performance in gross anatomy: What are the relationships? *FASEB Journal*, 29(1), supplement, 689.6.

Gamel, M. (2014). Impact of character development and empowerment program on grit and resilience growth in early and middle adolescents. *Dissertations, Theses and Capstone Projects*. Paper 646. http://digitalcommons.kennesaw.edu/etd/646.

Hattie, J., Marsh, H., Neill, J., and Richards, G. E. (1997). Adventure education and Outward Bound: Out-of-class experiences that make a lasting difference. *Review of Educational Research*, 67(1), 43–87.

Hawkins, J. D., Catalano, R. F., and Arthur, M. W. (2002). Promoting science-based prevention in communities. *Addict Behaviors*, 27(6), 951–976.

Hayashi, A., and Ewert, A. (2006). Outdoor leaders'emotional intelligence and transformational leadership. *Journal of Experiential Education*, 28(3), 222–242.

Hayashi, A., and Ewert, A. (2013). Development of emotional intelligence through an outdoor leadership program. *Journal of Outdoor Recreation, Education, and Leadership*, 5(1), 3–17.

Hochanadel, A., and Finamore, D. (2015). In education and how grit helps. *Journal of International Education Research*, 11(1), 47–50.

Hoerr, T. R. (2013). *Fostering Grit: How do I Prepare my Students for the Real World?* Alexandria, VA: ASCD Arias.

Holman, T., and McAvoy, L. (2005). Transferring benefits of participation in an integrated wilderness adventure program to daily life. *Journal of Experiential Education*, 27, 322–325.

Kirmeyer, S. L., and Lin, T. R. (1987). Social support: Its relationship to observed communication with peers and superiors. *Academy of Management Journal*, 30 138–151.

Kurosawa, K. (2004). A Survey of Outdoor Experience-type Recreational programs in Depopulated Areas of Hokkaido. *Journal of Environmental Information Science*, 32(5), 119–128.

Li, P., and Pan, G. (2009). The relationship between motivation and achievement: A survey of the study motivation of English majors in Qingdao Agricultural University. *English Language Teaching*, 2(1), 123–128.

Linley, P. A., and Joseph, S. (2004). Positive change following trauma and adversity: A review. *Journal of Traumatic Stress,* 17(1), 11–21.

Masten, A. (2001). Ordinary magic: Resilience processes in development. *American Psychologist,* 56(3), 227–238.

Mayer, John D. (2008). Human abilities: Emotional Intelligence. *Annual Review of Psychology.* 59, 507–536.

Mikulincer, M., and Florian, V. (1995). Appraisal and coping with a real-life stressful situation: the contribution of attachment styles. *Personality and Social Psychology Bulletin*, 21, 408–416.

Mikulincer, M., Florian, V., and Weller, A. (1993). Attachment styles, coping strategies, and posttraumatic psychological distress: The impact of the Gulf War in Israel. *Journal of Personality and Social Psychology*, 64(5), 817–856.

Neill, J., and Dias, K. (2001). Adventure education and resilience: The double-edged sword. *Journal of Adventure Education and Outdoor Learning,* 1(2), 35–42.

Ommen, O., Janssen, C., Neugebauer, E., Bouillon, B., Rehm, K., Rangger, C., and Pfaff, H. (2008). Trust, social support and patient type: Associations between patients perceived trust, supportive communication and patients preferences in regard to paternalism, clarification and participation of severely injured patients. *Patient Education and Counseling*, 73(2), 196–204.

Perkins-Gough, D. (2013). The significance of grit: A conversation with Angela Lee Duckworth. *Educational Leadership*, 71(1), 14–20.

Peterson, D. (2015). Putting measurement first: Understanding "grit" in educational policy and practice. *Journal of Philosophy of Education*, 19(4), 571–589.

Rhodes, H., and Martin, A. (2013). Behavior change after adventure education courses: Do work colleagues notice? *Journal of Experiential Education*, 36, 1–21.

Richman, J. M., Rosenfeld, L. B., and Bowen, G. L. (1998). Social support for adolescents at risk of school failure. *Social Work*, 43(4), 309–323.

Richardson, G. E. (2002). The metatheory of resilience and resiliency. *Journal of Clinical Psychology,* 58(3), 307–321.

Robertson-Kraft, C., and Duckworth, A. (2014). True grit: Trait-level perseverance and passion for long-term goals predicts effectiveness and retention among novice teachers. *Teachers College Record*, 116, 1–27.

Salovey, P., and Sluyter, D. J. (1997). *Emotional Development and Emotional Intelligence: Educational Implications* (1st edn). New York: Basic Books.

Shechtman, N., Debarger, A., Dornsife, C., Rosier, S., and Yarnall, L. (2013). *Promoting Grit, Tenacity, and Perseverance: Critical Factors for Success in the 21st Century*. Washington, DC: US Department of Education, Department of Educational Technology.

Sibthorp, J. (2003). Learning transferable skills through adventure education: The role of an authentic process. *Journal of Adventure Education and Outdoor Learning*, 3(2), 145–147.

Silvia, P., Eddington, K., Beaty, R., Nusbaum, E., and Kwapil, T. (2013). Gritty people try harder: Grit and effort-related cardiac autonomic activity during an active coping challenge. *International Journal of Psychophysiology*, 88(2), 200–205.

Singh, K., and Jha, S. (2008). Positive and negative affect, and grit as predictors of happiness and life satisfaction. *Journal of the Indian Academy of Applied Psychology*, 34, April, 40–45.

Tough, P. (2013). *How Children Succeed*. New York: Random House.

Von Culin, K., Tsukayama, E., and Duckworth, A. (2014). Unpacking grit: Motivational correlates of perseverance and passion for long-term goals. *Journal of Positive Psychology*, 9(4), 306–312.

Waaktaar, T., Christie, H. J., Borge, A. I. H., and Torgersen, S. (2004). How can young people's resilience be enhanced? Experiences from a clinical intervention project. *Clinical Child Psychology and Psychiatry*, 9(2), 167–183.

Waite, P. J., and Richardson, G. E. (2004). Determining the efficacy of resiliency training in the work site. *Journal of Allied Health*, 33(3), 178–183.

Walsh, V., and Golins, G. (1976). *The Exploration of the Outward Bound Process*. Denver, CO: Colorado Outward Bound.

Ward, W., and Yoshino, A. (2007). Participant meanings associated with short-term academic outdoor adventure skills courses. *Journal of Experiential Education*, 29(3), 369–372.

Wiesner, M., and Capaldi, D. M. (2003). Relations or childhood and adolescent factors to offending trajectories of young men. *Journal of Research in Crime and Delinquency*, 40, 231–262.

Wöran, B., and Arnberger, A. (2012). Exploring relationships between recreation specialization, restorative environments and mountain hikers' flow experience. *Leisure Sciences*, 34, 95–114.

Yamada, R. (2012). Current status and problems of first year education: Trends and issues of first year experience. *University Management*, 8(2), 2–7.

6

RELEVANT TECHNIQUES AND THEIR USE IN THE FIELD

Overview

This chapter is designed to explore relevant techniques that field instructors can utilize to mitigate and manage behavior in any Experiential Education setting. The techniques discussed in this chapter often focus on students who need behavioral intervention, but the readers should remember that the techniques are relevant for dealing with any student and can often be used in preventative ways. Wielding these techniques will help instructors prevent, manage, and create behavioral change within the clients they are experiencing. Some techniques outlined will provide a lens or new way of thinking about the students with whom the instructors are working. Additionally, we include validated methods adapted from the field for managing behaviors or dealing with difficult students who lack motivation for participation in OAE programs. By learning, understanding, and practicing the techniques in this chapter, the instructor will have a solid toolkit with which to handle most issues that arise when working with students in an OAE context.

Strengths-based practice

The idea for strengths-based practice is simple: focus on strengths and success and downplay failures and faults (Clark, 1998). However, when put into practice in an experiential education context, it does not always prove to be easy. The emphasis on the negative is how most people have been conditioned to interact with parents, teachers, and other authority figures who may have had an influence in their lives at an early age (Stavros and Hinrichs, 2011). Thus, they perpetuate the emphasis on the negative, and do not always utilize a strengths-based approach which focuses on what a student is capable of or the desirable qualities they possess.

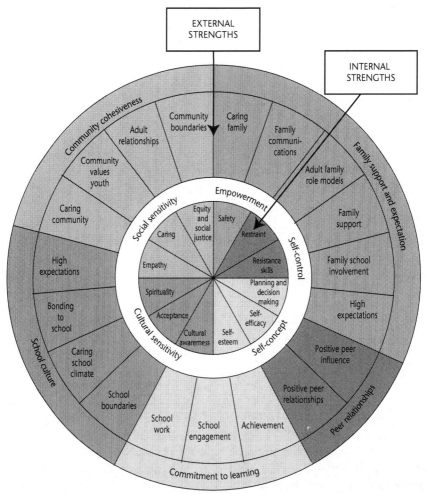

FIGURE 6.1 Various strengths which provide potential focal points to utilize the strengths-based approach

For example, think back to when you were in grade school. If you were a successful student, you probably brought home many more A and B papers than D and F. However, parents often emphasize the bad papers instead of praising every good paper that you earned. In this way, parents focused on the negatives of your achievement and de-emphasized the positives. This approach is the opposite of a strengths-based approach which starts by emphasizing the good attributes or character traits of a person before seeking to exploit, address, or change the deficits that they may possess (Clark, 1998).

Another way to think of the strengths-based approach is to look at a person's strengths first. This will provide a multitude of advantages for the instructor (Passarelli *et al.*, 2010). For starters, by only focusing on the positive, the person will feel valued and appreciated in a new way, and the instructor will have built solid rapport with which to work with the student. OAE programs lend themselves to this technique by providing a multitude of activities in which a person can find success. For example, if a student is not skilled at rock climbing, he or she may still be good at cooking, camp craft, or communication. Finding the strengths emphasize with a student is the first step to utilizing this approach. After identifying the strength, praising the individual, or helping them to understand this is one of their strengths, will progress the strengths-based process (Saleebey, 1996).

The strengths-based approach is also a lens through which to view people in addition to a technique to specifically practice (Gordon and Gucciardi, 2011). However, it can bleed over into all the techniques we utilized as instructors in the field. We want to help people change and grow, and we usually do that by focusing on their deficits. It is easy to forget all their strengths. But this approach reminds us that it can be pivotal for implementing the other techniques and strategies in this book. As you read the following sections, remember to keep in mind a strengths-based approach, and try and think of ways it blends in with all the techniques for having an OAE experience that is student centered, and a positive take on education and personal growth and development.

Natural and logical consequences

Natural and logical consequences are two very effective teaching and behavioral modification techniques (Dinkmeyer and McKay, 1989). If an instructor can properly utilize these ideas, he or she will find success in teaching the students relevant lessons with outcomes they desire. Further, the instructor will be able to promote or discourage behaviors that manifest within the student. This technique is most often utilized to decrease negative behaviors, but as you will see, it can also be utilized to promote pro-social and desirable behaviors.

Natural consequences occur when events transpire that reinforce or hinder a particular behavior. For example, if a student has been taught to keep all of their belongings inside of the tent at night, it is reasonable for them to accomplish this task. If they fail to do so, and a rainstorm comes and gets all their equipment wet, a natural consequence has occurred. Your job as the instructor is to help the student connect the dots so that they learn from this experience, and do not repeat the undesirable behavior. This is where expert facilitation comes into play.

Using this type of event to mitigate behavior requires patience. In the example of the student leaving their gear outside the tent overnight, the instructor must exercise patience while waiting on the rainstorm. It would be natural for the instructor to harass the student each night to put their gear in the tent, however this is a much less effective teaching technique and can strain the instructor/student relationship. If a student has to wear wet boots the entire next day, they are not likely to forget to put their belongings in the tent at nighttime again. This technique alleviates the necessity for the instructor to be a "policing force" during the OAE experience.

TABLE 6.1 Common student behavioral issues and potential consequence actions

Behavior	Consequence
Insults	Three compliments
Disrespects other students	Requires apology (verbal or written); create written contract; if continues, treat as noncompliant behavior
Refusal to clean pots	Loses privilege to eat food that utilize the pots and gets an alternative meal instead (i.e. peanut butter and jelly)
Leave personal gear out at night	Has to deal with wet gear (ensure hypothermia is not an issue)
Swearing	1st: Come up with three appropriate ways to say what they mean. 2nd: 3–5 minutes of silence. 3rd: Separation from the group for 30–60 minutes with journaling activity related to cursing. 4th: Treat as non-compliant behavior
Refusal to be quiet in cabin or tent at night	Stand quietly beside bunk, or just outside tent with staff; if continues, sleep outside with staff
Continually annoys other students	Other students won't interact with that student. Perform facilitation and teaching to increase social awareness
Continually displays unsafe behavior	Removed from activity, possibly course
Hovers around kitchen area during meal prep	Served last for the meal
Throws rocks in inappropriate circumstances or at other students	Must carry "pet" rock around; facilitate appropriate rock-throwing events
Engages in horseplay	Redirect to positive activities

Natural consequences for behavioral mitigation are sometimes a little less obvious to the student, which is why it is critical for the instructor to help the students make meaning of these lessons. As an example, let's consider a student who constantly complains about wearing their heavy backpack. A natural consequence of this behavior may be that the other students do not want to hike with that person anymore. In this example, the instructor may have to help the student make the connection between complaining and hiking alone. However, the natural consequence will be a good teacher for that student and a lesson in not complaining will be reinforced.

Logical consequences differ from natural consequences because they are imposed on the student by the instructor from a position of power. These consequences should be considered as a second resort to natural consequences because there are several factors at play when an instructor utilizes logical consequences. A power dynamic enters into the scene when an instructor chooses to use his or her authority to impose logical consequences. Additionally, logical consequences are not always a rational connection for the student and can result in distrust or resentment against the instructor who imposes the consequence. Therefore, expertise and caution must be utilized when employing this technique.

A logical consequence occurs when an instructor designs a "punishment" for the student because they have demonstrated an undesirable behavior (Dreikurs and Grey, 1990). Common occurrences for this in the OAE context are swearing, not following instructions, or inappropriate behavior. One classic example of the use of logical consequences is as follows. A student, after repeatedly throwing sand at other students was verbally reprimanded twice, and was informed that a

FIGURE 6.2 Students receiving instruction in swift water rescue techniques (photo: Ryan Hines)

third time would result in the use of a logical consequence. After throwing sand again, the student was then made to carry a bag of sand around for the remainder of the day, thus providing a logical consequence, and a tangible reminder not to engage in that behavior.

Because of the potential for this disconnect between the undesirable behavior and the logical consequence, the instructor should design the consequence to have some association with the behavior that they desire to alter. For example, let's say a student is repeatedly instructed to avoid insulting other students. A connected, logical consequence would be to then have the student provide three affirming statements in place of their insults to that student. The connection should be clear to the student that this consequence is a direct result of them saying hurtful things, even after this expectation was clearly stated in the rules of the program or within the context of their full-value contract.

When designing a logical consequence, instructors should be mindful of the three Rs for implementation: related; reasonable; and respectful. In the example of the person who threw sand, the consequence of carrying a bag of sand is directly related to the act of throwing it. Therefore, we would call this consequence related. Second, a reasonable consequence will limit the potential for the student to resent the instructor after the consequence has been imposed. Making a student do 100 pushups or carry all the group's food are not reasonable consequences. As in the old saying, "the punishment should fit the crime." Finally, a respectful consequence is probably the most important R of all. It is not appropriate to choose a consequence where shaming or embarrassment are used as an educational tool. For example, never make a student perform a dance for showing up to a group meeting late. This has the potential to damage an ego and is particularly dangerous when students are in the developmental years (12–22 years old). Using shame or embarrassment as a motivator or consequence is emotionally and socially dangerous and is never appropriate.

Natural and logical consequences are powerful tools and should be considered as effective methods for both teaching and managing student behavior. Hopefully, after reading this section you can come up with effective natural and logical consequences for managing undesired behavior. These ideas have their root in Reinforcement Theory (see Chapter 4) and are some of the most powerful techniques instructors wield. If used effectively, they will be the most impactful lessons you will have with your students.

Motivational Interviewing

Motivational Interviewing (MI) is a technique to be utilized by a facilitator, instructor, or any person who has the right rapport built with a student so that they can begin to talk about a change in behavioral patterns (Miller and Rollnick, 2012). MI is a proven technique to get people to talk about change across many different problems or issues, and spans cultural, age, and gender gaps as well. This technique has been shown to be effective with all kinds of behavior such as: drug use; academic habits; dieting; exercise; and many more (Rollnick and Miller, 1995; Rollnick *et al.*, 2009). It is important to keep in mind that change is often very difficult, and lack of change in behavior is not because of the person being lazy, lacking information, or being difficult. Lack of change is often due to dissonance, or a person wanting two different things simultaneously. Getting the person to transition out of this dissonance or ambivalence is when MI becomes most useful.

Before we get into the details of MI, it is important to understand the roots of MI and where it is grounded. It is because of this foundation that MI has been so successful across so many disciplines for helping people elicit change (Hettema *et al.*, 2005). This foundation is made up of four parts. First, "evocation" or the idea that the idea to change, and the strategies for doing so, come from the student. The instructional staff should avoid the idea that they are mandating for that person to change.

The second foundational element is compassion. It is important to always keep the student's best interest in mind. Further, this is their long-term best interest, and not merely the short-term interest. Instructors can want to change the student's behavior just for the duration of their time on course. They should keep in mind the client's long-term benefits from changing. Third, the instructor must come from a place of acceptance. This means, that they must be accepting if the student is not ready to change or refuses to implement the change. They must also accept their perspective, and opinions, even if the staff or organization disagrees with the student or client.

Finally, establishing a partnership is essential to MI. This means that an alliance is built with the instructor and the student in which there is mutual trust and

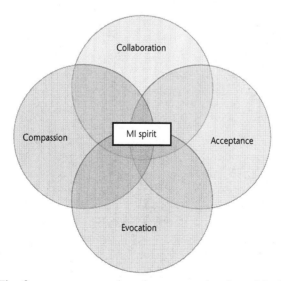

FIGURE 6.3 The four components thought to comprise the spirit of motivational interviewing

understanding. Without this partnership, the student will not view the instructor as a confidant and is much less likely to change their behavior. Instructors would be wise to remember that rapport building starts as soon as the student arrives and that great efforts should be made immediately for this process to be quick and efficient (for more on rapport building see later in this chapter).

After a solid understanding of the four foundational elements to MI, there are four key skills to understand and implement when moving forward with this technique: open questions; affirmations; reflections; and summaries (OARS skills). These skills are rooted in basic counseling techniques are great skills to have when working with people and facilitating a learning experience for them.

SPECIAL CONSIDERATIONS FOR FAITH-BASED GROUPS

Tom Smith, PhD, Summit Adventure, USA

Faith-based groups prolifically engage in experiential education (EE). In most ways, these groups are no different than their secular counterparts. People of faith desire challenge, expanded comfort zones, and improved relationships among colleagues, family members, and social groups. They enjoy gaining skills in new areas. And many are astonishingly passionate about protecting the environment that EE often calls home. There are, however, certain issues that set the sacred apart from the secular in EE. For those expressing particular religious commitments, addressing these core concerns is critical to achieving their goals.

First, worldviews of the truly religious are different from secular folk. Knowing this and acknowledging it publicly are the first steps in designing and implementing effective faith-based EE programs. A look at the twelve-step programs of Alcoholics Anonymous (AA) helps clarify foundational distinctions. According to AA, participants can effectively battle their destructive addiction to alcohol by first admitting that they are powerless to manage their lives on their own without help from a greater Power (or God as we understand God) (ACA, 2007).

For many people of faith, the starting point for human nature is that we inherently seek selfish ends and need the help of God (our greater Power) to overcome this tendency. This worldview is foreign to the secular mind, which often believes that human beings are inherently good, not selfish. And since we have this goodness within us, it follows that there is little or no need for help from God – we can do it ourselves.

Failure to account for these divergent approaches to human nature will undoubtedly cause confusion and mistaken programming objectives. Daily activities might be the same, but the transfer of learning from these program components would be quite different.

Let's take a day of rock climbing for example. This is a very common and powerful EE activity with myriad metaphors for participants to translate back to home, school, and work. A secular approach to human development might focus entirely on our potential to improve ourselves. Issues of trust, communication, risk, and skill would be discussed on the horizontal plane that exists between humans (more or less equal to one another) as they interact.

On the other hand, a faith-based group will interpret the climbing day very differently. The same issues of trust, communication, risk, and skill might well be discussed from a horizontal plane, but there is a "vertical" plane that exists in the relationship they have with God (who is typically viewed as being above or beyond them). Their discussions might include, for example, how trusting the rope is a metaphor for placing our faith in God who will not let us come to harm. And because rock climbing is a powerful activity, the metaphors of trust, faith, and risk in the context of a loving, protecting God become very relevant to religious persons.

The second core issue might perhaps seem to contradict the first, but within faith-based groups, differences among individuals will astonish the unprepared experiential educator. Though a group of people from a certain religious or spiritual commitment might agree on basic tenets of their common faith, they will also vary widely on other secondary issues. Take a volatile topic like capital punishment for example. Hearing one religious person say they favor the death penalty because that is the standard in the Old Testament crashes hard into the beliefs of another equally religious person adamantly asserting that Jesus was against killing of all sorts.

I have learned in nearly 35 years of work with thousands of groups, faith-based and secular, that judging and assuming certain things about the people that comprise these groups is risky business. Take for example, the use of the word "Christian" to describe a group or person. Popular media and our own experience can easily pigeonhole all people using that moniker into one stereotype and belief system. But even a quick check reveals that ten years ago there were at least 217 different Christian denominations in the US alone! Clearly there is no such thing as one kind of Christian.

The best recommendation that exists for working with faith-based groups is the same one that works for every other group: treat people compassionately and fairly as individuals and spend plenty of time really listening to them. Groups and people are all different – no two are the same. Recognizing that faith-based groups may well have a significantly different worldview than their secular counterparts can be the starting point for very fruitful discussions and powerful transfers of learning. Regarding each person in those groups as individuals with very different needs, feelings, and goals will cause us to seek out the best learning situations for everyone involved, regardless of religious affiliation.

Open questions

Open questions are those that will elicit more information from the student and will help the instructor make a more informed decision about the student (Davidson, 2013). For example, "are you hungry?" is a closed question. The instructor has limited the range of answers between "yes" or "no." A better and open-ended question would be something like, "how are you doing?" This type of open question enables the student to expand upon their answer and tailor it to their most relevant needs at the time the question is being asked.

This type of questioning is important to making the student feel like they can talk about their needs. Asking a question with "don't you want to ..." implies judgment on the part of the instructor and can make the student feel judged, ignorant, and break the trust between staff and student. Open questions also help the student drive the conversation and is more about meeting their needs as opposed to driving the instructor's agenda. These questions are great for MI and facilitating the experience.

Affirmations

Affirmations are statements pertaining to anything positive that the student has done. There is no limit to what an affirmation can consist of and they should be spread throughout the conversation so that the student feels encouraged, appreciated, and paid attention to. Affirmations can also help strike the balance of a conversation from being all about the negative things the student needs to change, to a more balanced discussion about what they've done well and behaviors they could work on. This will help the student avoid a defeatist attitude and walk away with more energy for implementing the changes discussed.

Reflections

The third skill, and considered the most important by some practitioners and scholars, is reflective listening. This skill takes the most practice for people, but is essentially trying to understand what the student is feeling or thinking, and then saying it back to them so that they know you understand. It is important to keep your reflections as statements, not questions. An example of a reflective statement would be:

> Student: I don't like being disrespected in the group and made fun of by others.

> Reflective statement: So, you want to change how you are perceived by the group.

These types of statements affirm that you have heard and understand the student and what they are trying to communicate with you.

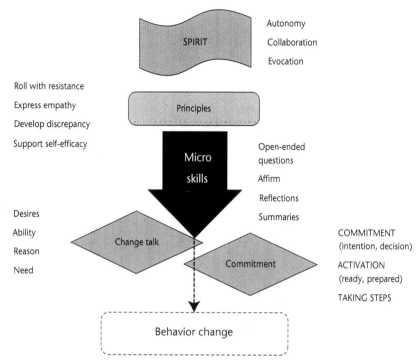

FIGURE 6.4 Progression through the steps of utilizing motivational interviewing

Using these statements also conveys empathy, helps build the alliance between instructor and student, and can help the instructor understand how the student sees the problem or issue. Having an empathetic, foundational understanding of the problem or behavior is essential before seeking change within the student. Only with this understanding can the adequate amount of trust be established for the student to move forward with changing their behavior.

Summary statements

Summary statements, can be used in concert with reflective statements. These types of statements, made by the instructor, distill the information that the student has conveyed, and establishes a place of mutual understanding. These statements can also help the student reach a moment of clarity. For example, if a student comes to an instructor with these three statements:

- "I hate the group"
- "I don't have any friends here"
- "Nobody likes me"

an appropriate summary statement from the instructor might be, "If I understand you, you don't like the group, are having trouble making friends, and are having trouble fitting in."

By selectively summarizing the student's statements, an instructor can then establish a platform for them to encourage the student to want to seize the opportunity to change. In the last example, after this summary statement, the student may come to the conclusion that they need to change their behavior to fit into the group. This revelation may come on their own, or there could be a follow-up reflective statement such as, "Are you making an effort to fit into the group or find friends?" In this way summary statements are a starting place to work with the student for behavioral change.

After a foundation in MI undertones and an understanding of the OARS process, the student and instructor can then move into the four processes for implementing change: engaging; focusing; evoking; and planning. These four processes follow an order after establishing a problem or point for change through the OARS process.

First, engaging the student is establishing a positive and trusting relationship. This can be done through taking an interest in that student's life, asking them questions, or trying to relate to them on a personal level. This process is essential if the instructor is to be a confidant and to help the student realize and then move through the change process. This process also involves time – it usually does not happen in an instant. During this time, remember to avoid judgments, questions that lead to implied judgment, telling them they have problems or need to change, or a power difference. For example, the instructor should try to avoid the fact that they are in a position to punish or reward the student, and should let the implicit power – that they have knowledge the student needs for participation on the course – be the only power dynamic present on the course.

Second, focusing is setting an agenda to establish change. This can be done in a myriad of ways: student contracts; behavioral plans; smart goals. The student and instructor should set the agenda together, but the student's motivation should drive the conversation. Establishing a change plan should be a collaborative process, and providing reflective statements that the students can act on. The instructor can make "soft" suggestions during this portion, only about specific behavioral change techniques, if it seems like the student lacks ideas for change implementation.

Third, evoking is defined as eliciting a student's own motivation for change. Returning to our example, reminding the student that they want to fit into the group is the perfect motivation for changing behavior. However, when this becomes difficult the student might need reminding of this motivation. During this phase, the instructor should key in on "change talk" or any quotes that convey desires by the student. "I want," "I wish," and "I can" are all change talk phrases to key on by the instructor and point out when facilitating conversations about behavioral change. Reinforce, encourage, and try to elicit change talk. During this phase, the instructor should ask questions to elicit as much change talk as possible so that the idea of change is reinforced in the student's mind.

Finally, planning is the final step in the MI process. This phase involves designing a specific plan in which the student can implement change. For

FIGURE 6.5 Students engaged in an evening "debrief" or meaning-making session (photo Ryan Hines)

example, a student who is having trouble making friends on the course might come up with a plan to ask three personal questions to each group member by the following night. In this way, the student and instructor have devised a specific, measurable, and timely plan for the student to try and increase their group membership status. It is important to remember that the student should devise these plans, or at the very least they should be collaborative utilizing the OARS skills.

MI is a powerful technique for implementing changes in student behavior. If utilized effectively and proper rapport is built, the instructor and student can come up with a solid plan to help the student accomplish any behavioral change idea they may experience in an EE setting. Learning the skills of the MI process will make any instructor a better teacher, facilitator, and confidant to help students become better human beings.

Behavioral contracts

A behavioral contract is a written or verbal agreement between the instructor and student to help reinforce a desired behavior. An effective behavioral contract includes three components:

1   The expected behaviors that the student will or will not display.
2   The positive or negative consequences for the behavior.
3   The timespan that the contract encompasses.

Behavioral contracts are a proven method for mitigating or altering behavior (Miller *et al.*, 1974). These contracts can be used to promote positive behavior in addition to influencing negative behaviors (Wolery *et al.*, 1998).

The first step to using a behavioral contract is to establish the behaviors that need to be altered. Keep in mind that this technique can be positive, like encouraging a student to voice his or her opinion. Or they can aim to decrease a negative behavior such as using swear words during their OAE experience. This means that the behaviors should be observable and measurable, and not vague. An example of a poor, vague behavior would be something like "Billy should be more of a leader." This type of behavior is hard to quantify and lacks specificity.

Developing behaviors to be altered should also be decided upon collaboratively using the motivational interviewing process. By involving the student in the decision to alter the behavior, the instructor will create investment in the process and, as a result, they will be more likely to improve their behavior. Simply mandating behavioral change should only be considered in extreme conditions like a student is being unsafe or violating key principles to the OAE program.

After the initial behavioral change is agreed upon, get the student to help you identify rewards that he or she can earn. Some examples of rewards that a student may be interested in are food rewards like chocolate, or something intangible like more free time may be appropriate. Go into the contract meeting prepared with some rewards in mind, but let the student be the driver of what he or she would like to earn. This too will create investment in the process and increase the likelihood of success of the behavioral contract. Also consider creating a list of rewards from which the student can periodically choose. This may also increase the investment of the student in the process.

The next step is to develop a clear outline of the direct actions the student must take to earn the reward. Remember to be as specific as possible when developing this section of the contract. Something that can be helpful is to create observable benchmarks that the student must meet. For example, in the case of the student who wants to exhibit leadership, an appropriate benchmark might be to speak their opinion at least three times per day. As an instructor, you should keep track of these benchmarks and write them down so that you can reference them with the student at a later time.

Before the final step of signing the contract, make sure to go over the contract thoroughly with your student to ensure that both of you know what is expected of that student and yourself, as the instructor. Be clear about how the behavior will be observed and measured, and how the reward or consequence system will be utilized. A misunderstanding in the execution of the contract can lead to major issues of trust between the student and the instructor. This type of misunderstanding should be avoided at all costs. Because of this issue, it is usually helpful to have the student write the components of their contract. This will cater to visual learners and make them think more about what they are about to agree to.

After signing the contract, the agreed upon behaviors, rewards, and consequence system should take effect. To increase the likelihood of success,

Name: _____   Date: _____

Length: _____

Starting time date: _____   Ending time/date: _____

What behavior do I accept responsibility for changing?

I can change my behavior best by choosing a more appropriate behavior to replace it.
What happens for me, or how are things better for me by choosing the new behavior?
My new behavior(s) will be:

What are at least 2 other specific things I can do to help change this behavior?

What are the reasons that I can think of for me not to follow my plan?

What are the negative consequences for my choosing not to follow my plan?

What are the positive consequences my choosing to follow my plan?

What is my plan when this contract is finished?

Student Signature: _____   Staff Signature: _____

FIGURE 6.6 An example of a behavioral contract from the Outward Bound field staff manual

make sure to reference the contract often. This could be as simple as pulling the student aside each morning and evening and looking at the contract together. If the student never sees the contract again, they will start to assume that you have forgotten about it. Looking at it frequently will help reinforce the contract and goals for the behavior of the student. Other options to consider are posting the contract where the student can see it, or making two copies, one for the instructors and one for that student to keep in their pocket.

If you find the behavioral contract is not being effective there are a few techniques you can try to increase the student's investment. First, try increasing the reward system in place. The immediate receiver of a reward will help reinforce the positive benefits of participating in the behavioral contract. Second, consider compartmentalizing the desired behavior. Making smaller, more achievable behavioral goals for students might increase their ability to accomplish the intended outcome. This can be particularly important when working with developmentally limited students like kids with ADD, ADHD, or LD.

Behavioral contracts are an important tool for an instructor to be able to utilize when dealing with students. Often, they should be utilized before a student is dismissed from the course, because they have been found to be a powerful and effective resource for promoting or discouraging behaviors. Remember to make the goals observable and measurable, create investment by using a collaborative process to develop the contract, and make the rewards and consequences meaningful for the student. Finally, keep the contract handy and reference it often. These contracts can often be the key piece a student needs in order to find success during their EE experience.

BEHAVIOR CONTRACT

Date: _____

I promise to work on these behavior expectations: _____
_____
_____

Choose 3 of the following or create your own.

- ☐ I will go to bed when asked
- ☐ I will not interrupt
- ☐ I will respect the property and privacy of others
- ☐ I will not give in to peer pressure
- ☐ I will present a positive attitude instead of being negative, pessimistic, or rude
- ☐ I will get ready for school on time
- ☐ I will limit my use of technology (television, cell phone, computer, video games, etc) to ___ hrs/day

- ☐ I will pick up after myself
- ☐ I will keep good hygiene
- ☐ I will be sensitive to the feelings of others
- ☐ I will avoid places and objects that are unsafe or dangerous
- ☐ I will complete my homework on time
- ☐ I will listen and be attentive when spoken to
- ☐ I will spend time with my family
- ☐ I will _____

- ☐ I will use good manners
- ☐ I will treat others with respect
- ☐ I will avoid behaviors that are aggressive, destructive, or dangerous
- ☐ I will take responsibility for my actions and not blame others
- ☐ I will eat healthy foods
- ☐ I will do my chores
- ☐ I will _____
- ☐ I will _____

Reward for meeting these expectations: _____
_____
_____
_____

Consequence for not meeting these expectations: _____
_____
_____
_____

Child Signature: _____ Date: _____

Parent Signature: _____ Date: _____

Kid Pointz™ Pointing Kids in the Right Direction
www.KidPointz.com

FIGURE 6.7 Another example of a behavioral contract

Caring environment/rapport building

Building rapport is considered by some to be the most foundational practice to preventing behavioral issues in experiential programs. Having a solid rapport between staff and students will increase the likelihood that all parties involved will find success. Rapport can lead to increased communication, trust, and increase the likelihood that people will get along. Building rapport is also paramount if instructors are interested in having the type of relationship with their students in which they can change their lives as so many of our programs often claim to do. This will also help the instructional staff establish a caring environment in which the course will become richer.

Building rapport is very much a skill just like paddle strokes or facilitation. It should not be assumed that staff automatically come in with an understanding of how to effectively build rapport with students. Training and guidance should be provided in staff orientation on how best to do this. Further, it would be wise to consider how staff match with the population they serve. For example, a United States based staff member working overseas in Korea may need additional training, not only in cultural competencies and norms, but also in how to build rapport effectively with those students.

There are many effective ways to build rapport with students. The purpose of this section is not to exhaust this topic, as whole books have been written on it. However, there are a few fundamental components to rapport building that we will mention. Following these basic steps will help ensure your staff knows the basics of building rapport and should help them successfully establish a relationship with students.

Authenticity is essential, as most people can effectively detect when somebody is not acting in a genuine manner. The screening for this happens in staff hiring, which is why it is essential to hire staff that are there to serve the students and the organization and not their own desires. One way to show authenticity is to ask questions of the students. Taking a genuine interest in where they are from, number of siblings, or what their parents do for work will help convey care and interest from the instructor to the staff.

While building rapport, one of the most powerful tools a person can use is active listening. This will show the student that you have an interest in their lives, and are making an effort to get to know them. Active listening includes:

1   Make eye contact.
2   Look and act interested.
3   Nod your head to show you understand.
4   Paraphrase what you think you've heard.
5   Ask clarifying questions.

Utilizing these skills can help build rapport quickly. Making this a priority isn't always easy to do with busy course starts, but it should be as it will lead to a much easier and more successful course in the long run.

Using names is another way to quickly and easily build rapport. Learning names, especially in a large group, can be difficult, but learning people's names shows that you have a genuine interest in who they are. Also, don't forget to use their names after you have learned them to demonstrate you know who that person is. There are several techniques for facilitating this process. Instructors should explore this idea at length and find a technique that works for them and their learning style. After learning a name, try using it at least two times the first day to make the learning stick, and show that you know it.

Finally, finding what excites the person and taking an interest in it can help build rapport. This one can be difficult when age or culture creates differences that are often misunderstood. The classic case is the outdoor instructor who is technologically averse, but has a group of students who love video games. The instructors should seize this as an opportunity to learn about an area that they don't know much about and see what types of games are out there. Furthermore, they can also use this knowledge to connect lessons, tailor the course, or facilitate peer to peer connections through common interests among students.

As stated, rapport building is a complex topic. Though it does not take a rocket scientist to build rapport with somebody, it does take effort and a genuine desire to get to know that person. Seeing a person as a valuable human being with knowledge and skill, regardless of how they differ from you, is essential to this process.

Intentionally designed experiences

Designing OAE programs with an intentionality to minimize behavioral and motivational issues can be exceptionally important to minimizing the issues instructors may experience on courses. Careful thought about who the students are and gleaning as much information about them before the course begins is essential to building a course that will accommodate the needs of the students. Techniques for this include reviewing provided paperwork thoroughly, talking with other staff who may have interviewed the students prior to the course, and making calls to parents, doctors, therapists, teachers, or to the students themselves. Beginning the experience with as much information as possible will help you design their course to achieve maximum success with minimal hiccups.

Additionally, designing the experience with incremental challenges is critical to fostering success (Ewert and Voight, 2012). Oftentimes, behavioral issues are the result of stress and anxiety. Ensuring that you are easing into your program in terms of skill acquisition or physical difficulty will help build the efficacy of the student and empower them to believe that they are capable of completing the course. Ewert et al. (2011) found that a student's number one fear is their ability to complete the course. Having components where the students can find success early in the course, like meeting the required miles of hiking for a day, or teaching them basic skills like stove use, will build confidence in the student and minimize behavioral incidents.

OAE programs are also intense in terms of time spent with other people. Instructors would be wise to consider this and recognize that, if they do not allow for students to recharge their social energy, they may soon find themselves dealing with interpersonal issues related to behavior. One technique for alleviating this is periodically building in solo time for students who are more introverted. This will allow social tensions to ease and gives all students, even the extroverts, time to regain patience, kindness, and the ability to deal with being in a large group for an extended, intense period of time.

Working with a pair of instructors, a minimum of two, is also part of intentionally designing an experience that may help assuage behavioral issues during an OAE experience. Working in tandem will allow for students to have double the chances of personally connecting with someone on the instructional team. As stated in the "building rapport" section, this rapport is often a critical component for having a meaningful, successful, OAE experience. Additionally, working as a minimum of two also allows for the establishment of roles within the instructional team with students. For example, one person can be the point person for consequences of a particularly difficult incident, while the second instructor can be the sympathetic ear who comes in later to mine the student for more information about the root cause of their issue. Gender differences within the instructional staff can also help the various students who feel it might be easier to connect with a particular gender do so within the OAE context.

Finally, designing your OAE experience to focus on group cohesion at the beginning of the course is essential to mitigating behavioral issues. Allowing time and space for the students to bond and learn about each other is critical. The most essential activity is the development of the group contract. Making this a collaborative, fun, and bonding activity will help bring the students together with a common understanding of the values you and your organization idealize and help ensure an inclusive OAE experience. Other activities can include any number of initiatives, free time, or a sharing circle in which all the students share some element of the life story. Remember to keep it fun and light at first so as not to burden the students with heavy, dreadful meetings from the onset of the course.

Carefully designing an OAE experience can be essential to minimizing the number of behavioral issues you and your students may experience on an OAE program. Instructors and programmers should give as much attention to behavior management issues when designing experiences as they do risk, cost, and location when they are choosing the elements for the OAE experience. Remember to be intentional about how you plan the experience and always have the student's best interest in mind, remembering that this is their first OAE experience (usually) and allowing time for proper learning and skill development will pay off for you in the long run.

Conclusion

This chapter, we have explored relevant techniques that are essential for a field instructor to be familiar with for managing and mitigating behavioral incidents that occur in the field. Additionally, some theoretical lens were provided to approach dealing with students to maximize instructor success in these situations. Hopefully, after practicing these skills, field staff will have resources and techniques with which to help students accomplish positive behavioral change.

Students from a major American Metropolitan area were brought to Wyoming for a summer camp that is one component of a year-round program promoting leadership development, interpersonal skills, and job training opportunities. These students are in their third year of this program. During the current year, students have the ability to partake in a two-week trip: the first half sea kayaking; the second half backpacking. During the backpacking portion of the trip the students are expected to perform at a high level and operate somewhat autonomously, and without instructor supervision.

On the backpacking trip, in which the students are operating relatively independently of the instructional staff, they arrived at the designated campsite after a five-mile hike. They are resting and relaxing, beginning to set up camp in a communal, leisurely manner. In a startling manner, gunshots ring out and are echoing off the mountain side in rapid succession. Upon hearing this, the group's demeanor suddenly changes as students revert back to an individualistic dynamic, tense with defensive fear. The leaders, hearing the gun shots, and watching the group change, became anxious deciding how to address this issue.

One leader addressed the group, stating various reasons for this sound and began a conversation asking in which situations students had heard gunshots before. The discussion allowed students to be vulnerable, share their perspective, and reinitiate trust. While this conversation was occurring, the other two leaders walked towards the sound to discover a group of target shooters. Upon the leaders' arrival and a quick greeting, both parties stated their purposes, with the leaders explaining the emotional and mental stress the gunshots were creating within their group. The target shooters apologized, asked if they could finish their rounds, and explained how in a national recreational area target shooting is allowed when groups are not within 500 feet. (The distance between the two parties was about a quarter of a mile.) The two leaders took this information back to the group, joined the tail end of the conversation, and followed up with each student individually. The next day, the group broke camp and headed out to their next destination.

1   What Ecological Systems are at play in the students' reaction to hearing gunshots that have affected their response?
2   How can Motivational Interviewing be useful for both confronting the hunters and having a meaningful conversation with the students?
3   How can this scenario be a catalyst for having meaningful conversations with the students after emotions have abated?

Main points

- Strengths-based approach can be used to focus on the strengths of an individual and build a platform of rapport with which to work with the student.
- By focusing on a student's strengths, an instructor can increase that student's self-esteem, locus of control, and confidence to make the necessary behavioral changes.
- With a foundation in Reinforcement Theory, an instructor can use natural and logical consequences to promote pro-social behavior or decrease undesirable behavior within an individual student or student group.
- Motivational Interviewing is a useful technique to dive into a student's background and behavioral issues. This technique, although complex, is extremely powerful and likely to yield very positive results.
- Behavioral contracts are a great way to define clear expectations and help a student work towards more pro-social behaviors.
- Building rapport might be the most important behavioral management technique an instructor can use with students. It is imperative that an instructor figure out techniques and styles that work effectively for them.

Discussion questions

1 What are the three most important considerations to remember when trying to build a rapport with a student?
2 How might you use motivational interviewing on a student who lacks the desire to complete their EE course?
3 A strengths-based approach requires finding the strengths in the student and then communicating that to that individual. What are some creative ways you could convey the strengths you have observed to those individuals beyond verbal praise?

References

Adult Children of Alcoholics (ACA) (2007). *Twelve Steps of Adult Children*. Torrence, CA: ACA World Service Organization.

Clark, M. (1998). Strength-based practice: The ABC's of working with adolescents who don't want to work with you. *Federal Probation*, 62(1), 46–53.

Davidson, C. (2013). *The Outdoor Facilitators Handbook* (1st edn). Lee Vining, CA: Go For Broke Publication.

Dinkmeyer, D., and McKay, G. (1989). *The Parent's Handbook: Systematic Training for Effective Parenting* (3rd edn). Circle Pines, MN: American Guidance Service.

Dreikurs, R., and Grey, L. (1990). *A New Approach to Discipline: Logical Consequences*. New York: Dutton Penguin.

Ewert, A., and Voight, A. (2012). The role of adventure education in enhancing health-related variables. *International Journal of Health, Wellness and Society*, 2(1), 75–87.

Ewert, A., Overholt, J., Voight, A., and Wang, C. C. (2011). Understanding the transformative aspects of the Wilderness and Protected Lands experience upon human health. In A. Watson, J. Murrieta-Saldivar, and B. McBride, comps. *Science and stewardship to protect and sustain wilderness values: Ninth World Wilderness Congress symposium. Proceedings RMRS-P-64* (pp. 140–146). Fort Collins, CO: U.S. Department of Agriculture Forest Service, Rocky Mountain Research Station.

Gordon, S., and Gucciardi, D. (2011). A strengths-based approach to coaching mental toughness. *Journal of Sport Psychology in Action,* 2(3), 143–155.

Hettema, J., Steele, J., and Miller, W. (2005). Motivational interviewing. *Annual Review of Clinical Psychology,* 1, 91–111.

Miller, P., Hersen, M., and Eisler, R. (1974). Relative effectiveness of instructions, agreements, and reinforcement in behavioral contracts with alcoholics. *Journal of Abnormal Psychology,* 83(5), 548–553.

Miller, W. R., and Rollnick, S. (2012). *Motivational Interviewing: Helping People Change.* New York: Guilford Press.

Passarelli, A., Hall, E., and Anderson, M. (2010). A strengths-based approach to outdoor and adventure education: Possibilities for personal growth. *Journal of Experiential Education,* 33(2), 120–135.

Rollnick, S., and Miller, W. (1995). What is motivational interviewing? *Journal of Consulting and Clinical Psychology,* 61, 455–61.

Rollnick, S., Miller, W., Butler, C., and Aloia, M. (2009). *Motivational Interviewing in Health Care: Helping Patients Change Behavior.* New York: Guilford Press.

Saleebey, D. (1996). The strengths perspective in social work practice: Extensions and cautions. *Social Work,* 41(3), 296–305.

Stavros, J., and Hinrichs, G. (2011). *The Thin Book of SOAR: Building Strengths-Based Strategy.* Bend, OR: Thin Book Publishing.

Wolery, M., Bailey, D., and Sugai, G. (1998). *Effective Teaching Principles and Procedures for Applied Behavior Analysis with Exceptional Students.* Boston, MA: Allyn & Bacon.

7

WORKING WITH
SPECIFIC POPULATIONS

Overview

Populations that experiential programmers work with are diverse and unique. These populations can range in age, gender, ethnicity, and have a variety of needs. Part of the beauty of experiential education programs today is the fact that these programs serve all types of ethnicities, races, and backgrounds. From people with terminal illnesses to veterans returning from war, experiential education can be beneficial to all these populations when staff have the proper training to accommodate their needs. The purpose of this chapter is to explore some commonly served populations and how the typical OAE instructional staff member can adjust their facilitation and instructional techniques accordingly, to best deliver the mission of their organization to these populations.

Adolescents

Working with adolescents can be particularly rewarding and frustrating at the same time because of the stage of life these students are experiencing. This specific population is difficult because of the range in maturity an instructor can experience between students who range in age from 12 to 18 years old. However, these students are engaged in an important developmental phase of life where identity formation, values, and beliefs are happening, and thus an experiential education program can be particularly powerful for these students (Baltes *et al.*, 2007). The following sections will provide some important considerations for working with this population.

First, consider the place of the adolescent in the societal context in which the OAE program is taking place. As stated in other parts of this book, an adolescent in one particular cultural setting can be drastically different from another. For example, they can have been subjected to different norms, parenting styles, and various ecological systems that influence every facet of their personality and character (see Ecological Systems Theory in Chapter 4) (Holmbeck *et al.*, 2000). Having some cultural awareness of the student, regardless of age, is always critical to providing a meaningful and impactful experiential education course for those individual students.

An additional consideration is to take into account the life stage in which these students may be involved at the time they are on their OAE course (Head, 2002). For example, a 12 year old is usually significantly less mature than an 18 year old, but not always. Likewise, even though they are both considered "adolescents" they are different in a myriad of ways. To speak in generalities, the older student is concerned with driving, getting into college, or pursuing romantic relationships more seriously. The younger student is closer to childhood, and thus possibly has different goals, priorities, and life experiences that are relevant to their OAE experience, and the types of learnings they can experience while participating in the program differ drastically.

First, it is important to establish some characteristics of adolescents. These stereotypes should be taken with a caution in the sense, that they are not applicable to every adolescent. However, these assumptions are grounded in the author's personal beliefs, experience, and relevant literature on these topics. These characteristics are as follows. First, adolescents are at a vulnerable and unique time in their life where their identity is being challenged and formed through constant social pressures and constraints. At this time, they are particularly vulnerable to outside influence such as adults that are important to them. Studies suggest that the number one influence on adolescents is a strong role model, and this will quite possibly be the "cool" instructor of their OAE program. Further, these impacts are timely when adolescents come on an OAE program because this can be an extremely impactful experience. Likewise, this vulnerable time in their life can be riddled with pitfalls, as the student learns to negotiate hardships, relationships, and their own personalities.

Adolescents seek autonomy and independence as they test their own limits and abilities (Holmbeck *et al.*, 2000). This may make experiential education programs ideal places for learning for adolescence. For example, having an autonomous student experience, where the students navigate off-trail independently, may

FIGURE 7.1   OAE students on a backpacking course in central Oregon (photo: Curt Davidson)

be particularly useful for instilling traits like resilience and grit into the learner. Instructors should allow for the appropriate amount of training before turning too much autonomy over to the students. Further, a good practice to create investment is to allow the adolescent to makes rules within the guidelines so that there is a sense of freedom inherent with the structuring of courses or activities.

Young adolescent's worldviews are expanding at the most rapid rate that will occur in their lives. Guidance, through conversations, about how they see the world and their place in it can strongly help these students grasp these concepts and will help them view their world in a positive light. Further, helping them make meaningful contributions through service, or discussions centered on how they can serve the greater community and become a productive member of a global citizenry, is paramount. Outdoor Adventure Education programs lend themselves to these conversations naturally because of the missions these organizations oftentimes have, the setting in which they take place, and the sense of community that is established during these programs with other participants.

Students who are in the adolescent phase of life also begin to question rules and authority that, until this point in their life, have been taken at "face value" (Holmbeck *et al.*, 2000). This has implications when structuring the course. For example, instructors should consider explaining the higher purpose behind rules rather than merely laying the rules out. One specific example is explaining that walking across a wet log is not safe, rather than just yelling at the student to "get off that log!" Providing a rationale for following norms can also help the student in other facets of life when society expects them to follow a certain behavioral code.

Growth is something that adolescents are constantly dealing with while they are in this stage of life. Therefore, their bodies have pent-up energy that can be problematic to deal with for an instructor. Adequate amounts of physical exertion and exercise are of great importance to these students so that they use up energy that otherwise could be misdirected. Additionally, having outlets for them to occupy their minds or to help the "fidget" when having a tough conversation can make these interventions more productive. Additionally, consider having one-on-one conversations with an instructor so the student builds a good, solid rapport.

Consider also that hormonal changes are occurring as students go through the adolescent phase of life, oftentimes exacerbated by the different medications with which these students come to OAE programs (Reiter and Root, 1975). These changes often include the increase in thinking about, and in some cases acting upon, their desire to have sexual experiences. These feelings should be addressed and clear expectations should be established from the onset of the course. Programs should consider a no-tolerance policy for sexual contact between two students. These can be awkward conversations, but structuring these types of behaviors is often the best way to prevent a larger problem down the road.

Finally, a sense of belonging and social acceptance is critical to understanding adolescent behavior (Hamm and Faircloth, 2005). You may have a student who appears to be acting irrationally, and this may be the underlying reason for their behavior. Their basic need to receive attention is not being met, and therefore they have resorted to extreme measures to get attention. These situations are best avoided by facilitating, early in the OAE experience, an expectation that all team members will get along and promote a sense of community through the instructor's actions, emphasis on "get to know you" activities at the start of course, and creating an open and safe community in which the students can express their needs.

Adolescents are an incredible age group with which to work in the OAE setting. Because of their unique time in life and openness to learn, research shows that OAE programs can have an important and lasting impact on these students. Their curiosity, energy, and fun nature oftentimes make these courses the most enjoyable ones that we as OAE facilitators get to serve. Try to take care of their ego and sense of self on course, and you can have an impact on these students that will last for the rest of their lives.

Intact and non-intact groups

Group membership and types of group are often extremely important consideration when determining behavioral norms and the ways in which you will want to facilitate your OAE experience for any given group (Sibthorp and Jostad, 2014). Generally, there are two types of group memberships; intact and non-intact groups. During your planning and preparatory phase, consider if you are working with an intact group that will stay together even after they leave your program or a non-intact group that will disband at the conclusion of the OAE experience. As you'll see from this section, the ramifications of working with these two types of groups manifest in a few critical ways.

To begin with, research has suggested that non-intact groups can be more committed to the OAE experience, be more forthcoming with personal thoughts and opinion, and often find freedom in the anonymity that comes with knowing that, when the course is over, they will likely not see any group members from their OAE experience afterward (Gillis and Bonney, 1989). As a facilitator, you can use this to your advantage by creating a safe space of anonymity for these students. You may also find that these students are less likely to have interpersonal behavioral issues manifest, particularly on shorter OAE experiences, which can be an advantage to the staff.

Intact groups present their own unique challenges and opportunities. These groups are interesting to work with because they come to the OAE experience with social structures and normative roles that have developed from being in a group together prior to their OAE experience. To compound this, groups from the corporate world may come to your programs and there may be many interesting dynamics to consider when facilitating the experience. One such consideration is the power dynamic that is present when a "boss" is around or there is an implicit hierarchical structure to manage. Consider that all these components will factor into a person's behavioral response to a given situation, with particular importance under stress.

A special consideration with intact groups is the facilitator's advantage of using booster sessions or other techniques to increase the long-lasting effects of their OAE experience. For example, one activity you could do with an intact group is to have them create an individual goal sheet for that upcoming year. Then, you could establish an "accountability buddy" within that group who will have weekly meetings to discuss their progress on the goals they created while on your course. This technique would be a powerful tool for increasing the durability of the learnings that the student experiences on the OAE program and provide a powerful way to transfer the learning they have received on course to other venues like their work environment.

One key consideration of non-intact groups is the temporal component to behaviors while managing a group. As suggested by Tuckman and Jensen's (1977) group development model, non-intact groups will typically go through five stages: forming; storming; norming; performing; and adjourning. Relative to behavior management, the forming and norming stages are the most important for preventing and discouraging undesirable behaviors, while storming presents the most likelihood for interpersonal conflict to occur.

During the forming stage, the instructor will want to be very present and attentive to what social norms and group hierarchical structures are beginning to unfold (Ewert and McAvoy, 2000). Although it is natural for group structures to form, these structures can slip into unhealthy or unsafe places very quickly if not facilitated and behavioral intervention strategies utilized. For example, this stage is often when people will test the group for what attributes they can contribute. It is oftentimes the student with less tangible skills to contribute at this stage that later becomes the scapegoat of the group who is blamed for dysfunctional group dynamics or other group-related issues.

During this phase, the instructors should strongly consider reframing conversations in which rules, norms, and behaviors are being assessed by group members and consider facilitating some activities that highlight the students with less tangible skills to contribute to the group. Additionally, the group's "full-value contract" can help set the stage for meaningful discussions and help ensure positive group norms (Henton, 1996). These conversations are critical to have at this stage and set the tone of the trip. You may also want to have the conversation about expectations and consequences with deviant students at this stage of the course.

Storming is the other critical stage of group development when it is important to pay special attention to behavior management (Bisson, 1999). A skilled facilitator should know that the storming phase is a natural process through which many students can experience significant learning. However, this stage also presents certain dangers if these conversations get too emotionally charged or are unhealthy and unproductive. As the instructor, you should be present for these conversations and be ready to interject if the conversation gets close to emotionally charged or if one person is being targeted in a negative way. Also consider if you have given the students the proper tools, like conflict resolution and positive communication styles, to have this conversation at the appropriate time. You can always use these moments to teach these, among other, lessons.

When family members come on course together the instructor also has a special opportunity to impact their collective lives. When this occurs, you get a unique glimpse into that family's life and structure and have the opportunity to facilitate discussions about their dynamics. This is also a time to exercise caution and be sure not to encroach on family values or established norms unless they've provided you with evidence and trust for doing so. Instructors will often find that these students are cagey and harder to get to open up in front of their family members. Sensitivity when excavating information about their family life should be high priority.

Attention deficit disorder and attention deficit/hyperactive disorder

Students with attention deficit disorder (ADD) and attention deficit/hyperactive disorder (ADHD) can be some of the most challenging and rewarding ones you can experience on an experiential education course. These students can be fun, energetic, and quite interesting. Students with ADD/ADHD often require extra preparation and effort on the part of the instructor. These considerations, as well as teaching and behavioral strategies, will be discussed at length in the following section to prepare you or your staff as best as possible for managing these students.

FIGURE 7.2   Military veterans celebrate at the top of a mountain hike (photo: Chad Spangler)

Bear in mind that, if your program serves youths and teens, you will likely experience students with ADD/ADHD even if they are not officially diagnosed.

Students with ADD/ADHD participate in many types of OAE programs. In fact, OAE experiences may be ideal places for these students as they are oftentimes more engaging, provide exciting activities, and utilize the natural environment, all of which have been shown to facilitate learning in these types of students. The most common symptom in students with ADD/ADHD is their lack of ability to focus their attention for extended periods of time (Leo, 2000). Having this condition has been described as equivalent to someone changing the television channel every few seconds just as you begin to focus on a particular channel. With this image, one can imagine how difficult it is to learn, particularly in an unengaging environment.

ADD/ADHD is oftentimes extremely difficult to diagnose, as the affliction can look very different in each individual (Cantwell, 1996). Compound this fact with the notion that parents may not want or have the ability to have their child tested and diagnosed. So the instructor may have students with ADD/ADHD on course, with no indication in their medical history form that they suffer from this. Current literature suggests that one in ten people under the age of 18 displays signs and symptoms of a person with ADD/ADHD (Kuo and Faber Taylor, 2004).

With the likelihood that the instructor may have at least one person per course with ADD/ADHD, coupled with the fact that many of these cases go undiagnosed or are not reported, it is important to be able to recognize the signs and symptoms. The following is a partial list of typical signs and symptoms you may experience working with this population:

1 The students oftentimes will miss or overlook details.
2 They may have trouble paying attention, particularly with verbal instructions or lessons.
3 They may be forgetful with tasks that should be undertaken on a daily basis (i.e. brushing teeth).
4 They get easily distracted while trying to learn new tasks or skills.
5 These students may be more prone to lose their belongings.
6 They avoid or dislike tasks that involve prolonged mental effort such as homework or filling out paperwork.
7 They may exhibit signs of difficulty when organizing the sequence of tasks. For example, when setting up a tent, they may have difficulty remember the sequence of groundsheet, stakes, rainfly, etc.
8 Following instructions, particularly a long list of detailed instructions, may be difficult for these students.
9 When you speak directly to these students, it may seem like they are not listening.

It is important to remember that these common signs and symptoms have been with these students their whole lives and may have impacted other aspects of their lives, particularly skills that could have been learned verbally or interpersonally. For example, social skill development may have been impeded within students with ADD/ADHD.

Relatedly, students who experience hyperactivity and impulsivity may exhibit the same signs and symptoms. However, these students may also experience or exhibit the following, in addition to those just listed:

1 Frequently intrude on others' conversations, activities, or games.
2 Experience hardship while waiting for their opportunity to participate.
3 Interrupt conversations and generally have an impulsive way of communicating (i.e. speaking out of turn).
4 Be extremely talkative.
5 Demonstrate an inability to be still. For example, they may always be fidgeting, pacing, etc.
6 Impulsively run, walk, or climb around when the situation is inappropriate for such behavior.

Below, instructional techniques to mitigate and modify these behaviors will be discussed. Instructors should remember that these behaviors may be indicative of ADD/ADHD behavior, but could also manifest in other students who are nervous. Regardless, the techniques suggested can be utilized for all students of any ability.

Gathering as much information about their condition and medication before the student arrives is paramount in any of the behavioral conditions discussed in this book and ADD/ADHD is no exception. As stated previously, each case and individual with this diagnosis can vary greatly. With this in mind, it's oftentimes a good idea to talk to parents before the student arrives about what nuances, tips, and strategies they have found to be successful with their child. Further, having a solid understanding of the medicine the student is taking at the time the OAE experience occurs, the effects of that medication, and a way to manage the medicine on course is critical for setting the student up for success (see Figure 7.3).

One strategy for working with students with ADD/ADHD is to keep a routine and schedule and stick to it. These students usually thrive when they know the plan of what's going to happen, as well as what is expected of them. Use visuals to communicate the plan for the day each morning such as a whiteboard. One useful trick is to write out the schedule of the day, and the items they will need to bring along on the whiteboard, and hang it in a common space so they can all check the board for information. This technique will help the student visualize how the day will progress and give them a clear picture of when they need to focus, and when they can relax.

As stated, students with ADD/ADHD can have issues with losing their belongings and staying organized. Early in their OAE experience, it's a good idea to label everything that belongs to those students. Seasoned instructors who work with this population will carry a marker on their person at all times for this use. Labeling all their equipment the first day of the course is a great way to get a jump start on this issue. Relatedly, keeping their belongings organized will help with their organizational issues. Teaching them a strategy for this early in the experience will help ensure their success. For example, showing them how to pack their backpack or organize belongings in their tent or cabin is a useful strategy. Additionally, this

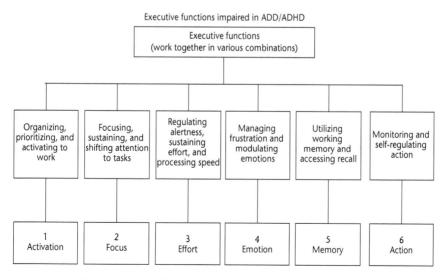

FIGURE 7.3   Consequences of having ADD/ADHD

gives the instructor a great platform for indicating how to carry that skill at home and stay organized when they leave their OAE experience.

Structuring a positive and conducive learning environment is crucial for delivering lessons, debriefs, or facilitating discussions with students with ADD/ADHD. The first step in doing this is to minimize distractions for these individuals. You'll find that a lesson where the students can see the ocean or watch traffic on a road will likely fall on deaf ears. In these scenarios, hike students away from places with distractions.

Somewhat conversely to limiting distractions, you may find that these students actually retain more information, and have an easier time limiting their distractions and paying attention, when you engage them with what other fields would call a "fidget toy." This can be any number of toys or items that you could carry, or have the student carry, for them to fidget with during discussions. These toys have been shown to calm the student during times when they should be focusing. It is also suspected that they increase concentration, reduce stress, and increase tactile awareness. One strategy is to teach a lesson, and then check for comprehension with the student and address how distracting he or she was to the other students throughout the lesson. Second, you could then teach a similar lesson, this time with the introduction of the fidget toy, and assess if the student performed better or worse based on attention span, limiting distractions, and information retained.

Additionally, having debriefs or meaning-making sessions with students with ADD/ADHD can be particularly challenging. Special consideration should be given to keeping these sessions short and productive. You may find that the traditional debrief techniques such as sitting around in a large group circle will be ineffective. Consider planning to debrief the students by having them move around, think critically, or rate themselves with numbers. For example, draw a line in the dirt where one end represents five and the other equals zero. Next, give the students a factor on which to rate their group's performance during the last activity such as communication. Next, have the student stand on the number that represents their assessment. Last, have a few students explain why they gave the number they choose.

You may also find that meaning-making sessions are more effective on an individual basis. For example, an instructor could use time hiking down the trail to ask a student about different learnings they have experienced on the course to date. This may be a powerful way to engage the students as many students find it easier to discuss sensitive information while hiking instead of sitting in a circle. This may also make it easier for the student to process the events of the course and help them transfer their learnings from the OAE experience to other facets of their life.

Finally, it is important to remember that a student who suffers from ADD/ADHD is no less intelligent than a person who has not been diagnosed with this affliction. A person's intelligence is in no way affected by this diagnosis. However, they may be developmentally behind their peers because of the system in which they are placed and are expected to learn that does not effectively cater to their needs. Our current educational system is ill equipped to deal with learners such as people with ADD/ADHD. This should inspire OAE instructors because they have the opportunity to engage these students in an environment where they can excel, and give them an empowering opportunity in which they can thrive.

Autism spectrum disorder

Autism, Asperger's syndrome, pervasive development disorder, and childhood disintegrative disorder were recently recategorized by the Diagnostics and Statistics Manual version five into one common condition: Autism Spectrum Disorder (ASD). Autism is a general term for a complex set of cognitive and brain development disorders (Robledo and Ham-Kucharski, 2005). Autism, even more so than ADD/ADHD, can manifest itself in a myriad of ways within individuals. Typically, autism will affect some aspect of social interactions, communication, and will often manifest with repetitive behaviors. When students with autism visit OAE programs, this presents a unique challenge and opportunity to work with a very fun population. Consider Figure 7.4 as we consider the description of some signs and symptoms that a person with autism will exhibit. Then, some strategies for managing behavior and facilitating the experience will be discussed at length.

It is estimated that ASD affects around 3 million people in the United States alone (Robledo and Ham-Kucharski, 2005). Until recently, scientists were unclear on what causes ASD, but research has revealed some possible culprits such as genetic predisposition and a lack of essential vitamins while the baby is in the womb. However, just like there is not one type of autism, there is (probably) not one cause for the disorder (Baron-Cohen *et al.*, 1994).

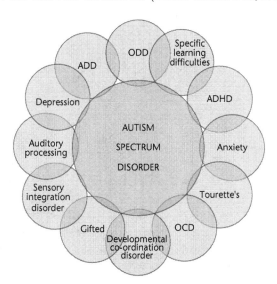

FIGURE 7.4 Autism spectrum disorder symptoms and conditions

ASD is merely a part of the individual and does not account for that person's entire personality or character. Knowing this, it's important to treat these students similarly to your other students. Keep in mind that 40 percent of people on the ASD spectrum have average or above average intelligence (Frith, 1989). Many possess extraordinary abilities in science, music, and mathematics. Famous people who had, or likely had, autism include Albert Einstein, Amadeus Mozart, Sir Isaac Newton, Thomas Jefferson, and Michelangelo. Consider the possibility that you could have the next genius on your OAE course!

People on the ASD scale oftentimes come across as mean or disgruntled. This is most commonly due to a defense mechanism that stems from their senses being out of sync with the surrounding environment, telling them that they are in danger. Their hearing may be really sensitive to certain frequencies. Also, light stimuli such as a flashlight in the eyes can set them off on a tantrum. Special considerations should be given relative to the hyper-sensitive nature of these sensory issues. For example, if their own body odor is causing them discomfort because of their heightened sense of smell, consider making special accommodations for showers or bathing options.

Students on the ASD spectrum should also receive special considerations when given instructions (Russell, 1997). For example, if you yell at them from across the room, they are likely not to understand. Commonly this gets interpreted by instructional staff as failure to comply with instructions. A wiser course of action is to walk over to the individual and speak plainly and frankly to them when giving instructions. Relatedly, consider the idea that people with autism interpret language literally and concretely. Sarcasm, idioms, and metaphors are often lost on these students or misinterpreted and confusing. Instead, speak plainly and say what you mean with this population. For example, instead of saying "we need to hike double time," consider the more concrete, "we need to hike faster," phrase instead. This plain speak is likely to have a more desirable outcome.

As stated, communication can be a major hurdle for people on the ASD spectrum. Consider all the myriad of ways that this population might be communicating. Pay special attention to body language, as people with autism typically have a difficult time communicating, and a really difficult time expressing themselves when something is wrong. These students will often feel the same emotions as other students such as hunger, fear, and joy, but they may express it in very different ways. For example, using movie quotes is a way some people on the ASD spectrum express themselves. Some possess a remarkable ability to remember certain aspects of life like movie scripts, quotes, or song lyrics.

Relatedly, students with autism can be very visually oriented and may require you to show them the same task several times. This patient practice and repetitive demonstration is likely to be far more effective than verbally reiterating the lesson you're trying to teach. Similarly, showing them a single, correct way is preferable to several nuanced ways to perform a given task. It is important to focus on what a person on the ASD spectrum can do, rather than what they cannot do. For examples of this, see the section on the strengths-based approach in Chapter 6.

Finally, because of several factors, students on the ASD spectrum can be prone to meltdowns or escalated events. Heightened senses or troubles with lack of social skills can be part of the root issue for these incidents. This is why it is critical to identify what can trigger a meltdown for these individuals. Again, a tried and true method for this is to call the parents before the student arrives to try to ascertain what these triggers may be. Additionally, de-escalation techniques for students with autism are related to the other section in this book on this topic (see Chapter 5).

Teaching and facilitating for this population can be exceptionally challenging. However, with a few key considerations, you can adapt your teaching style to include this population's learning style, and help them have an extremely powerful OAE experience (Koegel and Koegel, 1995). Here are a few considerations when teaching and facilitating these groups:

1   Avoid long strings of verbal instructions.
2   Use visuals and demonstration techniques at every possible opportunity (i.e. show them how to put a tent stake in instead of telling them).
3   Use art to help them make meaning of the experience. For example, have them draw pictures of ideas that they've learned while on the OAE experience.
4   People with ASD can get fixated on certain subjects like comic books, video games, trains, etc. Use this to your advantage by building rapport with this student through conversation. Additionally, if you can incorporate these fixations into lessons or debriefs you may find that they will be more engaged.
5   In some situations it may be helpful for them to wear heavy clothes or a personal floatation device while engaged in learning. The weight of the extra garments can help calm the person by calming the nervous system. If utilizing this technique, avoid letting the student wear it for more than 20 minutes as their nervous system will adapt to it.
6   Some ASD spectrum individuals are mono-channeled learners. For example, they physically cannot see and hear at the same time. If you encounter these individuals, be sure to only engage one sense at time by covering their eyes and teaching to their preferred method of learning.
7   For learning a large quantity of information, flashcards are often a very effective tool with this population.
8   Sequenced teaching is not usually effective with this population as they can have a hard time understanding how the two concepts fit together. For example, teaching how to use a compass and then teaching how the compass applies to the map will be challenging concepts if taught in a hierarchical fashion.

Students on the ASD spectrum need OAE programming just as much, if not more than most children. These students are often relocated to indoor activities, like video games, if they lack the coordination to find success in traditional sports. Their OAE experience is their opportunity to have a positive interaction with the natural environment. Take a little extra time to plan for these students and remember that patience is a must with them. Additionally, utilize visuals whenever possible, and keep in mind that they're not mean or disobedient, but likely are just defensive and do not totally understand the OAE process.

Youth at risk

With the invention and growth of wilderness therapy programming, OAE programming has probably seen the most growth in student numbers in this population. However, many OAE programs will find that they are serving youth at risk at some point in time. While it is true that a number of other textbooks could be written on youth at risk and wilderness therapy, the authors thought it wise to include this population into this book, as characteristics of youth at risk can and do emerge in almost all OAE programming at some point or another. Therefore, this section seeks to explore what it means to be a youth at risk, what factors contribute to these students, what behaviors they are likely to elicit, and then the application of various techniques for working with this population specifically.

Many instructors are reticent about working with youth at risk because of the unique challenges, and oftentimes difficult behaviors that they bring into our programs, we would posit, however, that these individuals are one of the populations most in need of our programming. Removing them from the ecological system, teaching and training them with life skills, empowering them

FIGURE 7.5 OAE students after completing their course (photo: Pete Allison)

by survival and challenges in the wilderness, and then returning these students as changed individuals to their home life is a unique opportunity to help an underserved population in our society.

Youth at risk come from all different demographics. Typically defined as a person who is less likely to transition into adulthood successfully, these students come from all geographic locations, socio-economic backgrounds, and family structures (Brendtro *et al.*, 2012). In this context, success is defined as the ability to avoid crime, achieve academic success, and/or become financially independent. Although there are a few factors that make a person more likely to join this category of people, there is no one formulaic scenario these persons are likely to come from. Lower socio-economic status, broken families, and growing up in high crime areas all increase a person's likelihood that they will join the "youth at risk" demographic. Instructors may find it useful to research the student's background as thoroughly as possible by interviews, parental interviews, and assessing the home time of the student before they come to the program. However, instructors should avoid stereotyping and forming preconceived notions about how a student might actual behave or with what issues they may enter into the program.

When working with this population, developing a caring relationship is of paramount importance (Fraser, 1997). Oftentimes, these students will not have had a positive role model either at school or in their home life, or if they have, they may have chosen not to listen to them for one reason or another. Just being an individual they can look up to can make a huge impact on their life. Additionally, showing care can help ally these individuals to you, as the instructor. Try and build rapport quickly and show that you care even beyond their OAE experience. Gather as much information about them as possible, including what they are good at as well as some of the struggles they experience. This relationship will be a key prerequisite to teaching and facilitating the experience for these individuals. Instructors should strongly consider using the strengths-based approach for establishing a positive, caring relationship.

Another consideration for work with youth at risk is setting realistic goals and expectations with them. These students can oftentimes come up with grandiose ideas about what they want to do with their lives based on mass media and popular culture. Helping them put this into perspective can formidably and positively alter their lives for the better. By forming a positive and personal relationship, you can help these students set realistic career and life goals based on their potential. Consider using the SMART goal setting strategy to help these students understand their potential, limitations, and the requisite work for setting them up to have a successful life.

Relative to these goals, the instructor can also act as a facilitator to help these students reach their goals. For example, if the student wanted to go to college, you may research the prerequisites for them to get into school. Similarly you may offer alternative paths for them to reach the goal that they hadn't considered, like starting at community college. Laying a clear pathway with them with measurable and realistic checkpoints can set at-risk students up for success after your OAE experience. You can even go so far as to write out a five-year plan with these students. Consideration for booster maintenance sessions should also be given, to check in with these students and encourage them to reach their goals or keep them on track. You can also utilize this technique for helping overcome those obstacles or setbacks they have experienced since graduating from your OAE experience.

Instructors should also do as much as possible to prepare these students to return to their existing ecological system. For example, a student who comes to OAE experience who has been using drugs may find it easy to stop using those drugs because of access issues and positive influence. However, when they return to their home or neighborhood, those temptations and access to negative influence are still going to be there. Be sure to alert them to this phenomenon and give them some strategies for dealing with the temptations or exposure to negative environmental factors upon returning home.

Another important consideration for working with this population is the frontloading and early establishment of expectations. This can take many forms, as some organizations will use the full-value contract as a way to democratize the formation of rules and norms. Youth at risk may need a little more structure when forming rules and norms for the formation of expectations for safety's sake (Capuzzi and Gross, 2014). More structure may mean that the guidelines for acceptable behavior are handed down to them from the organizational structure. This process should be done as soon as possible when the group forms, or when a new member is introduced, as is oftentimes the case in wilderness therapy. Having these clear expectations, regardless of whether they are generated by the students or by the organization, will help keep students physically and emotionally safe. Additionally, it allows the instructor to remove him or herself from the doling out of consequences when these rules aren't adhered to.

Consequences, as outlined in the previous chapter of this book, are a little more challenging with youth at risk (Muncie and Goldson, 2006). The way we normally think of consequences, particularly logical types of consequences, set yourself up for policing and trying to enforce something that does not hold relevance in the larger context of the OAE experience or the behavior management of the student. It also is really easy for a student to refuse to perform the consequence and you can quickly wind up with a power struggle on your hands (McWhirter et al., 1993). For example, if a student insults another student, consider instead asking the student to explain his or her intention as to why they insulted the individual in the first place. Afterward, ask yourself, "is there group culture the staff doesn't know about that are contributing to these behaviors?" or "are students upset with each other and need help discussing differences?" These types of inquiries will help you assess where your group is at and then address their needs to keep the course flowing smoothly.

You may find that students will self-regulate when you get them to a point when they are invested in your program. Instructors should also consider when and how to build and use rapport. For example, becoming emotionally connected to a student and having built strong rapport, you can oftentimes use them to motivate the group, particularly when that student is in a leadership role. For example, an instructor who has a strong rapport with a student can go to that student to help him or her influence the group's feelings about something. Say a long hike is coming up, you could elicit that student's help for getting the group energized about the upcoming challenge.

Knowing when to pick and choose our battles with this population is of exceptional importance. In other words, an instructor should consider when to address and/or redirect unallowed or undesirable behavior. If you make a lesson or dole out consequences at every breach of rule, you will be fighting a long uphill battle, and probably be disliked by the students because of your heavy-handed approach. Consider the following example; you walk up to a group of students who are having an inappropriate conversation about drug use. Two options would be to either make a big point about how that is against programmatic rules and dole out consequences. This course of action may be appropriate in many situations. However, an alternate course of action would be to redirect the students into talking about another topic that you know they'll be interested in. By redirecting the conversation, you've gotten the students to return to the adherence of program policies, while not alienating yourself by using an authoritarian leadership style in which you have to "punish" the offending students.

As with all students, youth at risk are a challenging, yet unique opportunity to meet the students where they are in life and have a positive influence on the people in your OAE program. As stated, it is critical to understand the environmental and personal factors that have brought the students to the place where they are in life, and try to empathize with the situation they have been placed into. From this place of empathy, showing compassion and caring is oftentimes all it takes to make a powerful alliance with these students to allow you to have a positive and successful course. Establish that you may not understand or relate to their place in life or upbringing but that does not discredit your desire to support them and help them find the best way to reach their goals.

Finally, for youth at risk having realistic expectations, a plan for their future, and an increased understanding of the world around them can have a significant impact on these students' futures. These students, usually, will respond to effort that you put into them in a positive way. Try to stay positive, see them for their strengths, and recognize that this is your chance to make a huge difference in their life. Oftentimes, instructors will remark about the impact these students have had on their lives, and increased understanding of the way society, culture, and behavior can impact a person's outlook on life, and potential for success.

Adjudicated youth

Recently, much attention has been given to adjudicated youth in the OAE through research and in popular culture. Through television shows such as *Brat*

Camp, wilderness therapy programs which serve these students were broadcast into homes around the country. Because of this, and other external factors, their popularity has soared. And now the research to show that these programs can be effective has followed and increased their visibility as a viable option for treatment for adjudicated and at risk youth.

This section will provide you with an understanding of what adjudicated youth are, what OAE can do for this population, and some relevant techniques to have them have a successful course. There is much overlap with mitigating behaviors of adjudicated, and at risk youth so be sure to reread the previous section for specific techniques that carry over. Adjudicated youth, which is defined as a youth who has been found guilty by a judge of committing a crime, by default falls into the "youth at risk" category.

Programs that serve adjudicated youth range in length, dosage, and course design. For example, there is a program in Washington State that takes adjudicated youth and trains them to do wildland firefighting. Conversely, adjudicated youth may be sent to existing wilderness therapy programs with other at-risk youth. Programs willing to work with adjudicated youth need to have the necessary infrastructure and staff training to handle this unique population. They may want to consider having licensed counselors or therapists on hand to handle the risky nature of these students. The focus of this section is what you, as an instructor, can do to increase the likelihood that these students will find success on your OAE experience.

As stated, the popularity of these programs has increased in large part because of the success that has been documented through the research efforts of a few organizations. For example, Gillis *et al.* (2008) found that adjudicated youth who participated in OAE programs had a statistically significant reduction in rates of rearrest over the following three-year period compared to other youth. Additionally, Russell (2006) found that adjudicated youth who go to jail instead of completing a wilderness program are two to three times more likely to commit additional crimes. Although further evidence is needed about the success of these programs, the initial results are promising.

Gass and Gillis (2010) also found seven key differences in programs that were successful at positively influencing behaviors after an OAE experience. By exploring these seven ideas, as an instructor or program designer, you can start to get a picture of the way in which OAE programs might positively affect adjudicated and at risk youth.

First, by utilizing action-oriented experiences the adjudicated youth start to feel empowered in their own experience. Through a sense of mastery, other positive attributes can start to be established in the OAE participants. For example, by learning how to cook over a fire, a student might also experience increases in their sense of control of their own life (locus of control). In this way, the action-oriented experience empowers the student over the outcome of their life, even after their OAE experience.

Next, an experience that is centered on the use of unfamiliar client environments will likely cause a few things to happen in the student (Feierman *et al.*, 2009). First, by being removed from external negative stimuli and temptations, they may be able to refocus their life. Second, the novelty of the wilderness will provide them with a time for introspection, and an investigation of their lives. Couple this with skilled facilitation, and you have the makings of a life-altering course. The novel environment plays a critical role for all students of the OAE process, but is particularly critical for at risk and adjudicated youth.

Finally, producing a climate of functional change through the positive use of stress is a critical element of a successful program for adjudicated youth (Coulter, 2004; Balcazar *et al.*, 1995). Creating challenge and stress engages the student, and allows for self-discovery to occur. This process can provide the life-changing opportunity for the student to turn their behavior towards a more positive avenue. For example, through the increased understanding that they are capable of living in the wilderness for an extended period of time, a student may come to understand that, if they can accomplish that, then resisting to shoplift is also a surmountable goal. This type of interpersonal growth and learning is paramount to creating an environment where the use of stress is positive, facilitating self-discovery.

It is paramount that OAE programs wishing to serve adjudicated youth work from a highly informed place of knowledge is above and beyond what is covered in this textbook. Each year, new insights from research are emerging from the OAE field as well as many others about positive treatments for working with adjudicated youth. By staying current on this research, programs can always become more effective at serving this population. Relatedly, a highly structured, transparent, and informed client assessment should be implemented with these populations. This will help ensure that positive growth occurs as a result of their participation in OAE, provide an ending point for these students if their graduation from the program hinges upon it, and give the student a framework for understanding what is expected of them, both in the program and, on a more grand scale, society.

Instructors will oftentimes find that small, supportive groups are the most appropriate dynamic for lessons, fostering a caring environment, and the best way to retain attention and increase learning and understanding. Instructional staff can easily split the group into two smaller groups. Consider either both instructors teaching the same lesson to their small groups, or each instructor teaching a unique lesson and then the students swap lessons. Small group processing is also usually easier for at risk and adjudicated youth. The students will often find that it is easier to open up and be vulnerable in smaller groups. These are some of the many advantages to small group processing and facilitation.

Instructors can also maximize their success with these populations by staying focused on solution oriented principles and techniques, similar to a strengths-based approach. These students are often overly vulnerable and react to elements that are beyond and out of their control (Wolery *et al.*, 1998). If it is explained to them that they are in control of their actions and their emotional responses, these students can begin to think about their behavior and learnings from the OAE experience. Sometimes just telling students what an appropriate emotional response would be is enough to help them begin to have proper emotional reactivity. Finally, giving them tools to help control their anger, understand and empathize with others, and any other way that will help these students find success will be a positive strategy on the part of instructional staff (Gass, 1995). Consider that these students have probably received little, if any, praise their whole life. This can go a long way with building rapport, managing behavior, and teaching tools they need to find success in life.

Military veterans

Nobody comes home from war unchanged and for many of our redeploying veterans, these changes can be characterized as negative, often debilitating, psychological wounds (Ewert, 2014). Since 2001, more than 3.5 million United States soldiers, sailors, marines, and airmen have been deployed to the Global War on Terror, including those involved in Operations Iraqi Freedom, Enduring Freedom, and New Dawn. A substantial number of these individuals have experienced physical wounds and psychological co-morbidity including a broad spectrum of health-related problems such as PTSD, substance abuse, destructive marital/family issues, domestic violence, depression, anxiety, and other mental illnesses (Resnik and Allen, 2007). In addition, there is considerable evidence that, when compared to the general population, redeployed veterans are at higher risk for other health-related issues such as obesity (Nelson, 2006).

The extent of these psychological issues often go underreported because these injuries are not easily observed and are often not reported until several months after redeployment (returning home). The military climate can stigmatize the admission of psychological health-related problems often present among returning veterans, thus reducing the likelihood of reporting these issues (Seal et al., 2008).

As a means of coping with the physiological and psychological issues resulting from deployment, military veterans engage in unhealthy or destructive behaviors such as increased substance use and abuse. For many veterans that have returned to the United States or their home country, effective interventions are needed to facilitate the development of resilience, self-efficacy, sense of coherence, social support, and self-regulation so that they have the necessary self-support skills to successfully deal with the stresses associated with reintegration into community or redeployment.

Traditional approaches for treating symptoms related to PTSD and similar issues have been pharmacological- (Olfson et al., 2002) or psychology-based, such as cognitive behavior therapy exposure-based interventions, supportive counseling, prolonged exposure therapy, emotional debriefing, and collaborative care. However, veterans, especially those that have been exposed to combat, can sometimes underutilize these types of health care services, and in particular, those associated with mental health (Hunt and Rosenheck, 2011). This underutilization by some veterans has prompted the need to develop alternative treatment modalities and interventions.

One such intervention, Outdoor Adventure Education (OAE), has evolved as a therapeutic tool used with redeployed (returning) military veterans in ameliorating post-deployment health issues such as depression and feelings of isolation (Gass *et al.*, 2012). Following the Vietnam War, programs using natural environments and adventure-based activities began to appear as either an alternative or adjunct to more traditional psychological counseling approaches (Hyer *et al.*, 1996).

Through the effective facilitation and reflection of different components of these types of programs, veterans often report being more resilient and capable of dealing with uncertainty, stress, and other potentially adverse circumstances. The use of a natural environment with real and concrete consequences, through active involvement of the participants, while dealing with issues of risk and uncertainty of outcome and within a context of purposeful use of incremental and specifically designed activities, constitute some of the key elements of this type of intervention.

A common program design for military veterans within a OAE/BGM program consists of some combination of hiking, camping, rock climbing, ropes course, and/or white-water or ocean kayaking. Each course typically will have two to three professional staff and involve six to twelve veterans. The courses are carefully planned with activities sequenced to produce a scaffolding effect whereby each course member has specific responsibilities, rotated leadership positions among all the participants, an expectation that all participants will actively support each other, and provide accurate and honest feedback to each other. Group decision-making, collective goal setting, and constructively resolving internal differences are integral to the BGM experience.

Moreover, the effective use of debriefings and facilitation is paramount to the success of the overall experience, by creating an atmosphere whereby military veterans can consider and change their behaviors relative to issues such as substance use and abuse. Through the effective facilitation and reflection of different components of the program, veterans emerge more resilient and capable of dealing with uncertainty, stress, and other potentially adverse circumstances. Studies utilizing this type of program model have documented significant positive effects on variables such as self-concept, locus of control, and sociability (Hattie *et al.*, 1997; Kennedy and Minami, 1993).

The theoretical pathway of the connection between the military veteran, the OAE/BGM experience, and the reduction in negative behaviors such as substance abuse (i.e. alcohol and tobacco use) is illustrated in Figure 7.6. Within this framework, the military veteran brings to the experience a number of attributes that can serve as moderating variables such as status (active duty or National Guard/Reserve), length and intensity of combat exposure, length of military service, rank (i.e. enlisted or officer), and gender. The implication of this theoretical pathway is that issues such as substance abuse can be influenced through a number of variables such as type of military status, length of service, rank, and exposure to combat. Moreover, the development of behaviors that result in decreased alcohol and tobacco use is facilitated through the OAE/BGM experience that allows an individual to develop a "stronger" perception of him or herself and a greater willingness to make changes related to substance abuse.

Thus, OAE/BGM programs provide purposive and discrete tasks that are designed to create positive emotional and psychological outcomes involving a high level of directed attention and a holistic involvement on the part of the individual veteran that requires mental, emotional, and physical resources. The overall goal of many of these programs is to address or prevent combat-related disorders by providing wilderness-based adventure recreation courses that are immersed in the therapeutic aspects of the natural world, teamwork, and challenge-based activities. Key issues that are often addressed include a reduction in feeling of isolation, lack of trust, and a sedentary lifestyle, and an increase in affirmation of self, a sense of empowerment, and relational skills.

There may be a number of factors that could account for this impact. For example, McKenzie (2000) attributes these outcomes to four characteristics common to many OAE experiences such as BGM programs: (a) the unfamiliar nature of the physical environment; (b) the incremental and progressive sequencing of the challenges presented through the adventure education experience; (c) the "processing" of the experience in order to identify and organize meaning for the participant; and (d) the use of small groups to facilitate issues such as reciprocity, group cohesiveness, interpersonal relationships, and the balance between group belongingness and individual autonomy. In addition to the four components of physical environment, sequencing, processing, and group size previously described by McKenzie, the adventure education experience also provides opportunities for outdoor physical activity, solving problems while being together, and being part of a shared experience that can facilitate future conversations and discussions.

Military veterans report that participation in OAE/BGM programs can create a sense of camaraderie and feeling part of a team (Van Puymbroeck *et al.*, 2012). In turn, this sense of teamwork can provide for mutual respect, communication, and developing trust (Johnson *et al.*, 1994). In addition, post-war structural social support (i.e. number of friendships and complexity of social attachment) appears particularly important to male veterans, while

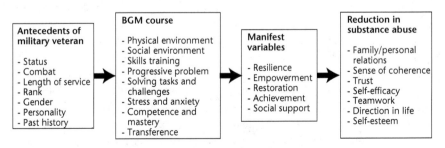

FIGURE 7.6 The OAE/BGM experience and the reduction in negative behaviors such as substance abuse

functional social support (i.e. perceived emotional support and assistance) is deemed important to both female and male veterans (Palmer, 2008). As an inherent component of the program, groups formed during an OAE/BGM experience are often encouraged to provide both emotional and physical support to each other.

The logic underlying this type of intervention is that, by successfully completing an OAE/BGM-type program, veterans can experience enhanced perceptions of their personal abilities such as leadership, teamwork skills, effective communication, resilience, and self-efficacy (see Figure 7.6). In addition, the small group context provided by the intervention promotes a level of social support that facilitates the veteran in making positive attitudinal and behavioral changes in his or her personal life, at home, or at work. The overall goal of many OAE/BGM programs for veterans is to transfer the outcomes realized at the end of the course to situations which may occur later in an individual's life. As discussed in Chapter 2, the concept of transference, or the applying of course outcomes to situations later in life, is considered a critical component in many OAE programs (Goldenberg *et al.*, 2005).

In particular, veterans have reported experiencing feelings of courage, bonding with others, increased self-determination, responsibility to self and others, and a sense of competence in times of uncertainty and challenge while engaged in their military duties. Through the use of a series of structured and challenging experiences designed to facilitate change while engaged in the program setting, these feelings can often be emulated through participation in programs such as OAE/BGM (Sheard and Golby, 2006).

Within this context, military veterans often report a number of beneficial outcomes, including:

1   A willingness to trust others again, starting with the other members of the group who, it should be stated, are usually complete strangers at the beginning of the OAE/BGM course or program.
2   A belief that they can change their life for the better.
3   Engaging in positive reinforcing activities while being "off the grid."
4   A reawakening of the energizing effects of nature, physical activity, and practicing learned skills, particularly as a result of being involved in adventure activities that are physically demanding, and necessitate using these learned skills within a setting that has consequential and real, rather than abstract, outcomes.

Thus, being in a group of other military personnel, within a unique adventure setting, often allows the participants to feel connected with other soldiers again and this connection can be clearly beneficial in their redeployment and integration process. For many veterans, "emptying out the rucksack" through an OAE/BGM experience is easier and more meaningful than on the clinician's couch.

OUTWARD BOUND VETERANS

Chad Spangler, Outward Bound USA

With roots that trace back to England at the beginning of World War II, Outward Bound is an organization that in many ways was created in response to conflict. As early as 1969, when they exchanged training materials with the US Army Infantry School, Outward Bound USA has worked to engage the military and veteran communities as a tangible demonstration of their organizational commitment to the value of service.

Beginning in 1983 that commitment has been expressed through fully funded custom Outward Bound expeditions for veterans, designed to assist veterans making the daunting transition from military to civilian lives. By drawing on the healing power of teamwork and challenge in some of our nation's most awe-inspiring environments, Outward Bound Veterans recreates many of the positive aspects of military service in a civilian context, and challenges those veterans that participate to attack challenges associated with leaving the military with the same vigor and resilience that served them so well while on active duty.

Initially created by retired Col. Bob Rheult the early expeditions were created in partnership with clinicians working at an in-patient unit at a Veterans Administration (VA) Hospital in Northampton, MA, that focused on treating Vietnam veterans hospitalized due to challenges related to post traumatic stress. The programs, and their strengths-based approach, quickly became an integral part of the Northampton VA's treatment for Vietnam veterans. Dr Richard Pearlstein, a clinical psychologist in charge of treatment, described the outcomes of these expeditions in this way:

> The thread that I see is a much needed affirmation of self, and an awakening of the sense of possibility that one can, in fact, change his life. He can do things that he thought impossible. There is a liveliness and a reawakening of a capacity to generally struggle as opposed to just going along with hospital routines in a vague hope that things will somehow get better. As a staff we consider the contribution of Outward Bound to be the single most powerful tool in our treatment.

While remaining small and experimental in nature, these early expeditions created the foundation on which Outward Bound would build their current day-programming as a response to the Global War on Terror. Beginning in 2005 by serving just ten of the nation's newest generation of combat veterans, the program swelled to a peak at just over 1,200 veteran participants in 2010, and currently serves between 500 and 700 veterans a year. In total since 2008 Outward Bound has delivered transformative wilderness courses to over 6,500 veterans free of charge.

Intentionally designed with the new generation of veterans in mind, current veterans programming at Outward Bound no longer focuses exclusively on post traumatic stress, and instead serves any veteran that has been deployed to a combat zone as part of their service.

Current veterans programming at Outward Bound consists of six to eight day programs where veterans take part in wilderness expeditions that are physically, mentally, and emotionally challenging in order to build the self-confidence, pride, trust, and communication skills necessary to successfully return to their families, employers, and communities following wartime service. These expeditions purposefully scaffold wartime experiences (carrying heavy backpacks, sore shoulders, rubbery legs, sleeping out, strange noises, sweat, dirt, frustration, and anger) with authentic achievements to create positive emotional and mental outcomes.

Wilderness activities are used as metaphors for daily life experiences in the pursuit of individual and group excellence, illuminating how the support and collaboration needed to meet Outward Bound goals can positively impact participants' interactions with others at home. Many veterans experienced courage, brotherhood, and a real sense of power and competence while in combat. Outward Bound gives veterans and service members the opportunity to re-experience these strengths in themselves in a different context.

As the program has grown and evolved, so too has Outward Bound's understanding of the unique needs and challenges facing the current veterans population, and how some of those challenges may present themselves in the context of a wilderness expedition. One of the more significant challenges Outward Bound staff faced when working with post-9/11 veterans was how to build trust, foster deep connections, and create a space where veterans would buy in completely to the Outward Bound process. With less than 1 percent of the population serving in the military since 9/11, the divide between the military and civilians is wider than at any time in our history.

Many veterans feel as though civilians couldn't possibly understand the experience, and oftentimes feel marginalized by a population that has continued living life with little, if any, awareness that men and women are fighting and dying on their behalf in Iraq, Afghanistan, and other far-away lands. Contracting older, more experienced staff that were willing to spend some time and effort to learn about the current conflicts, focusing on shared values of Outward Bound and the military, and quickly empowering veteran participants to create the dynamic for the group were strategies that helped to significantly break down barriers and ensure buy in.

Another challenge that presented itself was a culture within the military that embraces toughness and those willing to ignore pain for the good of the larger group. While undoubtedly a valuable trait in times of war, on wilderness expeditions that presented challenges for staff used to working with younger students. Minor injuries, that if treated early would have presented little challenge, occasionally were exacerbated to the point where a veteran needed to be evacuated from the field.

Managing appropriate student behavior on expeditions when working with veteran populations in a wilderness setting can also present challenges that were not initially anticipated by Outward Bound staff. Such things as swearing, tobacco use, and institutional safety guidelines occasionally presented staff with difficult decisions. Do you correct a 35-year-old former Marine who was deployed five times to combat zones for swearing? How might you explain to a former Special Forces soldier who has rappelled off of a helicopter in pitch black that they need to stay a minimum of one full body length from a cliff despite the beautiful view it would present?

Outward Bound staff learned ultimately that, to manage veterans successfully in the field, flexibility, knowledge, technical expertise, and taking the approach of a crew not a guide when it came time for expedition chores, were the best strategies in managing veteran students with the unique challenges that they can sometimes present.

Conclusion

In this chapter, special considerations were given to the different populations that frequent OAE programming. While students with these conditions present certain challenges, they often give you great opportunities to facilitate a positive OAE experience for them. It's possible that you are the first person to come along to provide a positive experience for these individuals, so take extra time to plan for these populations to have a successful course. Gather as much information as you can about the individual, their condition, and particularly how that condition manifests itself with that individual, when planning for these people to visit your program.

Remember that none of these conditions represents the individual's cognitive abilities or intelligence nor do these conditions define who they are as people or what hardships they have overcome before your OAE/BGM program. Consider the fact that our society does a poor job at incorporating and training people with these conditions. This is your chance to make a difference in their life, show them compassion, and teach them the valuable insights the natural environment and OAE/BGM can offer them.

Discussion questions

1   What are some key considerations for working with adolescents in an OAE setting? What are some preparation actions you can take before the experience begins to set yourself up for success?

2 How might you structure a course differently to accommodate students on the autism spectrum? Students who are at-risk? Students with ADD/ADHD?

3 When working with veterans, what emotional safety considerations might you want to incorporate into your group discussions?

SCENARIO

An urban based school has sought out an adventure-based experience for their 7th grade boys. Each grade of the school embarks on a separate experience for that class. During the previous year the school had provided feedback that the backpacking program based in Joshua Tree was too physically rigorous and that they would like the trip to cater to other goals and values that the school holds. They were particularly interested in a focus on service and social engagement.

The Program Director had previously designed and successfully implemented programming that involved service components in downtown Los Angeles in the "Skid Row" area as well as adventure experiences in Joshua Tree. When this combination was mentioned to the school they immediately gravitated toward this new model and were willing to undertake the "transition" that is typically associated with a new contract.

Although the Program Director had experience with the program design and model, many of the instructors had not worked primarily in a wilderness setting. Of the six instructors, three had previous experience working in urban environments but in San Francisco rather than in LA. Due to the unfamiliar environment, the Program Director led course-specific training over three days to familiarize the instructors with the course area and specifics of the program.

During the two-day LA portion of the program, student groups participated in a walking tour of downtown LA seeing cultural and historic city sights. They also participated in service at two of the missions on Skid Row. After the two full days in Los Angeles they would spend three days climbing and hiking in Joshua Tree National Park.

When the students arrived to the location where they would be staying it was immediately apparent that the program was not ideally suited for the student type. Despite the encouragement of the school that the students were exceptionally mature and prepared for an experience of this nature, their behavior suggested otherwise. There were multiple behavioral incidents on the first night that included bullying, name calling, ostracizing, and even physical fighting. One group of students described their surroundings as "the ghetto" and pretended they were gang members, even creating fake weapons and engaging in role-playing where they pretended to be inmates in a prison and were trying to escape. The instructors struggled to make meaningful connections with the experiences and many provided feedback after the course that it was not a good fit.

Actions taken

Certain individuals were moved from one group to another. There were multiple verbal contracts that students were put on. A couple of students were threatened with dismissal. During post-course discussion, it was determined that the experience was likely not appropriate for the age of the students and the following year the school returned to the standard backpacking itinerary.

Discussion questions

1   What factors contributed to the lack of success in this scenario before the course took place?
2   Instead of removing students from the group, what alternative actions could have been taken to promote success with this experience?
3   What theoretical applications apply to this scenario and how might understanding these theories have informed the decisions of the Program Director?

References

Balcazar, F. E., Keys, C. B., and Garate Serafini, J. (1995). Learning to recruit assistance to attain transition goals: A program for adjudicated youth with disabilities. *Journal for Special Educators*, 16(54), 237–246.

Baltes, P. B., Lindenberger, U., and Staudinger, U. M. (2007). Life Span Theory in Developmental Psychology. *Handbook of Child Psychology*, I:11.

Baron-Cohen, S., Tager-Flusberg, H., and Cohen, D. J. (1994). *Understanding Other Minds: Perspectives from Autism*. New York: Oxford University Press.

Bisson, C. (1999). Sequencing the adventure experience. In J. Miles and S. Priest (eds), *Adventure programming* (pp. 205–214). State College, PA: Venture.

Brendtro, L., Brokenleg, M., and van Bockern, S. (2012). *Reclaiming Youth at Risk: Our Hope for the Future*. Bloomington, IN: National Education Service.

Cantwell, D. (1996). Attention deficit disorder: a review of the past 10 years. *Journal of the American Academy of Child and Adolescent Psychiatry*, 35(8), 978–987.

Capuzzi, D., and Gross, D. (2014). *Youth at Risk: A Prevention Resource for Counselors, Teachers, and Parents*. Alexandria, VA: American Counseling Association.

Coulter, G. (2004). Using one-to-one tutoring and proven reading strategies to improve reading performance with adjudicated youth. *Journal of Correctional Education*, 55(4), 321–333.

Ewert, A. (2014). Military veterans and the use of adventure education experiences in natural environments for therapeutic outcomes. *Ecopsychology*, 6(3), 155–164.

Ewert, A., and McAvoy, L. (2000). The effects of wilderness settings on organized groups: A state-of-knowledge paper. In S. F. McCool, D. N. Cole, W. T. Borrie, and J. O'Laughlin (eds), *Wilderness Science in a Time of Change*, vol. 3, *Wilderness as a Place for Scientific Inquiry* (pp. 13–26). Proceedings RMRS-P-15-VOL-3R. Ogden, UT: US Department of Agriculture, Forest Service, Rocky Mountain Research Station.

Feierman, J., Levick, M., and Mody, A. (2009). School-to-prison pipeline ... and back: Obstacles and remedies for the re-enrollment of adjudicated youth. *New York Law School Law Review*, 54, 1115–1129.

Fraser, M. (1997). *Risk and Resilience in Childhood: An Ecological Perspective*. Washington, DC: NASW Press.

Frith, U. (1989). *Autism: Explaining the Enigma*. Oxford: Blackwell.

Gass, M. (1995). Adventure family therapy: An innovative approach answering the question of lasting change with adjudicated youth? *Monograph on Youth in the 1990s*, 4, 103–117.

Gass, M., and Gillis, H. L. (2010) Clinical supervision in adventure therapy: Enhancing the field through an active experiential model. *Journal of Experiential Education*, 33(1), 72–89.

Gass, M. A., Gillis, H. L., and Russell, K. C. (2012). *Adventure Therapy: Theory, Practice, and Research*. New York: Routledge.

Gillis, H., and Bonney, W. C. (1989). Utilizing adventure activities with intact groups: A sociodramatic systems approach to consultation. *Journal of Mental Health Counseling*, 11(4), 345–358.

Gillis, H., Gass, M., and Russell, K. (2008). The effectiveness of project adventure's behavior management programs for male offenders in residential treatment. *Residential Treatment for Children and Youth*, 25(3), 227–247.

Goldenberg, M., McAvoy, L., and Klenosky, D. B. (2005). Outcomes from the components of an Outward Bound experience. *Journal of Experiential Education*, 28, 123–146.

Hamm, J., and Faircloth, B. (2005). The role of friendship in adolescents' sense of school belonging. *New Directions for Child and Adolescent Development*, 107, 61–78.

Hattie, J., Marsh, H. W., Neill, J. T., and Richards, G. E. (1997). Adventure education and Outward Bound: Out-of-class experiences that make a lasting difference. *Review of Educational Research*, 67, 43–87.

Head, J. (2002). *Working with Adolescents: Constructing Identity*. London: Falmer Press.

Henton, M. (1996). *Adventure in the Classroom: Using Adventure to Strengthen Learning and Build a Community of Life-Long Learners*. Hamilton, MA: Project Adventure Inc.

Holmbeck, G. N., Colder, C., Shapera, W., Westhoven, V., Kenealy, L., and Updegrove, A. (2000). Working with adolescents: Guides from developmental psychology. In P. C. Kendall (ed.), *Child and Adolescent Therapy: Cognitive-Behavioral Procedures* (2nd edn, pp. 334–385). New York: Guilford Press.

Hunt, M. G., and Rosenheck, R. A. (2011). Psychotherapy in mental health clinics of the Department of Veterans Affairs. *Journal of Clinical Psychology*, 67, 561–573.

Hyer, L., Boyd, S., Scurfield, R., Smith, D., and Burke, J. (1996). Effects of Outward Bound experience as an adjunct to inpatient PTSD treatment of war veterans. *Journal of Clinical Psychology,* 52(3), 263–278.

Johnson, D. R., Feldman, S. C., Southwick, S. M., and Charney, D. S. (1994). The concept of the second generation program in the treatment of post-traumatic stress disorder among Vietnam veterans. *Journal of Traumatic Stress,* 7(2), 217–236.

Kennedy, B. P., and Minami, M. (1993). The Beech Hill Hospital/Outward Bound adolescent chemical dependency treatment program. *Journal of Substance Abuse Treatment,* 10, 395–406.

Koegel, R., and Koegel, L. (1995). *Teaching Children with Autism: Strategies for Initiating Positive Interactions and Improving Learning Opportunities.* Baltimore, MD: Paul H. Brooks Publishing.

Kuo, F. E., and Faber Taylor, A. (2004). A potential natural treatment for attention-deficit/hyperactivity disorder: Evidence from a national study. *American Journal of Public Health,* 94, 1580–1586.

Leo, J. (2000). Attention deficit disorder. *Skeptics Society and Skeptic Magazine,* 8(1), 63.

McKenzie M. (2000). How are adventure education program outcomes achieved? A review of the literature. *Australian Journal of Outdoor Education,* 5(1), 19–29.

McWhirter, J., McWhirter, B., McWhirter, A., and McWhirter, E. H. (1993). *At-Risk Youth: A Comprehensive Response.* Belmont, CA: Thomson Brooks/Cole Publishing.

Muncie, J., and Goldson, B. (2006). *Comparative Youth Justice.* London: SAGE.

Nelson, K. M. (2006). The burden of obesity among a national probability sample of veterans. *Journal of General Internal Medicine,* 21(9), 915–919.

Olfson, M., Marcus, S. C., Druss, B., Elinson, L., Tanielian, T., and Pincus, H. A. (2002). National trends in outpatient treatment of depression. *Journal of the American Medical Association,* 287, 203–209.

Palmer, C. (2008). A theory of risk and resilience factors in military families. *Military Psychology,* 20, 205–217.

Reiter, E., and Root, A. (1975). Hormonal changes of adolescence. *The Medical Clinics of North America,* 59(6), 1289–1304.

Resnik, A. J., and Allen, S. M. (2007). Using international classification of functioning, disability, and health to understand challenges in community reintegration of injured veterans. *Journal of Rehabilitation Research and Development,* 44(7), 991–1006.

Robledo, S., and Ham-Kucharski, D. (2005). *The Autism Book: Answers to your Most Pressing Questions.* New York: Penguin.

Russell, J. (1997). *Autism as an Executive Disorder.* New York: Oxford University Press.

Russell, K. (2006). *Examining Substance Use Frequency and Depressive Symptom Outcome in a Sample of Outdoor Behavioural Healthcare Participants (Research Report No 1).* Minneapolis, MN: Outdoor Behavioral Healthcare Research Cooperative College of Education and Human Development, University of Minnesota.

Seal, K. H., Bertenthal, D., Maguen, S., Gima, K., Chu, A., and Marmar, C. R. (2008). Getting beyond "Don't ask; don't tell": An evaluation of US Veterans Administration postdeployment mental health screening of veterans returning from Iraq and Afghanistan. *American Journal of Public Health,* 98(4), 714–720.

Sheard, M., and Golby, J. (2006). The efficacy of an outdoor adventure education curriculum on selected aspects of positive psychological development. *Journal of Experiential Education,* 29(2), 187–209.

Sibthorp, J., and Jostad, J. (2014). The social system in outdoor adventure education programs. *Journal of Experiential Education,* 37(1), 60–74.

Tuckman, B. W., and Jensen, M. A. C. (1977). Stages of Small-Group Development Revisited, *Group Organization Management*, 2(4).

Van Puymbroeck, M., Ewert, A., Luo, Y., and Frankel, J. (2012). The influence of the Outward Bound Veterans Program on sense of coherence. *American Journal of Recreation Therapy,* 10(5), 1–8.

Wolery, M., Bailey, D., and Sugai, G. (1998). *Effective Teaching Principles and Procedures for Applied Behavior Analysis with Exceptional Students.* Boston, MA: Allyn & Bacon.

8

STUDENT MEDICATION MANAGEMENT AND ISSUES

Overview

OAE programs are experiencing increases in students who come to programs who take prescription medications (Russell *et al.*, 2008). This is due to several factors. First, western medical programs are getting increasingly better at diagnosing children with depression, anxiety, obsessive compulsive disorder, etc. and thus increasing the percentage of the population who take these types of medications. Second, as the popularity of OAE programs continues to rise, parents are turning to these types of programs as supplements to the sole use of medications or as a trial period to examine how their child performs while not taking the medication, while not having to directly deal with the consequences themselves.

Programs need to have a very detailed and thorough plan and staff training for how to accommodate student medications and issues relative to this topic. Also important considerations are what to do if a student misses a medication while on course, or if there is an abuse of substances while an individual is under the care of the OAE program. In this section, how to accommodate student medications, tips and tricks for tracking medication usage, and best practices will be explored. By having a well considered plan for handling student medication, the burden on the instructor will be assuaged and there is the likelihood that an incident of abuse or missed dosage can be minimized.

Trends/issues

According to the Citizens Commission on Human Rights in 2014, the number of youth in the United States on psychotropic medication was 8,389,034 (CCHR International, 2014) – a staggering number that is hard to comprehend. However, the takeaway from this type of data is that it is inevitable that OAE programs will see students who take prescription medication on their programs. The number is likely to continue to rise in the following years as new diagnoses and ways to diagnose become available to doctors, psychiatrists, and therapists. An additional factor is the influence of the pharmaceutical industry on American society and the increasing norm of youth taking on medication, which diminishes the negative stigma.

Some interesting US statistics relative to youth and medications are as follows:

1   There are some 4,404,360 kids on ADHD drugs.
2   Around 2,165,279 are taking antidepressants.
3   Approximately 830,836 take antipsychosis medications like lithium.
4   The category with the highest increase in recent years is the 2,132,625 kids on anti-anxiety medications (CCHR International, 2014).

One major concern for practitioners should be the potential for abuse on the course (Stich and Gaylor, 1984). This can include a number of issues including not taking medications, selling medications, and/or taking an unhealthy dose of their own medication. Because of the potential for abuse, practitioners will want to have a detailed plan for keeping track of which students come to the program with medication, how many pills they have in their possession, dosage, and frequency. Details for a highly controlled medication plan as well as suggestions for best practices are outlined below.

Initially, programmers and practitioners will want to consult their local laws and guidelines for best practices within their state. Additionally, the denial of a student into your program based on medication issues is illegal in most states and the law should be considered before making the decision to exclude a student based on any medical issue. In light of this, it is important to come up with a comprehensive plan. The first steps in handling student medication is to ensure that you are setting yourself, or your instructor, up for success relative to medication issues. A detailed outline of your company's policies and procedures on how to accommodate students with medication should be distributed at staff training and thoroughly explained to all staff members. First, make sure you understand which students are coming with medication, what those medications are, and how often the student needs to take these medications. Second, talk to the parents before the OAE experience starts, if dealing with youth, about sending the correct amount of medication. Have the parent send enough medication for the length of the course, with about two extra doses in case the student drops or loses a pill in the administration process. When you receive the medication from the student, you will want to count and document the number of pills the student has brought to the course.

Programs should consider having a plan in place for lost, missed, or dropped medication. This could be a simple form with space that has a narrative with what happened. The potential repercussions of missing a medication for a student can be extremely hazardous to the health and wellbeing of an individual and is not something to take lightly. After you document the incident, if you have not had a discussion with parents or a physician beforehand, a call to some authority (parents or doctor) should be undertaken to ascertain if missing the medication requires additional treatment or action like evacuation from the field or admission to a hospital for rebalancing of the medication.

While talking to the parents before the OAE course beings, make sure you each have a thorough understanding of what the medications are for, and that the plan for their medication administration on course is the same as when the student is at home. Some cases have occurred of parents utilizing their son or daughter's participation on an OAE course to experiment with dosage of medications. Due to the higher stress and unfamiliarity of being on an OAE experience, this is not a good idea. Programs may also want to consider omitting students who have just stopped or started new medication within a few weeks of the beginning of the OAE course. Remember that some medications take over a month to start having an effect on the student.

One hazard that was identified by Stich and Gaylor (1984) relative to the management of student medication is mitigation from harmful external factors such as weather. Certain student medication needs should be protected from the various elements that might impinge on the effects of the medication. For example, many OAE programs choose to carry an epinephrine injector for allergic reactions. Programs operating in colder environments need to figure out a method for keeping the epinephrine above the manufacturer's recommendation or above (59° Fahrenheit). Be sure to check individual manufacturer's recommendations. Relatedly, some medications cannot be stored at high temperatures and thus warrant storage in a cooler with ice or some other refrigerating mechanism. Instructors and staff need to be diligent about checking these guidelines before the students show up for their program, and figure out how to manage the necessary precautions for handling student medications. Again preparation is the key to having a smooth course with student medications.

Programs also need to consider the appropriate method for storage and safekeeping of student medications. For example, when working with older clients, you may consider letting the students keep their own medication.

FIGURE 8.1   Students breaking after a day of mountain biking as part of their OAE course (photo: Pete Allison)

However, with youth, instructors may want to keep and oversee the distribution of these medications to prevent abuse or to help students remember to take their medications. Either way, a detailed plan should be formulated before the students arrive and be agreed upon by administrators and field instructors. An additional consideration that some programs choose is to let the students keep "over the counter medications" but not prescription drugs. Also, consider allowing the students to keep medication that may need to be administered quickly like inhalers or epinephrine. If choosing this method, the instructors should know where the students are keeping these devices in case they need to render assistance when administering the medication to the student (i.e. in the lid of their backpack).

Another sensitive issue can be male staff and medications relating to female menstruation. Although it can be interesting to challenge gender norms and have a male staff member facilitate the administration of these types of meds, female students are often more comfortable with female staff members being their contact for these issues. Regardless of how your program chooses to handle these types of medications, be intentional about how you go about distribution and oversight of these medications, always keeping the dignity of the student in mind. Special sensitivity should be given to the distribution and management of birth control as this can be of particular sensitivity with female students.

THE BACKCOUNTRY AS A THERAPEUTIC SETTING

Ken Gilbertson, PhD, University of Minnesota Duluth, USA

Building from the work of Bob Rhealt in using the backcountry as a therapeutic setting for Vietnam veterans diagnosed with post traumatic stress disorder (PTSD) a colleague and I set out to serve combat veterans from the Midwest in the Boundary Waters Canoe Area Wilderness (BWCAW) in Northeastern Minnesota. My colleague held a Masters of Social Work and specialized in treating combat veterans with PTSD. He also had access to several clients. I had the backcountry skills and access to equipment in addition to training in clinical counseling, but I was not licensed. Following is a story of the setting, the clients, and the necessary skills of the therapists using a wilderness setting for therapy.

The setting

Initially, we simply imagined the BWCAW as a great place to work with our clientele. Our goal was to use the backcountry as a way to help bring the veteran back home. With PTSD, the person is frozen in time from the source and/or place of the trauma that so severely affected the person. In this case, it was the constant intense stress of combat in the jungles of Vietnam. We believed that by immersing in a wilderness setting where the group of vets worked together to become comfortable in the woods we would achieve a means to bring them back home, to help them leave Vietnam. We ran our program for several years.

To a veteran who has been "in country," that is to say in harm's way in a military conflict, the backcountry is a place of danger and constant stress to survive. It is not a friendly setting for recreational pursuits. We quickly found that the vets were behaving just as they had when they left Vietnam. Some would stay up all night standing just outside the light of the campfire as if they were on guard duty. Others would sleep away from the group because they found that they "could more easily survive an enemy ambush targeting their group." Since this worked in combat, this was their habit in the BWCAW. Our goal was to enable them to experience the backcountry as a place of comfort rather than danger. Our means was to show and teach them simple backcountry skills like finding a campsite that provided respite rather than a place to elude enemy notice.

During our second year, we found ourselves crossing a portage that was quite overgrown with thick brush. The day happened to be very still, hot, and humid. A storm was approaching and this was that quiet moment before the storm. I mean this literally and metaphorically. It was day 2 of the trip and the group was working together to cross the portage. My colleague noticed the group getting very quiet and whispered for me to pay attention to their dynamic. Suddenly a white dog came bounding down the portage trail towards them. As it passed with its two owners the group seemed to do a collective sigh of relief. One group member quietly told me that, if he had a gun at that moment, that dog would not have lived. We realized that the conditions of the BWCAW were very similar to those in the jungles of Vietnam. We also realized that we had found our perfect setting for what our goals were.

I have seen this behavior with other combat vets who served in Afghanistan. On a different trip that was a leadership training course and not intended to be therapeutic I found a participant who had served in Afghanistan to be uncharacteristically quiet as we were hiking in the Badlands of the Western Dakotas. The hillsides were a chalky gray and white with steep ravines holding a few boulders here and there. As I was watching my student, he began to hold his camera tripod across his arms as if he were on patrol holding his weapon. He was on full alert. I walked alongside him and quietly asked if he was all right. He whispered that the valley we were walking in with the surrounding hillsides were very much like Afghanistan. "This is a good place to come under attack," he replied. In essence, he was having a flashback that had brought him back to his combat zone; he was not hiking in "the beauty" of the Badlands at that moment.

It is not practical to place every person suffering from PTSD in the setting where they experienced their trauma. Still, whether they are a combat veteran or not, the backcountry can become a very effective setting because it enables the therapist to work with the flashbacks and gently nudge the client to "come home" by allowing them to experience the backcountry as a friendly place and a source of physical and emotional comfort.

The clients

In order to be safe and effectively therapeutic, we required the clients to be assessed as outpatients. They needed to have recovered sufficiently that they would not be unsafe toward themselves and others while on trail. They could not be violent. We needed to trust that they wouldn't just attempt to leave the group and strike out on their own. Since substance abuse is a common symptom of a PTSD client, they needed to be sober for at least a week and had to be willing to confront their addiction. Certainly no alcohol or illegal drugs were tolerated while on the course (as is the case with any type of structured adventure activity).

Each client needed to be willing to address their PTSD and be willing to become a participating group member. What did not matter was the extent of their mobility. We have had clients who were paraplegic, were amputees, or just had poor mobility. We found that these kinds of "inabilities" were of no concern. We also found that group-building exercises to build a sense of team were a waste of time. These guys knew the importance of team. As veterans with a common experience, they were automatically a team, a brotherhood, or sisterhood.

I found this out by spending an afternoon rock climbing toward the end of the trip. I began with the classic line of explaining the importance of teamwork and trust between the climber and the belayer. The knowledge that the belayer was holding the climber's life in their hands was important to building that trusting relationship. After I began this explanation, I found the group chuckling over my serious pronouncement. I asked what was so funny. One of the vets let me know that they were quite used to entrusting their lives to their comrades. They didn't really need that line. Their response was, "why don't we just try rock climbing and leave it at that."

While the length of time spent in the backcountry varies, we found that five days was ideal. It wasn't too long, yet it provided enough time to acclimatize to the setting, build necessary skills to travel and camp, and to work on issues related to their PTSD, and then discuss how they would transition back to their home lives. A shorter time period – even four days – was simply not enough to be able to cover those areas effectively.

The therapists

The skills, knowledge, and more importantly, the mindset of the therapists are essential. Having a licensed practicing counselor (e.g. MSW or LPC) who has experience working with combat veterans and/or PTSD is very helpful. Yet, the team of leaders do not all need to be combat veterans nor is it necessary to have experienced the same kind of trauma as the clientele. Initially I was very worried about this. I had the training and experience in counseling, but I was not a veteran. I had worked in emergency care so I understood traumatic experiences first hand. What is required is to be genuine, empathetic, and a good listener, to not be afraid of the clients because they have experienced some severe traumatic experience. In the case of Vietnam veterans, it was critical to avoid having an agenda toward or against the military and/or combat. Vietnam was an unpopular war, so vets carried a stigma that today's veterans do not.

On the other hand, not having the training or skill in clinical counseling can be a problem if the client does experience a flashback and the leader doesn't have the skills to help bring the client back emotionally – and then have the skill to process the experience to turn it into a learning moment rather than yet another moment to reinforce the PTSD.

I found that I was quickly accepted by my group members and soon felt as one among them, even though I did not spend any time in combat. I did find that they watched me closely to see if I really was good at getting along in the woods. They would jokingly test my knife-blade for its sharpness, they would want to teach me how to "really" flip a pancake. That joking was an important part of the therapy. Humor truly does unite a group as much as challenge and dissonance.

I did find that simple acts, like baking a cake in a Dutch oven, were profound because they demonstrated comfort in the woods. That cake brought one man to tears. On another occasion our group had climbed to the top of an overlook. As we sat on the granite outcrop and scanned down on our camp and across to another lake in the distance, I explained to them that they were literally sitting on the bedrock of North America, known as the Canadian Shield. Again, I discovered that by sharing a simple insight about the land we were traveling in and making a connection to them through the metaphor, the vets could feel that sense of North America – of home.

After the moment on the portage of the calm before the storm, the group got out onto the water. It was taking a bit of time because some members were amputees and took longer than others to get situated in their canoe. As we drifted away from the portage we could see a black wall of fast approaching clouds. The storm was about to break. One of the group members had casually thrown a fishing line into the water and quickly caught a fish, which surprised him to the point that he fell out of his canoe. Now we had two people in the water, the wind picking up as the front approached, and canoes drifting apart. With some clear directions and decisive action some canoes towed the swamped canoe and its paddlers in to shore. Others pulled their packs out of the water. As we got to shore some members quickly got dry clothes out for the wet paddlers, another team strung a tarp, a third team got a stove lit and soon had hot water for coffee. Then the rain hit. By now we were well sheltered, comfortable, and laughing at our mishap when moments earlier the group was in a "combat" mode on the portage. No better therapeutic moment could be contrived outside of the backcountry. That night we discussed all of the events of the day. It made for some great insights into the effects of war and the feeling of being home.

Were we effective? For the most part, I can say yes. While I can't claim that anyone was "healed," I can say that the experience was very healing. We were deliberate in our setting, our sequence of experiences, and our approaches to one-on-one and group therapy sessions. We were pleasantly surprised by our insights into what made the setting so very important – more so than simple talk therapy in an office. Some of our clients are still very close friends 20 years after the trip. One is one of my closest friends – a brother. A few have died from suicide (more combat vets die from suicide when they return to America than die in combat – this has held true from Vietnam through to the wars in the Middle East). Still, as a mode of therapy for combat veterans, my colleague and I are still certain that the backcountry was the best therapeutic setting for these clients.

FIGURE 8.2 Students kayaking during an outdoor program (photo: UMD Recreational Sports Outdoor Program 2016)

Diet and course food

Recently, trends surrounding the altering of the diets of students on course are starting to emerge. For example, a recent study found that avoiding sugar and unhealthy fats can significantly decrease a child's symptoms of ADD/ADHD (Parletta, 2016). Consider that your student on your OAE course may have very unhealthy and erratic eating behaviors at home. This may be a factor, particularly at the start of the course, as a student may have trouble adjusting to the type of food served on OAE course and thus exacerbate the symptoms of their condition.

TABLE 8.1 Recommended foods to eat or avoid

Foods to eat	Foods to avoid
Beans	Candy
Cheese	Corn syrup
Eggs	Honey
Meat	Sugar products
Nuts	White flour products
Fruits	White rice
Vegetables	Potatoes
Tuna	Caffeine
Salmon	
Olive oil	

Note: ADHD, ODD symptoms, stubbornness, temper tantrums, and provocative behavior, which were present in 50% of the children, decreased significantly (Hurt and Arnold, 2014; Hurt et al., 2011; Nigg and Holton, 2014).

Careful planning and consideration of dietary accommodations for student can greatly increase your chances of reducing student behavioral issues while on course. This approach can also help teach students what foods are best for managing their conditions, while showing them an approach to supplement their medications. This strategy should only be used as a supplement to their medication and is not a replacement for the medications that the students are taking at the time of the OAE experience.

Managing withdrawal

Managing a withdrawal from a student who has been addicted to medication can be extremely dangerous and should be treated with the utmost caution. A common rule for managing withdrawal is that, typically, the harder the substance, the more dangerous the withdrawal process can be (Stewart and Brown, 1995). For example, heroin is one of the most dangerous abusive substances and, relatedly, one of the most dangerous during the withdrawal process. Other examples of drugs from which students can experience withdrawal symptoms include methamphetamine, heroin, cocaine, and benzodiazepines (i.e. valium).

The first step in managing withdrawal is to ascertain what substance the person has been abusing. This information will then determine if a field evacuation is necessary or preferable. After this information is obtained, be sure to reliably assess and validate the information. You may consider calling the student's parents to inform them of the situation, gain background information, and see if they prefer the situation to be handled under medical professionals. Staff may also want to contact their consulting physician to make sure the field staff can safely handle the situation, give advice, and communicate best practices for the substance with which the staff are dealing.

There will be some signs and symptoms that student is going through withdrawal. These signs may be masked by the administration of over the counter medication that the staff may have available to them. So, if you suspect a student may be beginning withdrawal (i.e. they have a history of substance abuse), staff will want to increase the monitoring of this student. At first, signs and symptoms of withdrawal may be mistaken for cold and flu like symptoms. For example, a student may experience sore muscles, sleeplessness, and a runny nose. Be sure to continue monitoring these students closely. These are all phase one types of symptoms. Remember that symptoms of withdrawal vary greatly with the individual and the substance involved.

Phase two of drug withdrawal oftentimes is harder to mistake for cold and flu symptoms. Phase two symptoms can include diarrhea, rapid heartbeat, and dilated pupils. These two phases can last anywhere from a week to a month depending on the individual, abuse length, and degree of addiction. If these unbearable symptoms last for longer than a week, programs will want to strongly consider evacuating the student, as they are not likely to find success on an OAE program not designed to accommodate such students. Dehydration is also a major issue for

TABLE 8.2 Common symptoms of substance abuse withdrawal

Phase 1	Phase 2
Muscle aches	Diarrhea
Restlessness	Abdominal cramps
Anxiety	Nausea and vomiting
Agitation	Dilated pupils
Tearing eyes	Rapid heartbeat
Runny nose	Goosebumps
Excessive sweating	Rhinorrhea
Sleeplessness	Dysphoria
Excessive yawning	Arthralgia
Low energy	Elevated blood pressure
Lack of appetite	

Source: Cemek *et al.*, 2011

students going through withdrawal because of vomiting and diarrhea. Consider hydrating as a number one priority with the addition of sports drinks.

Some over the counter medications can help in the withdrawal process. For example, consider giving the student Imodium to treat the symptoms of diarrhea. Similarly, Ibuprofen can be administered to help treat sore muscles and headaches. Other medications are options for students but would require leaving the field unless a consulting physician could prescribe them to be administered. This would include substances like methadone, buprenorphine, or clonidine, all of which can make the withdrawal period easier on the individual. However, it is not likely that these can be administered in the field unless special circumstances apply.

Finally, if you do have a student who suffers from withdrawal, the final task of the instructor will be to help that student continue on the path to stay drug-free. Becoming familiar with and utilizing support service and groups back in their home town will be of paramount importance.

Refusal to take medication

Sometimes, an OAE instructor may face the issue of a student refusing to take their medication. Commonly cited reasons for this are when the student reports that they "feel fine" or "I want to see what happens if I do not take my medication." OAE settings, without parents or doctors, are not places to experiment with dosage changes or a change to the medications a student takes prior to the experience. Therefore, an instructor should do everything in their power to get the student to electively take the medication.

If a student refuses to take their medication at the prescribed time, the following actions can be taken. First, ask the student why they do not want to take their medication. The denial of the medication might be an indicator of a different behavioral issue occurring. Consider their interactions with other group members. Another possible solution is that the student is having difficulty socially, emotionally, or physically in the OAE setting.

Second, ask the student if they remember why the treatment is necessary. If they cannot remember, be sure to remind them. This act may establish a basis of understanding in which you can both move forward, with you convincing them that taking the medication is the right course of action. If they still refuse, remind them of the ramifications of not taking the prescription. For example, this may mean they will experience withdrawal, become ill, or possibly be removed from the OAE experience (caution that this may be their underlying motivation).

Third, wait a little for the student to de-escalate. They may not positively respond to the pressure that you are imposing upon them by encouraging them to take the medication. Medications have a "time frame" in which the student needs to take them. In light of this, you can wait within that time frame for the student to see the necessity in taking his or her medication. Most time frames are about one hour on either side of the recommended time.

Finally, if they continue to refuse, document the missed medication dose and the reason for the issue. You should then follow your institution's policies and procedures for moving forward with this incident. Administrators should consider contacting parents and doctors for advice on how to move forward. Again, it should be emphasized that the refusal of medication is likely a wider issue than the refusal of a particular dose. Use motivational interviewing techniques to ascertain the reason for this student's undesirable behavior and possible bid for attention.

FIGURE 8.3 Students ascend a steep slope in the early morning (photo: George Armstrong)

Best practice/policy

As previously suggested, OAE programs will want to work diligently to develop policies and practice that work best for their program. Some considerations for the development of these policies and practice should include the age of the participants, the types of clients they're seeking to serve, and the policy surrounding the admission of students based on an assessment of their mental health. For example, it may be in the best interest of the program not to admit a person diagnosed with a severe condition like schizophrenia who takes lithium. These types of extreme conditions are both a personal liability if the staff do not have the capacity to handle an individual student's condition, and a programmatic liability if something happens while this student is on course.

To aid in the development of best practices and policies, these authors would like to offer a few methods that have been developed by other programs. The reality is, your program will want to decide how to handle student medications based on a spectrum that ranges from allowing the students to have total control of their own medication, which may be appropriate for high functioning adults, to absolute oversight by staff which is probably best suited for working with adjudicated youth. These practices will be guided by the populations your programs serve, the location in which you operate, and the advice of your consulting physician. Your insurance provider may also have guidelines surrounding the administration, storage, and distribution of medications to your students while they are under your program's supervision.

The SUESS program that operates in North Carolina and Idaho serves youth at risk and adjudicated youth. This program utilizes a method that takes absolute control over student medication with the intention to ensure the students are taking the medication and to prevent abuse. The medication is kept in a locked Pelican Case Box and the key to the box is kept on a lanyard around the instructor's neck. The instructional staff is responsible for the distribution of

TABLE 8.3 Common behavioral diagnosis and prescription medications

Behavioral diagnosis	Common medications
ADD/ADHD	Amphetamine (Adzenys XR ODT, Evekeo) Amphetamine/Dextroamphetamine (Adderall and Adderall XR) Dextroamphetamine (Dexedrine, ProCentra, Zenzedi) Dexmethylphenidate (Focalin and Focalin XR) Lisdexamfetamine (Vyvanse) Methylphenidate (Concerta, Daytrana, Metadate CD and Metadate ER, Methylin, Methylin ER, Ritalin, Ritalin LA, Ritalin SR, Quillivant XR)
Anxiety	BENZODIAZEPINES Alprazolam (Xanax) panic, generalized anxiety, phobias, social anxiety, OCD

Behavioral diagnosis	Common medications
Anxiety (cont.)	Clonazepam (Klonopin) panic, generalized anxiety, phobias, social anxiety
	Diazepam (Valium) generalized anxiety, panic, phobias
	Lorazepam (Ativan) generalized anxiety, panic, phobias
	Oxazepam (Serax) generalized anxiety, phobias
	Chlordiazepoxide (Librium) generalized anxiety, phobias
	BETA BLOCKERS
	Propranolol (Inderal) social anxiety
	Atenolol (Tenormin) social anxiety
	TRICYCLIC ANTIDEPRESSANTS
	Imipramine (Tofranil) panic, depression, generalized anxiety, PTSD
	Desipramine (Norpramin, Pertofrane and others) panic, generalized anxiety, depression, PTSD
	Nortriptyline (Aventyl or Pamelor) panic, generalized anxiety, depression, PTSD
	Amitriptyline (Elavil) panic, generalized anxiety, depression, PTSD
	Doxepin (Sinequan or Adapin) panic, depression
	Clomipramine (Anafranil) panic, OCD, depression
Bipolar disorder	Olanzapine (Zyprexa)
	Quetiapine (Seroquel)
	Risperidone (Risperdal)
	Ariprazole (Abilify)
	Ziprasidone (Geodon)
	Clozapine (Clozaril)
Depression	Sertraline (Zoloft)
	Fluoxetine (Prozac, Sarafem)
	Citalopram (Celexa)
	Escitalopram (Lexapro)
	Paroxetine (Paxil, Pexeva, Brisdelle)
	Fluvoxamine (Luvox)
	Trazodone (Oleptro)
	Desvenlafaxine (Pristiq, Khedezla)
	Duloxetine (Cymbalta)
	Levomilnacipran (Fetzima)
	Venlafaxine (Effexor XR)
	Amitriptyline
	Amoxapine
	Clomipramine (Anafranil)
	Desipramine (Norpramin)
	Doxepin
	Imipramine (Tofranil)
	Nortriptyline (Pamelor)
	Protriptyline
	Trimipramine (Surmontil)
	Bupropion (Wellbutrin, Forfivo, Aplenzin)

medicine at the appropriate times, and performs oral checks to ensure these medications are in fact being taken. Due to these precautions, it is highly unlikely that students can abuse the medication.

The Success Oriented Achievement Realized (SOAR) Program exercises moderate control over student medication. While the instructors retain control over the medication, they are kept in the instructor's first aid kit. Students are then administered the medication over the course of the day by the instructors. There's no lock and key system to prevent these students from stealing the medication; however, they are kept in the instructor's possession at all times. This method serves for both prescription medication and any over the counter medication the students may bring.

If you suspect a student is not taking his or her medication, it may be necessary to use a high degree of supervision when administering the oral medication. Students may spit out or "cheek" their medication for a myriad of reasons. However, if you start the course with a rigorous procedure to ensure they are taking their medication, you can avoid a larger issue later upon discovering they have not been taking their pills. Different guidelines for this vary but one way to ensure the student is swallowing their medication is as follows:

1 Have the student bring a clear water bottle to the administration of the medication.
2 Give the pill to the student and have them show you the pill placed on their tongue.
3 After swallowing the pill with water, inspect the water bottle to ensure they did not spit it into the bottle.
4 Visually inspect inside the cheeks and under the tongue of the student.
5 Have the student blow their lips (like their mimicking a horse's ninny) to ensure the pill is not stuffed behind the lips.

With these techniques, it is important to establish ground rules and fair treatment of all the students. For example, if you're going to go through the visual check for one student, it is a good idea to do it for all the students, even if you trust the others to not abuse the system. This will prevent the singling out of any one individual and reduce the building of resentment.

The use of a check sheet is also highly recommended to track the administration of student medication. These sheets, which have the student names, medications, and times they receive the medication, are also handy for tracking and remembering when it's time for the student to take the medication. This sheet should also include a count of the number of pills with which the student started the OAE course, and then at the end of the course, the number of pills deducted should equal the number of times it was administered.

Because there is a myriad of medications that have different requirements, it is imperative that an instructor have a good system for remembering, tracking, and administering student medication. One trick is to have the instructors

KIDS MEDICATION TRACKER

Day	✓	Medication	Dose	Time	✓	Medication	Dose	Time	✓	Medication	Dose	Time
Example	☐	Ritalin	5mg	7:00	☐	Ritalin	5mg	12:00	☐	Ritalin	5mg	8:00
Monday	☐				☐				☐			
	☐				☐				☐			
Tuesday	☐				☐				☐			
	☐				☐				☐			
Wednesday	☐				☐				☐			
	☐				☐				☐			
Thursday	☐				☐				☐			
	☐				☐				☐			
Friday	☐				☐				☐			
	☐				☐				☐			
Saturday	☐				☐				☐			
	☐				☐				☐			
Sunday	☐				☐				☐			
	☐				☐				☐			

Medication Name:			
Monday Count:			
Sunday Count:			
Pills Taken:			
Refill Needed?:	Y / N	Y / N	Y / N

Parent Signature: _____   Kid Signature: _____

www.FreePrintableMedicalForms.com

FIGURE 8.4 An example of a medication tracking sheet

carry watches with multiple alarms. This will allow the instructor to set alarms whenever it's time to administer medication. Middle of the day medication times are often the most difficult to remember because of all the activities that are occurring during an OAE program.

Programs will want to have some way of documenting an incident where a student misses the administration of medication. It is also important to talk to the student, parent, and sometimes healthcare provider, before the course begins to understand what needs to happen if a student misses their appointed time to take their medication. For example, the missing of some medication requires hospital admission to rebalance the student's chemical composition.

In sum, medications for either students or staff present an often complex and multi-dimensional challenge for the instructor or group leader. In addition to the different time schedules for medication, the instructor is often faced with questions about the medication's intended use, potential side effects, and special considerations in an OAE/BGM setting. Table 8.4 provides a sample of the complexity of issues surrounding medications with some often-prescribed medications. Despite these challenges, instructors and programs in OAE/BGM should expect an increase in the presence of medications and medicated students. Increasingly, part of the responsibility of the BGM staff will be to understand, monitor, and manage student medications as well as understanding the symptoms of withdrawal, abuse, and interactions with other drugs and the outdoor environment.

TABLE 8.4 Drugs and medications commonly seen in OAE/BGM

Generic name	Use	Potential side effects	Considerations in OAE/BGM setting
Prozac, Zoloft, Wellbutrin	Mild to moderate depression	Irregular/rapid heartbeat, chest pain	• Possible interactions with other drugs • Food during solo
Ritalin, Adderall	ADHD and depression	Changes in blood pressure	• Caffeine can increase anxiety • Hydration important • Possible interactions with other drugs
Lithium, Seroquel	Bipolar disorder, depression, and aggression	Irregular heartbeat, vomiting, seizure, and reduced coordination	• Must have food during solo • Hydration • Interaction with other drugs
Xanax, Klanopin	Anxiety, panic attacks, and sleep disturbance	Rapid heart rate, double vision, and constipation	• Food on solo • Interaction with other drugs

Main points

- It is imperative to have a detailed plan for the storage, administration, and track of student medication before the course starts. Gather as much information as you can from parents and physicians about medications and know what to do if a student misses a medication dose.
- Having a working knowledge of what each medication is before your students arrive is best practice. This will give you a sense of the student's condition, and what you should do if the student refuses or misses their medication.
- Having written policies about the storage of medications (i.e. all prescription medications will be kept safeguarded by staff) will help field instructors frontload the transactions and establish policies surrounding medication before the OAE experience.
- If a student refuses their medication, try to figure out the reason why. Gently encourage them to do so with logic and reason and the understanding that maintaining their medication is the best course of action and that OAE settings are not the appropriate place to experiment with dosage and medication changes.

Discussion questions

- What can you do, the next time you're in the field, to increase the likelihood that you will not have an issue with student/client medication?
- If you were creating a program, what policies around medication would you be sure to incorporate?
- What are the steps to ensure a student has successfully taken their medication?

SCENARIO

It is a frosty morning and the wet air is trapped by the canopy of rhododendron and poplar. As she sits drinking coffee before the students arise, she hears zippers opening, feet shuffling into shoes, and whispers, "I'm going to go to the bathroom." The whispers grow into chatter and laughter brings us to full morning. Together the group gathers in a huddle, dangling their empty water bottles and trying to discreetly hold their toothbrushes by their side that they forgot to put in the bear hang the night before.

As the group gets ready to walk to the kitchen she notices Sarah sitting by the smoldering morning-after fire poking it with a stick with a pout on her face. "Are you ready for breakfast, Sarah?" I ask. She glares and retorts, "I'm not going." *It's going to be that kind of morning* – the instructor thinks. In that moment she recognizes that she can not only choose her own emotions, but also has the ability to direct the day by the choices she makes as an instructor.

One option is for her to get openly frustrated and express that to Sarah in front of the group. This option has the potential to morph into a back-and-forth with a teenage girl before breakfast and put her in a defensive position. Rather than indulge her in the attention the instructor assumes Sarah is looking for, she ignores the pout and chooses to acknowledge her desire to wrestle with whatever emotion she is currently feeling in peace. "OK Sarah. When you get hungry feel free to come on over we will get your breakfast ready for you. Let us know if we can do anything for you."

The instructor tries to maintain a distance but stay within eye and ear shot of Sarah in case she takes a turn, for better or for worse. Outside of the circle she tells the co-instructor to be aware of Sarah's position and that they can take turns checking-in if she needs it but to give Sarah a chance to clean her slate herself.

Once breakfast is ready the group sits down to eat and the instructor takes Sarah and her breakfast back to camp and sits down next to Sarah. She doesn't talk for a while and just eats her breakfast and pokes at the fire with her. The instructor breaks the silence, "I added some brown sugar to your oatmeal hope that's alright." She proceeds to entertain her with a crazy dream from the night before as Sarah eats some of her oatmeal – still pouting. When the instructor asks her if she ever dreams in her sleep Sarah says that she misses her bed and wants a shower. "Well that's a dream that will be coming true very soon," she assures her. Instead of trying to distract her from her homesickness the instructor asks about her home and what she loves about it and asks if she knows that she can shower in the woods too. She laughs when the backcountry shower is described. The instructor continues to ask questions about her day-to-day life and how fascinated her friends and family will be when they hear about all that she's done. As they talk the instructor stands up and, distractedly, Sarah follows her to the group cleaning their bowls from breakfast.

The group, recognizing the difficult morning Sarah had, brings her into their conversation and they carry their things back to camp and begin to pack up. By this time the frost has melted and evaporated and the sun peaks through the pines.

Discussion questions

1   In this scenario, the instructor is utilizing several techniques described elsewhere in this book. What are some of these techniques and what effect does knowing and using them have on this scenario?
2   What's the most significant factor in this situation: NOT escalating into a tantrum or a larger issue?
3   What was the point in the instructor moving to the student and not confronting the brooding individual in front of the other group members?

References

CCHR International (2014). Number of children and adolescents taking psychiatric drugs in the U.S. Retrieved 16 September 2016, from www.cchrint.org/psychiatric-drugs/children-on-psychiatric-drugs.

Cemek, M., Büyükokuroğlu, M. E., Hazman, Ö., Bulut, S., Konuk, M., and Birdane, Y. (2011). Antioxidant enzyme and element status in heroin addiction or heroin withdrawal in rats: Effect of Melatonin and Vitamin E plus se. *Biological Trace Element Research*, 139(1), 41–54.

Hurt, E., and Arnold, L. (2014). An integrated dietary/nutritional approach to ADHD. *Child and Adolescent Psychiatric Clinics of North America,* 34(4), 955–964.

Hurt, E., Arnold, L., and Lofthouse, N. (2011). Dietary and nutritional treatments for attention-deficit/hyperactivity disorder: current research support and recommendations for practitioners. *Current Psychiatry Reports,* 13, 323–332.

Nigg, J., and Holton, K. (2014). Restriction and elimination diets in ADHD treatment. *Child and Adolescent Psychiatric Clinics of North America,* 23(4), 937–953.

Parletta, N. (2016). Can diet and nutrition affect our learning, behaviour and mental health? *Nutridate,* 27(4), 10–16.

Russell, K. C., Gillis, H. L., and Lewis, T. G. (2008). A five-year follow-up of a survey of North American Outdoor Behavioral Healthcare programs. *Journal of Experiential Education*, 31(1), 55–77.

Stewart, D. G., and Brown, S. A. (1995). Withdrawal and dependency symptoms among adolescent alcohol and drug abusers. *Addiction*, 90(5), 627–635.

Stich, T. F., and Gaylor, M. S. (1984). Risk Management in Adventure Programs with Special Populations: Two Hidden Dangers. *Journal of Experiential Education*, 7(3), 15–19.

9

SUBSTANCE ABUSE, RULE VIOLATION, AND INAPPROPRIATE BEHAVIORS

Overview

While unfortunate, substance abuse, rule violation, and inappropriate behaviors do happen during OAE programs. There is no recipe or formula for how to handle these situations as there are many variables that factor into these events, including past behaviors, environmental factors, and social settings. This is one of the ideas that makes behavior management much more of an art form than a technical skill like Wilderness First Responder. The complexity of each situation is varied and the unique individuals involved require delicacy, insight, and training. In this chapter, we will explore various options and issues relative to these difficult topics so that you and your staff can make the best informed decisions possible. These topics are merely a guide to give you a framework with which to work with the student. These concepts are predicated on other ideas in this book, such as having built rapport with the student and having a working background knowledge of the student's ecological system (see Chapter 4).

Substance abuse

Substance abuse occurs when any student overuses, underuses, or misuses a controlled substance. Most often, this happens when students sneak extra medications or illegal substances on course. Most programs will want to strongly consider their policies and practices when substance abuse happens during an OAE program and be sure to adhere to that policy for liability reasons. There are a few major considerations for substance abuse issues on OAE programs. For example, extreme caution must be taken to secure the safety of the student. This likely means admission into a hospital or care facility to provide oversight when these issues occur, in case the types of dosages and amounts of the substance the student has ingested or used put them in danger. Their safety and that of the rest of the students on the OAE experience are always the number one priority and, unfortunately, this sometimes means evacuating and dismissing the student from the OAE program.

Second, a thorough review of your program's policies and procedures, relative to controlled substances, needs to be undertaken by administrators before every season and especially following any violation. To start with, evaluate how your program secures controlled substances when the students arrive and confirms with parents and students beforehand of the expectation the program has toward this issue. Also, consider how the instructional staff talk to parents before the OAE experience and ask if their student will be coming with medications and if so, the type of medication, dosage, quantity, etc. In some cases, like in wilderness therapy settings, it may be helpful to know if the student comes with a history of substance abuse or illegal substance consumption which can be ascertained by a conversation with the family before the students arrive. Extra precautions may be undertaken when these students arrive to ensure you are setting them up for success in your OAE experience.

If a violation of your policies and procedures does happen, administrators should consider how the student got possession of the substance. Did they hide it in their personal equipment when packing their gear for the course or was it taken from the instructional staff or first aid kit? These questions will provide insight into what policy changes need to be undertaken to prevent future substance abuse issues. Consider ramping up efforts to secure and control substances you do not want to be abused and strengthening policies and procedures regarding this issue (see Chapter 8 for more issues relative to medication). If this is a repeated occurrence, consider hiring an outside consultant for guidance on this issue from a similar program that may be able to highlight flaws in your program's policies for handling medications.

One way to try and prevent substance abuse from occurring is to establish clear expectations, and do a thorough check at the beginning of the course of the equipment that the student brings. For example, consider that, when students get off the bus, one of the first expectations stated is a clear explanation of a zero tolerance policy of illegal substances. You can also lay out the consequences for any violation – however be cautious of saying this is an automatic ticket home as this may be a reason for violating these rules and then putting administrators in a tricky spot. Second, consider providing an opportunity for students to turn over these items or throw them away without reprimand. This unique approach will surprise the student and allow you to deal with this issue in an open and constructive manner. This can also provide an amazing platform to have conversations with the students about illegal drug use as it gets the topic and their using out in the open. Finally, figuring out some way to inspect every article the students are bringing into the field is a surefire way to limit their ability to sneak illegal substances on course. Programs located in states where recreational marijuana is now legal will have to be extra considerate when explaining their rationale for disallowing these substances and making these policies clear before the students arrive. Clear and explicit policies can help affirm and confirm instructors when they are providing the norms and expectations to the students.

In all but a few wilderness therapy programs, substance abuse should be considered as a reason for dismissing the students from the OAE experience. This behavior, when present in the student, is likely to indicate larger issues within the student's behavioral process and the majority of instructors in the OAE field do not have enough training to handle these situations and keep these students physically and emotionally safe. In all cases, the parents should be informed of this incident so that they are aware that they need to get additional help and counseling for their child to help them through this issue. With addictions and substance abuse, these are often lifelong issues that take dedicated professionals and controlled environments to help the student. This is a time to be realistic about your program's limitations and concede that this student is likely not a good fit for your program. Additional consideration should be given to your program's liability limitations and realize that keeping this student on the experience might be a breach of your insurance policy.

Strong consideration should be given to this issue as increasingly students are coming to OAE experience on and with medications (see Figure 9.1). See Chapter 8 for more specific guidance on the handling and mitigation of mediations while students are on your OAE experience. Do not underestimate substance abuse

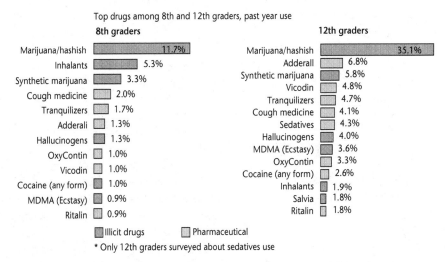

Top drugs among 8th and 12th graders, past year use

8th graders		12th graders	
Marijuana/hashish	11.7%	Marijuana/hashish	35.1%
Inhalants	5.3%	Adderall	6.8%
Synthetic marijuana	3.3%	Synthetic marijuana	5.8%
Cough medicine	2.0%	Vicodin	4.8%
Tranquilizers	1.7%	Tranquilizers	4.7%
Adderali	1.3%	Cough medicine	4.1%
Hallucinogens	1.3%	Sedatives	4.3%
OxyContin	1.0%	Hallucinogens	4.0%
Vicodin	1.0%	MDMA (Ecstasy)	3.6%
Cocaine (any form)	1.0%	OxyContin	3.3%
MDMA (Ecstasy)	0.9%	Cocaine (any form)	2.6%
Ritalin	0.9%	Inhalants	1.9%
		Salvia	1.8%
		Ritalin	1.8%

■ Illicit drugs   ▢ Pharmaceutical

* Only 12th graders surveyed about sedatives use

FIGURE 9.1 Drug usage among American teenagers

FIGURE 9.2 A student rows an oar rig down the Deschutes River with the group contact (flag) flying behind (photo: Meredith Strunk)

and student medication issues as they are likely to arise on the course. From finding drugs while in the wilderness to "cheeking" them to take later, these issues, if they manifest in the wrong way, can cause a program serious headaches, lawsuits, and to shut down entirely if it results in a student death from overdose.

Rule violation

Rule violation is a common issue on OAE courses and it is difficult to lay blanket statements about this because minor rule violations can often be overlooked while major rule violations are sometimes grounds for dismissal from the OAE program. While some strategies for this have been outlined elsewhere in this book, instructional staff should consider the severity and the consequences of the rules that have been violated. A surefire way to alienate yourself or your staff is to punish a student beyond the appropriateness of the rule that has been violated in the eyes of the students. Many issues factor into the decision to punish the student, including rapport, expectations, previous offense, to name but a few. Also, be aware of your limitations when implementing consequences to rule violation. It is inappropriate and illegal to strike, spank, or verbally assault a student. More subtly too, instructors should consider avoiding verbal abuse when students make errors or break rules. For example, saying, "You are really dumb because you did that," is not a helpful remark to the student or an appropriate way to respond to the situation. In any event, these are not effective behavior management strategies or techniques.

Most importantly with rule violation, it is important to consider that the incidents can oftentimes be indicators for other issues. For example, when a student runs away or locks themselves in a restroom, they are likely crying out because some larger issue is occurring. When we asked a friend who has worked in this industry for years about how to best manage behaviors, he replied that the single most important technique for this is to "get to the underlying problem and treat the cause, not the symptoms." Treating the cause and not the symptoms of these deviances in "normal" behavior is critical to helping the students have a positive OAE experience and make strides to improve their behavior both during and after the course.

Other suggested actions before punishment is doled out to the student would be to simply ask them if they knew they were breaking a rule. Sometimes a student genuinely does not know they are engaging in an inappropriate behavior. You may avoid having to punish the student if it was a simple misunderstanding. On a similar line of thinking, you may also want to make sure the rules are completely understood. For example, if a student is using inappropriate words that you thought would fall under the language of "cuss words," you may want to clarify with the student that those words are considered by both parties to be inappropriate. It is important for both parties to come from a place of mutual understanding before punishment is delivered to the student and irreparable damage is done to the student/staff relationship.

Other issues can arise when staff are relaxed about a rule or guideline and then later try to enforce it more strictly. It is difficult to come back from a place of lackadaisical oversight and establish the norm after letting the students break the rules. For example, if staff, at first, let a group of students talk about sex and then later try to punish a student for this conversational topic, they are likely going to have a hard time. One successful technique can be to have a meaningful conversation about the topic in a structured format where students can ask questions. Back to the example, you may want to point out that it is inappropriate to talk about this topic in a casual way as it can be very serious and offense to certain people. Another point to make is that, if the students are wasting their time talking about inappropriate topics, they are not getting to know each other and having meaningful conversations.

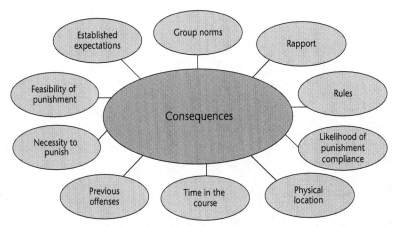

FIGURE 9.3 Factors that contribute to the use of punishment and consequences

In some cases you may want to document the rule violation. This can also be part of the behavior management plan that you negotiate with the student and is particularly useful for repeated behaviors. For example, if a student continually engages in a socially risky behavior, like verbally assaulting another student, the instructor might document the incidents and have the student initial the document certifying that they are aware of the rule violation. This can help later down the road if more serious action is taken against the student for repeated violations. This process can also help you investigate the rule violation. Using the verbal assaulting scenario as an example, you may find out that all the incidents were triggered by the other student first violating a different rule or norm.

Remember that all this process is happening to inform and modify the undesirable behavior. During this time, consider educating the student on alternative behavioral responses to the scenarios given, since they may not know how to respond more appropriately. Additionally, they may need other social and emotional skills for handling these scenarios like de-escalation or effective communication strategies. This is the perfect time to interject and teach these life skills as opposed to getting angry with the student and providing punishment.

GROUP MANAGEMENT FOR PARTICIPANTS WITH SPECIFIC NEEDS

Alison Voight, PhD, Indiana University, USA

In today's world it is more likely than not that an outdoor leader will have among his or her participants a person who may have certain physical limitations, emotional issues or challenges, or be perceived as socially different from others in the group. This can often create an uncomfortable or unfamiliar path for an outdoor leader, especially if he or she has not led many groups involving persons who have specific differences. However, these participants are seeking the same types of experiences as any other person who may sign up for an outdoor adventure program; and more to the point, they are not necessarily interested in "specialized" or segregated outdoor adventure activities. What can you do, as an outdoor leader, to manage and accommodate a diverse group with physical or emotional differences?

An important first consideration is to be aware of the "legal" rights that persons with differences, or disabilities, may have to be a part of your outdoor program. With the advent of many human rights programs, such as the Americans with Disabilities Act (ADA), passed in the US in 1990, the EU's Charter of Fundamental Rights (CFR), as well as the UN Convention on the Rights of Persons with Disabilities (CRPD) accepted in 2010, discrimination on the ground of disability is prohibited, thereby mandating that any participant who may have a disability must be accommodated, if he or she desires this. There may be, however, certain parameters surrounding participation, such as "essential eligibility rules" associated with the ADA, and it behooves any outdoor agency and/or outdoor leader to be fully aware of accommodations mandated by disability rights organizations in their country, such as the ADA, CFR, and CRPD.

Additional considerations regarding accommodations would include the following:

1   Making sure ALL participants are made aware of the potential risks, strength, endurance, or stamina that are required or associated with the adventure activities on the course – in advance, if possible. Obviously, not every outdoor challenge or contingency can be accounted for, but most outdoor leaders know what the demands and rigors of the outdoor adventure course may entail. When participants know what may be required of them on an outdoor adventure course, they can better make informed choices.

2   If certain levels of skill or physical strength are required of participants, for their safety as well as the group's then some form of assessment of the participant may be needed in advance of participation on the course. Keep in mind, however, that any pre-assessment of a potential participant must be given to ALL participants, not just those that may acknowledge a physical limitation. For example, singling out persons with a disability or limitation for assessment would be considered discriminatory under the civil rights law of the ADA. Assessments of participants should be given prior to the beginning of an outdoor adventure course as a standard protocol for everyone, thereby allowing an outdoor leader to better facilitate his or her group. Various forms of assessments may be used, including self-report forms, and/or skills testing, or demonstration, both before and during the outdoor adventure course. A final point to reiterate is that any assessment information should not be used to exclude or discriminate against a person's participation, unless expectations are clearly stated, in writing, prior to the course. In other words, if the outdoor adventure activity will require that a participant be able to lift at least 20 pounds, or hike five miles per day, or endure adverse conditions of weather and terrain, then, and only then, could a participant be advised against, or excluded from, the activity. These requirements, however, should be clearly indicated in writing, or verbally transmitted prior to the beginning of the course. While a group leader may "legally" be able to exclude a person based on assessment, every effort should be made to see where accommodations for that person could be made instead, perhaps with the assistance of the rest of the group, and by general consensus of the group.

3   When managing a diverse group of participants, a key step is to ask what specific needs or accommodations can be made for individuals. This will allow for greater facilitation of a diverse group. Some general

recommendations for various limitations might include more visual cues or hand signals for the deaf, as well as finding alternative or preferential means of communicating, such as sign language, lip reading, or written methods. Sign language interpreters are provided at the expense of the (outdoor) agency (in the US), where feasible, not the client. For visual impairments, greater verbal cues and descriptions are recommended, as well as touching objects, and modeled tactile demonstrations. Physical limitations can vary widely, and every participant will have different strengths and weaknesses, as is true for those without a physical disability. Never assume persons with the same physical limitation (e.g. multiple sclerosis) have the same level of disability. Be sure physical expectations on the course are well understood by the participant in advance, as well as being aware of access issues and possible modifications (i.e. less steep terrain or easier rock face, etc.) for more successful outcomes. Older adults are also an extremely diverse group in terms of strength, endurance, interests, and ability. Many older adults seeking adventure or risk related activities have done so their entire lives, and see no reason to let age stop them. A high level of motivation is often a common characteristic of older adults seeking adventure, where only some extra time or a slower pace is needed to accommodate them. Never patronize or assume an older participant needs or desires extra assistance. They will likely let you know if they do.

4   Allow persons with a disability or physical/emotional limitation the dignity of risk in an outdoor adventure program. Simply assuming that a participant with a limitation could not, or would not wish to engage in a high-risk activity is not a valid reason for preventing him or her from trying. Moreover, this presumption of inability to perform, and therefore preventing involvement, is also discriminatory. Most outdoor leaders are aware of group management techniques, such as "challenge by choice," or "full value contract," which permits participants to engage in risk associated with an outdoor adventure activity, to the fullest extent they feel comfortable. These same concepts must also be extended to persons with a physical or emotional limitation. If a person wishes to try, to the best of his or her ability, to participate in a high-risk activity, an outdoor leader should do everything feasible to safely involve all participants in the rewarding outcomes of outdoor adventure.

5   The following web links provide more specific information regarding the legal rights for accommodation of persons with disabilities:

• ADA = https://adata.org/factsheet/ADA-overview
• CFR = http://ec.europa.eu/justice/fundamental-rights/charter/index_en.htm
• CRPD = www.un.org/disabilities/convention/conventionfull.shtml

FIGURE 9.4   Therapeutic outdoor students practice skills learned in class (photo: Alison Voight)

Inappropriate behaviors

Inappropriate behaviors happen for a myriad of reasons. As with rule violation, the first critical consideration for handling this issue is to consider why the student is lashing out, and how might you find the cause of the inappropriate behavior instead of just punishing the student. For example, the smearing of fecal matter on bathroom walls has been positively linked to physical abuse at home. Consider working with these students from a place of empathy first, as opposed to anger about the student exhibiting inappropriate behaviors.

Inappropriate behaviors can also cause victims among other students which should be handled with delicacy. For example, if a student shows his or her privates to another student, both sets of parents (assuming they are under 18) should be notified of the incident.

Increased supervision can help mitigate issues surrounding inappropriate behaviors. For example, programs may want to have an instructor at the front and at the back of a bus or van to help supervise what is happening with the students on long journeys. While it is commonplace for staff to sleep between opposite gendered tents, it should also be considered to have established directions in which the two genders go for bathroom usage. This can prevent any inappropriate behaviors from happening while students are out of supervision range for legitimate reasons (bathroom).

Some common reasons for inappropriate behaviors include:

1   Inappropriate expectations
2   Misunderstood expectations
3   Immature self-control
4   Boredom

5   Fatigue or discomfort
6   Rebellion
7   Frustration
8   Discouragement
9   Attention seeking behavior
10 Dehydration

Oftentimes when students are exhibiting inappropriate behaviors, motivational interviewing is the preferred method to start the investigation into why students are eliciting certain behaviors. This technique, although typically utilized to elicit change behavior, this technique can also be utilized to help better understand why the student is behaving in a particular manner. As stated above, the number one consideration when these types of behaviors happen is to find the underlying root cause of the problem. It is likely that the student is exhibiting undesirable behavior for an ulterior motive. This may include attention seeking, power grabs, or confidence issues to name a few.

When dealing with inappropriate behaviors, it is important to remember a few techniques, regardless of the type of intervention you are going to utilize. For starters, always come from a place of respect. Remember that the student is acting out for a reason and that those reasons are legitimate in the eyes of the student. Do not try to invalidate the way they are feeling because, although it may be difficult for you to understand, those feelings and attitudes are legitimate.

Second, encourage the student to talk about the issue. It's likely that you are the only person that has listened to this person in their entire life! Remember that this is a privilege and take it seriously. Be intentional about making time and space to spend with that student and listen to their problems (Davidson, 2013). Utilize

FIGURE 9.5   OAE students rig gear in a canoe (photo: Ryan Hines)

active listening skills and don't try to "fix" the problem right away by offering your opinion and solutions. Relatedly, do not get angry at the student for these behaviors. Most likely they have been learned or instilled in the student from their parents, and to them it may be an appropriate way to respond to these issues.

Finally, remember that these inappropriate behaviors are ways of communicating. These actions should signal to you that something is going on within that student that needs to be addressed. If you feel like you cannot handle what the student has reported to you (i.e. sexual or physical abuse), make sure to tell your supervisors. Be sure to check the reporting laws in your state for how you should handle these types of situations. In cases where abuse is happening, make sure the student understands that you are a mandatory reporter for these types of issues and you will have to speak up if they tell you this type of information.

As with rule violation, make sure that the punishment fits the crime relative to handling inappropriate behaviors. Consider also the student may not have known their behavior was going to be considered inappropriate before they carried it out. Remember that oftentimes OAE programs work with youth and teens when they are learning how to be rational and functional members of society and that they may be acting out as a function of ignorance instead of malice.

Before

Outcomes	Timing	Learning styles	Setting
What outcomes should my students be getting from this experience?	Would it be best to debrief right after this activity or let the students process for awhile?	What learning styles do need to cater to during this debrief?	Where is the best setting for this that is free from distractions?

During

T - Trigger	**Dynamic debriefing**
R - Recall/Remember	90/10 rule
A - Affect/Effect	Active listening
C - Connection	Avoid judgments
T - Transference	Ask follow-up questions
	Take notes

Closing

Closing	Booster
Use a quote or summation to provide a definitive ending or closing on an experience or debrief	Consider creating a booster or tangible ways to help the students remember the learning after the experience

FIGURE 9.6 Borrowed from facilitation styles and techniques, the TRACT method can also be a useful structure to help guide discussions after students break rules or elicit inappropriate behaviors

Conclusion

Many practitioners debate about the rational and ethical nature of dismissing students from their OAE programs. These authors tend to lean in the direction that it is not only okay but is sometimes most appropriate and sometimes even beneficial to send students home. We feel this way for a few reasons. First, seasonal staff, working as camp counselors or instructors, oftentimes do not have the skills or training to deal with serious problems that sometimes OAE students come to the course with. Second, sometimes sending a student home from the OAE experience can be a wakeup call for them to get their life together. Third, it is not appropriate to sacrifice the remainder of the OAE experience for the other students in order to keep one or two students on course despite their deviant behavior. These decisions are not easy to make for practitioners and instructors. However, taking into consideration all these components should factor into the decision to keep or dismiss a student from the OAE experience.

These instances of deviance and violation are often the least fun part of working with an OAE program. Unfortunately, if you work in this field long enough you will find yourself having to dole out consequences or remove a student from the OAE experience because of some issue relative to behavioral issues. Remember to work from a place of empathy and compassion, and that a problem behavior is a problem to fix and that one deviant behavior does not define who someone is as a person.

Discussion questions

1   What are three techniques you can use as an instructor to lessen the likelihood of having an issue with substance abuse before the OAE course starts?
2   What are three techniques you can use as an administrator to lessen the likelihood of having an issue with substance abuse before the OAE experience begins?
3   What are the two most important factors to consider when administering consequences to a student after they have broken norms or rules?
4   Why is it the most important consideration treating the underlying cause of the behavioral issue and not the behavior itself?
5   When dismissing a student, why might it be more effective for behavior management, and more efficacious to the student, to dismiss the student from the OAE program?

Reference

Davidson, C. (2013). *The Outdoor Facilitators Handbook* (1st edn). Lee Vining, CA: Go For Broke Publication.

SCENARIO

On a 15-day course with 10 students. Oliver and Bethany are the instructors for the group. Oliver has worked three summers at this program and is the lead instructor for this course. Bethany, who touts herself as a "people person" has had two summers working for the organization. Each have their Wilderness First Responder training and have gone through all the necessary training with the organization to work their summer courses.

Those involved in this incident consist of six males and four females. There is nothing atypical about this group except that they have trouble making decisions. There is visible tension when they must make decisions and usually the loudest voice wins, which is usually a male student aged 16 named George. This is clearly starting to frustrate the group, especially another boy aged 14 named James. In his impatience James has started to mutter under his breath during group discussions whenever George has spoken up, been loud, or made decisions without consulting the group.

James has a mild form of autism and would be said to be "on the spectrum." This cognitive limitation hinders his ability to fully integrate with the group and has impaired him from learning various social skills. It also causes him to become frustrated with the group. He misses social cues about when to stop talking or that he is talking about inappropriate topics of conversation.

George comes from a home in which his parents are divorced. George frequently talks about how his dad yells and the instructors suspect physical abuse. It was his mother's idea for him to come on this course and his dad was not in support of his attendance. He is an only child and clearly used to getting his way in most matters. He loses his temper easily and yells. George is also physically a larger child for his age and uses this to intimidate the other students.

On day 5 of the course, James comes over to the kitchen clearly upset, with a red mark on his face. He informs the instructor team that there was an argument about what to cook for dinner in which he stood up to George's boisterous personality. James informs the instructors that during the confrontation George punched James one time on the right side of his head.

The instructors corroborated the story with two other students before finally calling George over to get his side of the story. George didn't deny any of the events and was calm and very matter-of-fact when recounting what had happened. He says that he punched James because he was always used to getting his way and that he didn't like it when people disagreed with him. The instructors sat him down and talked to him about why he can't always have his way. They discussed how compromise and discussing options is an essential part of this course and life and that he's going to have to learn that skill, without punching people, sooner or later. They tried to discern where or why he thought that behavior was appropriate and George said that his dad probably played an influence in his using that type of behavior. To finalize the intervention, the instructors then called James over to discuss his role in the issue. They informed James that he can come off as insensitive and that he had a role in aggravating George in the way he approached the situation. The two students shook hands and the incident seemed to be over.

The next day as the students were choosing a place to camp the instructors were about 100 yards away. Upon hearing raised voices they turned to see George punching James again. The instructors ran over to separate the boys. They learned that there had been a disagreement about where to make camp that night and the boys again had a heated conversation which led to George punching James. The boys were separated, one with the instructors while the other was put on a "solo" a little way out of camp but still in sight of the instructors. While this happened three of the other students came up to the instructor team and indicated that they were scared of George, that he yelled at them during their independent travel that day, and that they too were afraid of getting punched or hurt by him.

Next, the instructor team confronted George to try to get his side of the story. He indicated that he was not sorry for punching James and that this is the way he deals with his frustration. After many long discussions he indicated no willingness to change because this is what worked for him at home to get what he wants. He indicated that he used intimidation on his mother to get any video game or junk food he desired.

At this point the instructors made the decision, based on the fact that the whole group was scared of this student and the fact that he showed no indication or desire for changing his behavior, to expel him from the course. This involved hiking him out the 14 miles they had traveled and splitting the instructional team, since there was no overseeing course director. The following day he left the course.

The rest of the course went well and the morale of the group improved drastically. The other students felt safer and thus had a better course experience. The group became more high functioning and efficient in the process. The other instructor returned to the group two days later.

Discussion questions

1   As a student screener, what information could you have gathered primitively when screening these students?
2   As an instructor, how could you have intervened earlier to prevent this situation?
3   As a course director, how could you have facilitated a program to create success for BOTH of these students?
4   If he had stayed on the course, what theories or intervention techniques would you implement to increase the likelihood of a successful experience?
5   As the contact for the parents of each of these students, what considerations would you think about before you contacted them to give them an update of the situation?

10

OTHER RESOURCES

Overview

To date, most OAE programs and experiential educators have relied solely on internal training, investigation, and resources for understanding and preparing to handle behavioral issues within their programs. However, recently the field of OAE has become much more sophisticated and serious about how to handle behavioral issues. In this chapter, we provide related literature, research and training sites, and other resources you and your program can utilize to help prepare yourself, and your staff to mitigate and manage even the most complex and difficult behaviors.

Related literature

Probably the closest parallel to the information in this book comes from the classroom management textbooks and educator training pamphlets. Today, classroom educators are faced with many hardships relative to behavior management, and deal with these behavior issues on a daily basis. It can be important to find books about prevention, and about behavior management. Some books you may want to look into include:

1 *Conscious Discipline* by Becky Bailey
2 *Dream Class* by Michael Linsin
3 *Whole Brain Teaching* by Chris Biffle
4 *Positive Discipline* by Teresa LaSala, Jody McVittie, and Suzanne Smitha
5 *The Classroom Management Secret* by Michael Linsin
6 *The End of Molasses Classes* by Ron Clark
7 *Win-Win Discipline* by Dr Spcnccr Kagan
8 *Teach Like a PIRATE* by Dave Burgess
9 *Conscious Classroom Management* by Rick Smith
10 *The First Days of School* by Harry K. and Rosemary Wong

Periodically, researchers in the OAE field will publish new work based on their current research efforts. Typing keywords into Google Scholar like "behavior management," "mental first aid," or "behavior modification" will bring up the most recent articles related to this topic. Although there are only a handful, checking journal websites relative to the OAE field is also a good way to check to see if any new information is coming out of the academic world relative to behavior management. These journals include the *Journal of Experiential Education*, the *Journal of Recreation and Outdoor Leadership*, and the *Journal of Clinical Psychology*. Other journals that might be useful can be sought in the fields of education, social psychology, and social work.

Relatedly, many of the theories and practices for this book came from the field of social work. It was the thought of the authors that this field provided a

FIGURE 10.1 Map reading and navigation can be a great tool to build high function groups (photo: Ryan Hines)

happy medium between psychology and education and from which we could borrow relevant behavioral management techniques. Similarly, these techniques were also more practical and a little easier to grasp than borrowing straight from the field of psychology. There are countless books and articles relative to all types of behavior management that certainly carry-over to the OAE world. Some useful sites include www.socialworktoday.com, www.humanserviesedu.org, and www.socalworkers.org. These sites often have updates on new practices and techniques that may be useful for your program.

Researchers and trainers

As part of the impetus of this book, the Alpenglow Education Institute (www.alpengloweducation.com) is currently undergoing a process to certify outdoor behavioral healthcare providers as "Behavioral First Responders." This certification and training program is expected to become available in the summer of 2017. By providing high-quality educational training, Alpenglow hopes to train and certify staff in all the necessary facets to mitigate and manage behaviors in the OAE context. Much of the content will be based on the information in this textbook. Please check the website for additional details and consider honoring this certification within your program, as it is designed specifically for the field of OAE and is expected to drastically increase an instructor's ability to mitigate and manage all types of behaviors encountered on OAE programs.

Perhaps the most useful place for this topic, and certainly one of the first is the Outdoor Behavioral Healthcare Council at http://obhcouncil.com. Although this site is largely for wilderness therapy professionals, the resources and literature available on the site certainly provides information for all subcategories of experiential education. The mission of the organization is "a community of leading outdoor behavioral healthcare programs working to advance the field through best practices, effective treatment, and evidence-based research." This website is often a great starting place for recent literature and other avenues to find information regarding a behavioral management issue you or your program are experiencing.

Peak Experience run by Scott Bandoroff is another resource that can provide you with further information, and training from Dr Bandoroff himself. He is both a psychologist and adventure therapy instructor and can provide unique insight into how the two worlds can blend together to complement one another. According to his website, he can provide facilitation training, consulting, and therapy. Dr Bandoroff can be found at www.peakexperience.org.

Behavior management also comes under the auspices of crisis prevention and crisis management. Several programs around the country exist and provide training in these types of behavior management strategies. For example, the Crisis Prevention Institute is capable of providing material for you to train or sending their own experts to your site for training for you and your staff. Programs with considerable behavioral issues and/or programs that are seeking to serve particularly risky populations may consider this type of expert training.

Traditional education

Perhaps the most formal and effective training in this topic will be with formal credentialing and educational training in a related field like social work, psychology, or counseling. Majors in these areas are certainly capable of handling the types of behavioral issues that most practitioners will see on their courses. However, to date, the only school yet to incorporate the two concepts is the University of New Hampshire with their dual masters in Social Work and Adventure Therapy. This program is specifically designed for individuals who want to work in wilderness therapy. However, as behavior management issues increase, it is likely that there will be an influx of these types of programs. Additionally, many schools are now offering a behavior management course in their OAE curriculum which will help prepare instructors ready to enter the field to mitigate and manage behavioral issues.

Training sites

Behavioral Healthcare Training Network (BHC Training) is a continuing education program provider that can offer a variety of training options for professional and nonprofessional behavioral intervention strategists such as OAE staff. Much of their training is online and would be appropriate for OAE staff members. This program can also send training to your site and provide training specifically for your program.

FIGURE 10.2 Students receiving instruction before launching down the river (photo: Ryan Hines)

Likewise, mental health first aid is an eight-hour course that teaches you how to identify, understand, and respond to signs of mental illnesses and substance use disorders and was designed by the National Council for Behavioral Health. These trainings can give an introduction to the skills you need to reach out to all ages and provide initial help and support to someone who may be suffering from a mental health or substance use problem or experiencing a crisis.

As the reader might anticipate, there are many websites, institutes, and books relative to behavior management and behavioral modification. Because this field is so vast, this book is only a guide and an introduction to behavioral modification techniques. There are many subdisciplines and other fields that whole textbooks exist to explore. The following is a partial list that may help the reader hone in on a particular issue they are experiencing and some terminology to help you find additional resources.

1   Crisis prevention
2   Culture of emotional safety
3   Empathic listening
4   Crisis management
5   Managing problem behaviors
6   Classroom management
7   Student management
8   Positive behavior
9   Responding to unpredictable behavior
10 Preventing problematic behaviors
11 Bullying behavior

Perhaps the most important takeaway from this book is that behavioral issues are complex and difficult. When in doubt, defer to somebody who is a professional, as the mental health and safety of the student, and others, may be at stake.

Conclusion

Increasingly, the field of OAE programming is becoming aware of the necessity to mitigate and manage behavioral intervention techniques. No longer is it advisable to rely solely on in-house training. With this textbook and the other resources provided in this chapter, we hope that you can formulate a plan to educate yourselves and your staff for the coming behavior management issues you will face. Please keep checking the website for the forthcoming behavior management certification, and consider taking this or other relevant certifications that you find yourselves.

FIGURE 10.3   A group of students cross a chilly river in early spring (photo: Ryan Hines)

References

Alpenglow Education Institute. (n.d.). Alpenglow Education. Retrieved 5 May 2017, from www.alpengloweducation.com/

Bailey, B. A. (2000). *Conscious Discipline: 7 Basic Skills for Brain Smart Classroom Management.* Oviedo, FL: Loving Guidance.

Biffle, C. (2013). *Whole Brain Teaching for Challenging Kids: (and the rest of your class, too!).* Yucaipa, CA: Whole Brain Teaching LLC.

Burgess, D. (2012). *Teach Like a PIRATE: Increase Student Engagement, Boost Your Creativity, and Transform Your Life as an Educator.* San Diego, CA: Dave Burgess Consulting, Inc.

Clark, R. (2012). *The End of Molasses Classes: Getting Our Kids Unstuck –101 Extraordinary Solutions for Parents and Teachers.* New York: Simon and Schuster.

Kagan, S. (2007). *Win-Win Discipline: Strategies for All Discipline Problems.* San Clemente, CA: Kagan Publishing.

LaSala, T., McVittie, J., and Smitha, S. (2013). *Positive Discipline.* New York: Harmony.

Linsin, M. (2009). *Dream Class: How to Transform any Group of Students into the Class You've Always Wanted.* Berlin: JME Publishing.

Linsin, M. (2013). *The Classroom Management Secret: And 45 Other Keys to a Well-Behaved Class.* Berlin: JME Publishing.

Outdoor Behavioral Healthcare Council. (n.d.). Outdoor Behavioral Healthcare Council. Retrieved 5 May 2017, from https://obhcouncil.com/

Peak Experience. (n.d.). Peak Experience. Retrieved 5 May 2017, from www. peakexperience.org

Smith, R. (2004). *Conscious Classroom Management: Unlocking the Secrets of Great Teaching.* Fairfax, CA: Conscious Teaching, LLC.

Wong, H. K., and Wong, R. T. (2009). *The First Days of School: How to Be an Effective Teacher.* Mountain View, CA: Harry K. Wong Publications.

REFERENCES

Adult Children of Alcoholics (ACA) (2007). *Twelve Steps of Adult Children*. Torrence, CA: ACA World Service Organization.

Ai, A. L., and Park, C. L. (2005). Possibilities of the positive following violence and trauma. *Journal of Interpersonal Violence*, 20(2), 242–250.

Ajzen, I. (1991). The theory of planned behavior. *Organizational Behavior and Human Decision Processes*, 50, 179–211.

Allison, P., Stott, T., Felter, J., and Beames, S. (2011). Overseas youth expeditions. In M. Berry and C. Hodgson (eds), *Adventure Education: An Introduction* (pp. 187–205). London: Routledge.

Alpenglow Education Institute. (n.d.). Alpenglow Education. Retrieved 5 May 2017, from www.alpengloweducation.com/

Arthur, R. (2014). *Evaluation of Prince's Trust Fairbridge Programme – Holme House Prison Project*. Middlesbrough: Teeside University, Social Futures Institute.

Bailey, B. A. (2000). *Conscious Discipline: 7 Basic Skills for Brain Smart Classroom Management*. Oviedo, FL: Loving Guidance.

Balcazar, F. E., Keys, C. B., and Garate Serafini, J. (1995). Learning to recruit assistance to attain transition goals: A program for adjudicated youth with disabilities. *Journal for Special Educators*, 16(54), 237–46.

Baldwin, C., Persing, J., and Magnuson, D. (2004). The role of theory, research, and evaluation in adventure education. *Journal of Experiential Education*, 26(3), 167–183.

Baltes, P. B., Lindenberger, U., and Staudinger, U. M. (2007). Life span theory in developmental psychology. *Handbook of Child Psychology*, I:11.

Bandura, A. (1977). Self-efficacy: Toward a unifying theory of behavioral change. *Psychological Review*, 84(2), March, 191–215.

Bandura, A. (1986). *Social Foundations of Thought and Action: A Social Cognitive Theory*. Englewood Cliffs, NJ: Prentice-Hall.

Bardwell, L. (1992). A bigger piece of the puzzle: The restorative experience and outdoor education. Paper presented at the Coalition for Education in the Outdoors, *Research Symposium Proceedings* (pp. 15–20), Bradford Woods, IN, January 17–19.

Baron-Cohen, S., Tager-Flusberg, H., and Cohen, D. J. (1994). *Understanding Other Minds: Perspectives from Autism*. New York: Oxford University Press.

Bell, S, Tyrväinen, L., Sievänen, T., Pröbstl, U., and Simpson, M. (2007). Outdoor recreation and nature tourism: A European perspective. *Living Reviews in Landscape Research*, 1, 1–46.

Berger, C. R., and Calabrese, R. J. (1975). Some explorations in initial interaction and beyond: Toward a developmental theory of interpersonal communication. *Human Communication Research*, 1(2), 99–112.

Biffle, C. (2013). *Whole Brain Teaching for Challenging Kids: (and the rest of your class, too!)*. Yucaipa, CA: Whole Brain Teaching LLC.

Bisson, C. (1999). Sequencing the adventure experience. In J. Miles and S. Priest (eds), *Adventure Programming* (pp. 205–214). State College, PA: Venture.

Bolles, R. C. (1972). Reinforcement, expectancy, and learning. *Psychological Review*, 79(5), 394.

Bowman, N. A., Hill, P. L., Denson, N., and Bronkema, R. (2015). Keep on truckin' or stay the course? Exploring grit dimensions as differential predictors of educational achievement, satisfaction, and intentions. *Social Psychological and Personality Science*, 6(6), 639–645.

Bradberry, T., and Greaves, J. (2005). *The Emotional Intelligence Quick Book*. New York: Simon & Schuster.

Brendtro, L., Brokenleg, M., and van Bockern, S (2012). *Reclaiming Youth at Risk: Our Hope for the Future*. Bloomington, IN: National Education Service.

Brownlee, M. (2015). Parks and protected areas: A platform for adventure activities. In R. Black and K. Bricker (eds), *Adventure Programming and Travel for the 21st Century* (pp. 53–67). State College, PA: Venture Publishing.

Bunyan, P. (2011). Models and milestones in adventure education. In M. Berry and C. Hodgson (eds), *Adventure Education: An Introduction* (pp. 5–23). London: Routledge.

Burgess, D. (2012). *Teach Like a PIRATE: Increase Student Engagement, Boost Your Creativity, and Transform Your Life as an Educator*. San Diego, CA: Dave Burgess Consulting, Inc.

Campbell, J., Bell, V., Armstrong, S. C., Horton, J., Mansukhani, N., Matthews, M. H., and Pilkington, A. (2009). The impact of the Duke of Edinburgh's Award on young people. (Unpublished) http://nectar.northampton.ac.uk/2447.

Cantwell, D. (1996). Attention deficit disorder: a review of the past 10 years. *Journal of the American Academy of Child and Adolescent Psychiatry*, 35(8), 978–987.

Capuzzi, D., and Gross, D. (2014). *Youth at Risk: A Prevention Resource for Counselors, Teachers, and Parents*. Alexandria, VA: American Counseling Association.

Catalano, R. F., and Hawkins, J. D. (1996). The social development model: A theory of antisocial behaviour. In J. D. Hawkins (ed.), *Delinquency and Crime: Current Theories* (pp. 149–197). New York: Cambridge University Press.

CCHR International. (2014). Number of children and adolescents taking psychiatric drugs in the U.S. Retrieved 16 September 2016, from www.cchrint.org/psychiatric-drugs/children-on-psychiatric-drugs.

Cemek, M., Büyükokuroğlu, M. E., Hazman, Ö., Bulut, S., Konuk, M., and Birdane, Y. (2011). Antioxidant enzyme and element status in heroin addiction or heroin withdrawal in rats: Effect of Melatonin and Vitamin E plus se. *Biological Trace Element Research*, 139(1), 41–54.

Clark, M. (1998). Strength-based practice: The ABC's of working with adolescents who don't want to work with you. *Federal Probation*, 62(1), 46–53.

Clark, R. (2012). *The End of Molasses Classes: Getting Our Kids Unstuck –101 Extraordinary Solutions for Parents and Teachers*. New York: Simon and Schuster.

Cobb, S. (1976). Social support as a moderator of life stress. *Psychosomatic Medicine*, 38(5), 300–314.

Cohn, M., Fredrickson, B., Brown, S., Mikels, J., and Conway, A. (2009). Happiness unpacked: Positive emotions increase life satisfaction by building resilience. *Emotion* (Washington, DC), 9(3), 361–368.

Coulter, G. (2004). Using one-to-one tutoring and proven reading strategies to improve reading performance with adjudicated youth. *Journal of Correctional Education*, 55(4), 321–333.

Cutrona, C. E. (1996). *Social Support in Couples. Marriage as a Resource in Times of Stress.* Thousand Oaks, CA: Sage.

Cutrona, C. E., and Russell, D. (1990). Type of social support and specific stress: Toward a theory of optimal matching. In B. R. Sarason, L. G. Sarason and G. R. Pierce (eds), *Social Support: An Interactional view* (pp. 319–366). New York: Wiley.

D'Amato, L. G., and Krasny, M. E. (2011). Outdoor adventure education: Applying transformative learning theory to understanding instrumental learning and personal growth in environmental education. *Journal of Environmental Education*, 42(4), 237–54.

Davidson, C. (2013). *The Outdoor Facilitators Handbook* (1st edn). Lee Vining, CA: Go For Broke Publication.

Davidson, C. and Ottley, G. (2014). *Examining Outdoor Training and Certification Standards by Incident Data*. Poster presented at the Wilderness Risk Management Conference. Stone Mountain, GA.

Deci, E. L., and Ryan, R. (eds) (2002). *Handbook of Self-Determination Research*. Rochester, NY: University of Rochester Press.

Deci, E. L., and Vansteenkiste, M. (2004). Self-determination theory and basic need satisfaction: Understanding human development in positive psychology. *Ricerche di Psicologia*, 27, 17–34.

Dinkmeyer, D., and McKay, G. (1989). *The Parent's Handbook: Systematic Training for Effective Parenting* (3rd edn). Circle Pines, MN: American Guidance Service.

Donaldson, G. W., and Donaldson, L. E. (1968). *Outdoor Education: A Book of Readings.* Minneapolis, MN: Burgess.

Dreikurs, R., and Grey, L. (1990). *A New Approach to Discipline: Logical Consequences.* New York: Dutton Penguin.

Duckworth, A., and Gross, J. (2014). Self-control and grit: Related but separable determinants of success. *Current Directions in Psychological Science*, 23(5), 319–325.

Duckworth, A., and Quinn, P. (2009). Development and validation of the short grit scale (grit-s). *Journal of Personality Assessment*, 91, 166–174.

Duckworth, A., Peterson, C., Matthews, M., and Kelly, D. (2007). Grit: Perseverance and passion for long-term goals. *Journal of Personality and Social Psychology*, 92(6), 1087–1101.

Duckworth, A., Quinn, P., and Seligman, M. (2009). Positive predictors of teacher effectiveness. *Journal of Positive Psychology*, 4(6), 540–547.

Duerden, M., and Witt, P. (2010). The impact of direct and indirect experiences on the development of environmental knowledge, attitudes, and behavior. *Journal of Environmental Psychology*, 30(4), 379–392.

Dulewicz, V., and Higgs, M. (2004). Can emotional intelligence be developed? *International Journal of Human Resource Management*, 15(1), 95–111.

Eells, E. (1986). *A History of Organized Camping: The First 100 Years*. Martinsville, IN: American Camping Association.

Ewert, A. (2014). Military veterans and the use of adventure education experiences in natural environments for therapeutic outcomes. *Ecopsychology*, 6(3), 155–164.

Ewert, A., and Heywood, J. (1991). Group development in the natural environment: Expectations, outcomes, and techniques. *Environment and Behavior,* 23(5), 592–615.

Ewert, A., and McAvoy, L. (2000). The effects of wilderness settings on organized groups: A state-of-knowledge paper. In S. F. McCool, D. N. Cole, W. T. Borrie, and J. O'Laughlin (eds), *Wilderness Science in a Time of Change,* vol. 3, *Wilderness as a Place for Scientific Inquiry* (pp. 13–26). Proceedings RMRS-P-15-VOL-3R. Ogden, UT: US Department of Agriculture, Forest Service, Rocky Mountain Research Station.

Ewert, A., and Sibthorp, J. (2014). *Outdoor Adventure Education: Foundations, Theory, and Research.* Champaign, IL: Human Kinetics.

Ewert, A., and Voight, A. (2012). The role of adventure education in enhancing health-related variables. *International Journal of Health, Wellness and Society,* 2(1), 75–87.

Ewert, A., and Wu, Guan-Jang. (2007). Two faces of outdoor adventure leadership: Educational adventure programs and guided trips. *Journal of Wilderness Education Association,* 18(1), 12–18.

Ewert, A., and Yoshino, A. (2011). The influence of short-term adventure-based expereinces on levels of resilience. *Journal of Adventure Education and Outdoor Learning,* 11(1), 35–50.

Ewert, A., Overholt, J., Voight, A., and Wang, C. C. (2011). Understanding the transformative aspects of the Wilderness and Protected Lands experience upon human health. In A. Watson, J. Murrieta-Saldivar, and B. McBride, comps. *Science and stewardship to protect and sustain wilderness values: Ninth World Wilderness Congress symposium. Proceedings RMRS-P-64* (pp. 140–146). Fort Collins, CO: U.S. Department of Agriculture Forest Service, Rocky Mountain Research Station.

Ewert, A., Van Puymbroeck, M., Frankel, J., and Overholt, J. (2011). Adventure education and the returning military veteran: What do we know? *Journal of Experiential Education,* 33(4), 365–369.

Feierman, J., Levick, M., and Mody, A. (2009). School-to-prison pipeline ... and back: Obstacles and remedies for the re-enrollment of adjudicated youth. *New York Law School Law Review,* 54, 1115–1129.

Fillmore, E., and Helfenbein, R. (2015). Medical student grit and performance in gross anatomy: What are the relationships? *FASEB Journal,* 29(1), supplement, 689.6.

Foster, K. R., and Spencer, D. (2011). At risk of what? Possibilities over probabilities in the study of young lives. *Journal of Youth Studies,* 14(1), 125–143.

Fraser, M. (1997). *Risk and Resilience in Childhood: An Ecological Perspective.* Washington, DC: NASW Press.

Frith, U. (1989). *Autism: Explaining the Enigma.* Oxford: Blackwell.

Gamel, M. (2014). Impact of character development and empowerment program on grit and resilience growth in early and middle adolescents. *Dissertations, Theses and Capstone Projects.* Paper 646. http://digitalcommons.kennesaw.edu/etd/646.

Gass, M. (1995). Adventure family therapy: An innovative approach answering the question of lasting change with adjudicated youth? *Monograph on Youth in the 1990s,* 4, 103–117.

Gass, M., and Gillis, H. L. (2010) Clinical supervision in adventure therapy: Enhancing the field through an active experiential model. *Journal of Experiential Education,* 33(1), 72–89.

Gass, M. A., Gillis, H. L., and Russell, K. C. (2012). *Adventure Therapy: Theory, Practice, and Research.* New York: Routledge.

Gilbertson, K., Bates, T., McLaughlin, T., and Ewert, A. (2006). *Outdoor Education: Methods and Strategies.* Champaign, IL: Human Kinetics.

Gillis, H. L. (1992). Therapeutic uses of adventure challenge-outdoor-wilderness: Theory and research. In K. Henderson (ed.), *Proceedings of the Coalition for Education in the Outdoors Symposium* (pp. 35–47). Cortland, NY: Coalition for Education in the Outdoors.

Gillis, H., and Bonney, W. C. (1989). Utilizing adventure activities with intact groups: A sociodramatic systems approach to consultation. *Journal of Mental Health Counseling*, 11(4), 345–358.

Gillis, H., Gass, M., and Russell, K. (2008). The effectiveness of project adventure's behavior management programs for male offenders in residential treatment. *Residential Treatment for Children and Youth*, 25(3), 227–247.

Goldenberg, M., McAvoy, L., and Klenosky, D. B. (2005). Outcomes from the components of an Outward Bound experience. *Journal of Experiential Education*, 28, 123–146.

Gordon, S., and Gucciardi, D. (2011). A strengths-based approach to coaching mental toughness. *Journal of Sport Psychology in Action*, 2(3), 143–55.

Grant, D. A. (1964). Classical and operant conditioning. In A. W. Melton (ed.), *Categories of Human Learning* (pp.1–31). New York: Academic Press.

Hahn, K. (1958). Address at the forty-eighth annual dinner of the old centralians, London. *The Central: The Journal of Old Centralians*, 119, 3–8. Retrieved 16 September 2016, from www.KurtHahn.org/writings/writings.html.

Hamm, J., and Faircloth, B. (2005). The role of friendship in adolescents' sense of school belonging. *New Directions for Child and Adolescent Development*, 107, 61–78.

Hattie, J., Marsh, H. W., Neill, J. T., and Richards, G. E. (1997). Adventure education and Outward Bound: Out-of-class experiences that make a lasting difference. *Review of Educational Research*, 67, 43–87.

Hawkins, J. D., Catalano, R. F., and Arthur, M. W. (2002). Promoting science-based prevention in communities. *Addict Behaviors*, 27(6), 951–976.

Hayashi, A., and Ewert, A. (2006). Outdoor leaders' emotional intelligence and transformational leadership. *Journal of Experiential Education*, 28(3), 222–242.

Hayashi, A., and Ewert, A. (2013). Development of emotional intelligence through an outdoor leadership program. *Journal of Outdoor Recreation, Education, and Leadership*, 5(1), 3–17.

Head, J. (2002). *Working with Adolescents: Constructing Identity*. London: Falmer Press.

Henton, M. (1996). *Adventure in the Classroom: Using Adventure to Strengthen Learning and Build a Community of Life-Long Learners*. Hamilton, MA: Project Adventure Inc.

Heppner, P., Wampold, B., and Kivlighan Jr., D. (2007). *Research Design in Counselling*. Boston, MA: Cengage Learning.

Hettema, J., Steele, J., and Miller, W. (2005). Motivational interviewing. *Annual Review of Clinical Psychology*, 1, 91–111.

Hochanadel, A., and Finamore, D. (2015). In education and how grit helps. *Journal of International Education Research*, 11(1), 47–50.

Hoerr, T. R. (2013). *Fostering Grit: How do I Prepare my Students for the Real World?* Alexandria, VA: ASCD Arias.

Holman, T., and McAvoy, L. (2005). Transferring benefits of participation in an integrated wilderness adventure program to daily life. *Journal of Experiential Education*, 27, 322–325.

Holmbeck, G. N., Colder, C., Shapera, W., Westhoven, V., Kenealy, L., and Updegrove, A. (2000). Working with adolescents: Guides from developmental psychology. In P. C. Kendall (ed.), *Child and Adolescent Therapy: Cognitive-Behavioral Procedures* (2nd edn, pp. 334–385). New York: Guilford Press.

Hunt, J. (1990). *In Search of Adventure*. Guildford: Talbot Adair Press.

Hunt, M. G., and Rosenheck, R. A., (2011). Psychotherapy in mental health clinics of the Department of Veterans Affairs. *Journal of Clinical Psychology*, 67, 561–73.

Hurt, E., and Arnold, L. (2014). An integrated dietary/nutritional approach to ADHD. *Child and Adolescent Psychiatric Clinics of North America,* 34(4), 955–964.

Hurt, E., Arnold, L., and Lofthouse, N. (2011). Dietary and nutritional treatments for attention- deficit/hyperactivity disorder: current research support and recommendations for practitioners. *Current Psychiatry Reports,* 13, 323–332.

Hyer, L., Boyd, S., Scurfield, R., Smith, D., and Burke, J. (1996). Effects of Outward Bound experience as an adjunct to inpatient PTSD treatment of war veterans. *Journal of Clinical Psychology,* 52(3), 263–278.

IOL. (1998). *The Outdoor Source Book.* Penrith: Adventure Education.

James, T. (1980). *Education at the Edge.* Denver, CO: Colorado Outward Bound.

Johnson, D. R., Feldman, S. C., Southwick, S. M., and Charney, D. S. (1994). The concept of the second generation program in the treatment of post-traumatic stress disorder among Vietnam veterans. *Journal of Traumatic Stress,* 7(2), 217–236.

Kagan, S. (2007). *Win-Win Discipline Book: Strategies for All Discipline Problems.* San Clemente, CA: Kagan Publishing.

Kane, M., and Trochim, W. M. (2009). Concept mapping for applied social research. In L. Bickman and D. J. Rog (eds), *Applied Social Research Methods* (pp. 435–474). Los Angeles, CA: SAGE.

Kennedy, B. P., and Minami, M. (1993). The Beech Hill Hospital/Outward Bound adolescent chemical dependency treatment program. *Journal of Substance Abuse Treatment,* 10, 395–406.

Kingham, R. J. (1958). Alcoholism and the reinforcement theory of learning. *Quarterly Journal of Studies on Alcohol,* 19, 320–330.

Kirmeyer, S. L., and Lin, T. R. (1987). Social support: Its relationship to observed communication with peers and superiors. *Academy of Management Journal,* 30 138–151.

Koegel, R., and Koegel, L. (1995). *Teaching Children with Autism: Strategies for Initiating Positive Interactions and Improving Learning Opportunities.* Baltimore, MD: Paul H. Brooks Publishing.

Kottman, T., Ashby, J. S., and DeGraaf, D. (2001). *Adventures in Guidance: How to Integrate Fun into your Guidance Program.* Alexandria, VA: American Counseling Association.

Kuo, F. E., and Faber Taylor, A. (2004). A potential natural treatment for attention-deficit/hyperactivity disorder: Evidence from a national study. *American Journal of Public Health,* 94, 1580–1586.

Kurosawa, K. (2004). A Survey of Outdoor Experience-type Recreational programs in Depopulated Areas of Hokkaido. *Journal of Environmental Information Science,* 32(5), 119–128.

LaSala, T., McVittie, J., and Smitha, S. (2013). *Positive Discipline.* New York: Harmony.

Leo, J. (2000). Attention deficit disorder. *Skeptics Society and Skeptic Magazine,* 8(1), 63.

Li, P., and Pan, G. (2009). The relationship between motivation and achievement: A survey of the study motivation of English majors in Qingdao Agricultural University. *English Language Teaching,* 2(1), 123–128.

Linley, P. A., and Joseph, S. (2004). Positive change following trauma and adversity: A review. *Journal of Traumatic Stress,* 17(1), 11–21.

Linsin, M. (2009). *Dream Class: How to Transform any Group of Students into the Class You've Always Wanted.* Berlin: JME Publishing.

Linsin, M. (2013). *The Classroom Management Secret: And 45 Other Keys to a Well-Behaved Class.* Berlin: JME Publishing.

Long, T. (2011). Cognitive-behavioral approaches to therapeutic recreation. In N. J. Stumbo and B. Wardlaw (eds), *Facilitation of Therapeutic Recreation Services: An Evidence-*

Based and Best Practice Approach to Techniques and Processes (pp. 289–306). State College, PA: Venture.

Masten, A. (2001). Ordinary magic: Resilience processes in development. *American Psychologist,* 56(3), 227–38.

Mayer, John D. (2008). Human abilities: Emotional Intelligence. *Annual Review of Psychology,* 59, 507–36.

Mazur, J. (2002). *Learning and Behavior.* Upper Saddle River, NJ: Pearson Education.

McKenzie M. (2000). How are adventure education program outcomes achieved? A review of the literature. *Australian Journal of Outdoor Education,* 5(1), 19–29.

McWhirter, J., McWhirter, B., McWhirter, A., and McWhirter, E. H. (1993). *At-Risk Youth: A Comprehensive Response.* Belmont, CA: Thomson Brooks/Cole Publishing.

Metcalfe, J. (1976). *Adventure Programming.* Austin, TX: National Educational Laboratory Publishing.

Metsähallitus (2006). Institutional homepage. http://metsa.fi.

Mikulincer, M., and Florian, V. (1995). Appraisal and coping with a real-life stressful situation: the contribution of attachment styles. *Personality and Social Psychology Bulletin,* 21, 408–416.

Mikulincer, M., Florian, V., and Weller, A. (1993). Attachment styles, coping strategies, and posttraumatic psychological distress: The impact of the Gulf War in Israel. *Journal of Personality and Social Psychology,* 64(5), 817–856.

Miller, W. R., and Rollnick, S. (2012). *Motivational Interviewing: Helping People Change.* New York: Guilford Press.

Miller, P., Hersen, M., and Eisler, R. (1974). Relative effectiveness of instructions, agreements, and reinforcement in behavioral contracts with alcoholics. *Journal of Abnormal Psychology,* 83(5), 548–553.

Mitten, D. (1994). Ethical considerations in adventure therapy: A feminist critique. In E. Cole, E. Erdman, and E. Rothblum (eds), *Wilderness Therapy for Women: The Power of Adventure* (pp. 55–84). New York: Harrington Press.

Mitten, D. (2009). Under our noses: The healing power of nature. *Taproot Journal,* 19(1), 20–26.

Muncie, J., and Goldson, B. (2006). *Comparative Youth Justice.* London: SAGE.

Neill, J., and Dias, K. (2001). Adventure education and resilience: The double-edged sword. *Journal of Adventure Education and Outdoor Learning,* 1(2), 35–42.

Nelson, K. M. (2006). The burden of obesity among a national probability sample of veterans. *Journal of General Internal Medicine,* 21(9), 915–919.

Nichols, G. (1999). Is risk a valuable component of outdoor adventure programmes for young offenders undergoing drug rehabilitation? *Journal of Youth Studies,* 2(1), 101–115.

Nigg, J., and Holton, K. (2014). Restriction and elimination diets in ADHD treatment. *Child and Adolescent Psychiatric Clinics of North America,* 23(4), 937–953.

Norcross, J. C., Krebs, P. M., and Prochaska, J. O. (2011). Stages of change. *Journal of Clinical Psychology,* 67(2), 143–154.

Olfson, M., Marcus, S. C., Druss, B., Elinson, L., Tanielian, T., and Pincus, H. A. (2002). National trends in outpatient treatment of depression. *Journal of the American Medical Association,* 287, 203–209.

Ommen, O., Janssen, C., Neugebauer, E., Bouillon, B., Rehm, K., Rangger, C., and Pfaff, H. (2008). Trust, social support and patient type: Associations between patients perceived trust, supportive communication and patients preferences in regard to paternalism, clarification and participation of severely injured patients. *Patient Education and Counseling,* 73(2), 196–204.

Outdoor Behavioral Healthcare Council. (n.d.). Retrieved 5 May 2017, from https://obhcouncil.com/.

Palmer, C. (2008). A theory of risk and resilience factors in military families. *Military Psychology*, 20, 205–217.

Palmer, B., Walls, M., Burgess, Z., and Stough, C. (2001). Emotional intelligence and effective leadership. *Leadership and Organization Development Journal*, 22(1), 5–10.

Paquette, D., and Ryan, J. (2001). Bronfenbrenner's ecological systems theory. *Children*, 44, 1–105.

Parletta, N. (2016). Can diet and nutrition affect our learning, behaviour and mental health? *Nutridate*, 27(4), 10–16.

Passarelli, A., Hall, E., and Anderson, M. (2010). A strengths-based approach to outdoor and adventure education: Possibilities for personal growth. *Journal of Experiential Education*, 33(2), 120–135.

Peak Experience. (n.d.). Peak Experience. Retrieved 5 May 2017, from www.peakexperience.org

Perkins-Gough, D. (2013). The significance of grit: A conversation with Angela Lee Duckworth. *Educational Leadership*, 71(1), 14–20.

Peterson, D. (2015). Putting measurement first: Understanding "grit" in educational policy and practice. *Journal of Philosophy of Education*, 19(4), 571–589.

Pouta, E., Sievänen, T., and Heikkilä, M. (2000). National outdoor recreation demand and supply in Finland: An assessment project. *Forestry*, 73(2), 103–105.

Premack, D. (1965). Reinforcement theory. *Nebraska Symposium on Motivation*, 13, 123–180.

Priest, S. (1986). Redefining outdoor education: A matter of many relationships. *Journal of Environmental Education*, 17(3), 13–15.

Priest, S., and Gass, M. (2005). *Effective Leadership in Adventure Programming* (2nd edn). Champaign-Urbana, IL: Human Kinetics.

Priest, S., Gass, M., and Gillis, H. L. (1999). *Essential Elements of Facilitation*. Online at: https://openlibrary.org/publishers/Tarrak_Technologies

Raynolds, J., *et al.* (2007). *Leadership the Outward Bound Way*. Seattle, WA: Mountaineer Books.

Reiter, E., and Root, A. (1975). Hormonal changes of adolescence. *The Medical Clinics of North America*, 59(6), 1289–1304.

Resnik, A. J., and Allen, S. M. (2007). Using international classification of functioning, disability, and health to understand challenges in community reintegration of injured veterans. *Journal of Rehabilitation Research and Development*, 44(7), 991–1006.

Rhodes, H., and Martin, A. (2013). Behavior change after adventure education courses: Do work colleagues notice? *Journal of Experiential Education*, 36, 1–21.

Rhodes, H. M., and Martin, A. J. (2014). Behavior change after adventure education courses: Do work colleagues notice? *Journal of Experiential Education*, 37(3), 265–284.

Richardson, G. E. (2002). The metatheory of resilience and resiliency. *Journal of Clinical Psychology*, 58(3), 307–321.

Richman, J. M., Rosenfeld, L. B., and Bowen, G. L. (1998). Social support for adolescents at risk of school failure. *Social Work*, 43(4), 309–323.

Roberts, S. (2011). Beyond "NEET" and "tidy" pathways: Considering the "missing middle" of youth transition studies. *Journal of Youth Studies*, 14(1), 21–39.

Robertson-Kraft, C., and Duckworth, A. (2014). True grit: Trait-level perseverance and passion for long-term goals predicts effectiveness and retention among novice teachers. *Teachers College Record*, 116, 1–27.

Robledo, S., and Ham-Kucharski, D. (2005). *The Autism Book: Answers to your Most Pressing Questions*. New York: Penguin.

Rogers, S. D., Loy, D., and Brown-Bochicchio, C. (2016). Sharing a new foxhole with friends: The impact of outdoor recreation on injured military. *Therapeutic Recreation Journal*, 50(3), 213–227.

Rollnick, S., and Miller, W. (1995). What is motivational interviewing? *Journal of Consulting and Clinical Psychology*, 61, 455–461.

Rollnick, S., Miller, W., Butler, C., and Aloia, M. (2009). *Motivational Interviewing in Health Care: Helping Patients Change Behavior*. New York: Guilford Press.

Russell, J. (1997). *Autism as an Executive Disorder*. New York: Oxford University Press.

Russell, K. (2006). *Examining Substance Use Frequency and Depressive Symptom Outcome in a Sample of Outdoor Behavioural Healthcare Participants (Research Report No 1)*. Minneapolis, MN: Outdoor Behavioral Healthcare Research Cooperative College of Education and Human Development, University of Minnesota.

Russell, K. C., and Hendee, J. C. (2000). Wilderness therapy as an intervention and treatment for adolescent behavioral problems. In A. E. Watson, G. H. Aplet, and J. C. Hendee (eds), *Personal, Societal, and Ecological Values of Wilderness: Sixth World Wilderness Congress Proceedings on Research, Management, and Allocation* (vol. 2, pp. 136–141). Proc. RMRS-P-14. Ogden, UT: US Department of Agriculture, Forest Service, Rocky Mountain Research Center.

Russell, K. C., Gillis, H. L., and Lewis, T. G. (2008). A five-year follow-up of a survey of North American Outdoor Behavioral Healthcare programs. *Journal of Experiential Education*, 31(1), 55–77.

Saleebey, D. (1996). The strengths perspective in social work practice: Extensions and cautions. *Social Work*, 41(3), 296–305.

Salovey, P., and Sluyter, D. J. (1997). *Emotional Development and Emotional Intelligence: Educational Implications* (1st edn). New York: Basic Books.

Seal, K. H., Bertenthal, D., Maguen, S., Gima, K., Chu, A., and Marmar, C. R. (2008). Getting beyond "Don't ask; don't tell": An evaluation of US Veterans Administration postdeployment mental health screening of veterans returning from Iraq and Afghanistan. *American Journal of Public Health*, 98(4), 714–720.

Shank, J., and Coyle, C. (2002). *Therapeutic Recreation in Health Promotion and Rehabilitation*. State College, PA: Venture.

Sharp, L. B. (1947). Basic considerations in outdoor and camping education. *The Bulletin of the National Association of Secondary-School Principals*, 31(147), 43–48, The Department of Secondary Education of the National Education Association, Washington, D.C.

Sheard, M., and Golby, J. (2006). The efficacy of an outdoor adventure education curriculum on selected aspects of positive psychological development. *Journal of Experiential Education*, 29(2), 187–209.

Shechtman, N., Debarger, A., Dornsife, C., Rosier, S., and Yarnall, L. (2013). *Promoting Grit, Tenacity, and Perseverance: Critical Factors for Success in the 21st Century*. Washington, DC: US Department of Education, Department of Educational Technology.

Shore, A. (ed.) (1977). *Outward Bound: A Reference Volume*. Greenwich, CT: Outward Bound.

Sibthorp, J. (2003). Learning transferable skills through adventure education: The role of an authentic process. *Journal of Adventure Education and Outdoor Learning*, 3(2), 145–147.

Sibthorp, J., and Jostad, J. (2014). The social system in outdoor adventure education programs. *Journal of Experiential Education*, 37(1), 60–74.

Silvia, P., Eddington, K., Beaty, R., Nusbaum, E., and Kwapil, T. (2013). Gritty people try harder: Grit and effort-related cardiac autonomic activity during an active coping challenge. *International Journal of Psychophysiology*, 88(2), 200–205.

Singh, K., and Jha, S. (2008). Positive and negative affect, and grit as predictors of happiness and life satisfaction. *Journal of the Indian Academy of Applied Psychology*, 34, April, 40–45.

Smith, R. (2004). *Conscious Classroom Management: Unlocking the Secrets of Great Teaching*. Fairfax, CA: Conscious Teaching, LLC.

Stavros, J., and Hinrichs, G. (2011). *The Thin Book of SOAR: Building Strengths-Based Strategy*. Bend, OR: Thin Book Publishing.

Stewart, D. G., and Brown, S. A. (1995). Withdrawal and dependency symptoms among adolescent alcohol and drug abusers. *Addiction*, 90(5), 627–635.

Stich, T. F., and Gaylor, M. S. (1984). Risk Management in Adventure Programs with Special Populations: Two Hidden Dangers. *Journal of Experiential Education*, 7(3), 15–19.

Stipek, D. J. (1993). *Motivation to Learn: From Theory to Practice*. Needham Heights, MA: Allyn & Bacon.

Stumbo, N., and Folkerth, J. (2013). *Study Guide for the Therapeutic Recreation Specialist Certification Examination*. Urbana, IL: Sagamore.

Tuckman, B. W., and Jensen, M. A. C. (1977). Stages of Small-Group Development Revisited, *Group Organization Management*, 2(4).

Tough, P. (2013). *How Children Succeed*. New York: Random House.

Van Puymbroeck, M., Ewert, A., Luo, Y., and Frankel, J. (2012). The influence of the Outward Bound Veterans Program on sense of coherence. *American Journal of Recreation Therapy*, 10(5), 1–8.

Voight, A., and Ewert, A. (2015). Integrating theory with practice: Applications in adventure therapy. In C. Norton, C. Carpenter, and A. Pryor (eds), *Adventure Therapy around the Globe: International Perspectives and Diverse Approaches* (pp. 243–250). Champaign, IL: Common Ground Publishing.

Von Culin, K., Tsukayama, E., and Duckworth, A. (2014). Unpacking grit: Motivational correlates of perseverance and passion for long-term goals. *Journal of Positive Psychology*, 9(4), 306–312.

Von Neumann, J., and Morgenstern, O. (2007). *Theory of games and economic behavior*. Chicago, IL: Princeton University Press.

Waaktaar, T., Christie, H. J., Borge, A. I. H., and Torgersen, S. (2004). How can young people's resilience be enhanced? Experiences from a clinical intervention project. *Clinical Child Psychology and Psychiatry*, 9(2), 167–183.

Waite, P. J., and Richardson, G. E. (2004). Determining the efficacy of resiliency training in the work site. *Journal of Allied Health*, 33(3), 178–183.

Walsh, V., and Golins, G. (1976). *The Exploration of the Outward Bound Process*. Denver, CO: Colorado Outward Bound School.

Ward, W., and Yoshino, A. (2007). Participant meanings associated with short-term academic outdoor adventure skills courses. *Journal of Experiential Education*, 29(3), 369–372.

Watson, J. B. (1913). Psychology as the behaviorist views it. *Psychological Review*, 20, 158–177.

Waughfield, C. (2002). *Mental Health Concepts* (5th edn). Albany, NY: Delmar.

Wiesner, M. and Capaldi, D. M. (2003). Relations or childhood and adolescent factors to offending trajectories of young men. *Journal of Research in Crime and Delinquency*, 40 231–262.

Wilson, R. (1981). *Inside Outward Bound*. Charlotte, NC: East Woods Press.

Wolery, M., Bailey, D., and Sugai, G. (1998). *Effective Teaching Principles and Procedures for Applied Behavior Analysis with Exceptional Students*. Boston, MA: Allyn & Bacon.

Wong, H. K., and Wong, R. T. (2009). *The First Days of School: How to Be an Effective Teacher*. Mountain View, CA: Harry K. Wong Publications.

Wöran, B., and Arnberger, A. (2012). Exploring relationships between recreation specialization, restorative environments and mountain hikers' flow experience. *Leisure Sciences*, 34, 95–114.

Yamada, R. (2012). Current status and problems of first year education: Trends and issues of first year experience. *University Management*, 8(2), 2–7.

Zimmerman, M. A. (1990). Taking aim on empowerment research: On the distinction between individual and psychological conceptions. *American Journal of Community Psychology*, 18(1), 169–177.

INDEX